128-95

THE TRAINING TECHNOLOGY PROGRAMME

Volume 1

THE SYSTEMATIC DESIGN OF TRAINING COURSES

TRAINING TECHNOLOGY PROGRAMME
Produced by the North West Consortium

Volume 1

THE SYSTEMATIC DESIGN OF TRAINING COURSES

Bob Wilson

Supported by OPEN TECH **MSC**

Parthenon Publishing

THE PARTHENON PUBLISHING GROUP LIMITED

To my wife, Pat

The Training Technology Programme is published on behalf of the North West Consortium by:

In the U.K. and Europe

    The Parthenon Publishing Group Ltd
    Casterton Hall
    Carnforth
    Lancashire LA6 2LA
    England

ISBN 1-85070-158-X

In the U.S.A. at

    The Parthenon Publishing Group Inc
    120 Mill Road
    Park Ridge
    NJ 07656
    U.S.A.

ISBN 0-940813-30-0

Editorial Note
The male pronoun has been used throughout the Training Technology Programme for stylistic reasons only. It covers both masculine and feminine genders.

THE TRAINING TECHNOLOGY PROGRAMME

The Training Technology Programme (TTP) aims to provide materials which will help improve training and learning.

The Programme is presented by the North West Consortium, consisting of Lancashire Polytechnic, S. Martin's College and Lancashire College.

TTP is a set of distance learning materials in two versions. There is a choice between a hard-back Volume edition and a soft-back Package edition.

PROGRAMME PRODUCTION

Project Manager .... *Bob Wilson*
Co-ordinator .... *John Stock*
Programme Co-ordinator .... *Kath Litherland*
Video Advisor .... *Fred Fawbert*
Audio Advisor .... *Peter Darnton*
Main Illustrators .... *Angela Pour-Rahnema*
David Hill & Lesley Sumner
Editors .... *Andy Davies & Derek Oliver*
Production Team Members .... *Lynne Hamer, Judith Hindle*
Caroline Nesfield (Programme Secretary)
Susan Western, Bobby Whittaker

ACKNOWLEDGEMENTS

With gratitude and appreciation to the many who have supported the Programme including the Directorate, Principals and mangement of Lancashire Polytechnic, S. Martin's College and Lancashire College; David Bloomer, Norma Brennan, Cyril Cavies, Ryland Clendon, Noel Goulsbra, Stanley Henig, Tony James, Peter Knight, Joe Lee, Ken Phillips, Alan Sharples, Ross Simpson; The Director and members of MSC Open Tech, especially Steve Emms, Les Goodman, Fiona Jordan; last, but certainly not least, The Authors' Families.

FOR FURTHER INFORMATION

Write to Bob Wilson, Programme Director,
Training Technology Programme, Lancashire Polytechnic,
PRESTON, PR1 2TQ. Tel. (0772) 22141

Foreword
to the Training Technology Programme

Today we see technology being applied to every department of civilised living. It comes in many forms and its applications are virtually limitless. What we see today, although it is transforming society, is but the beginning, and the extent and pace of change is likely to increase many times.

It is most fitting and timely therefore that a systematic effort is being made to apply technology to training. The techniques available are very varied ranging from computers to audio visual equipment. It will enable training to be undertaken privately at home or at the work place in a group, in the remote croft or in the city.

Technology is revolutionising training; I welcome therefore this Training Technology Programme developed by the North West Consortium and Parthenon Publishing, supported by the Manpower Services Commission. It brings training in technology, through the medium of technology, to more people than ever before.

I commend it and I am delighted to have been invited to contribute this foreword.

John Banham
Director General CBI

Contents

Study Unit 1

The Systematic Design of Training Courses

START

STUDY UNIT ONE

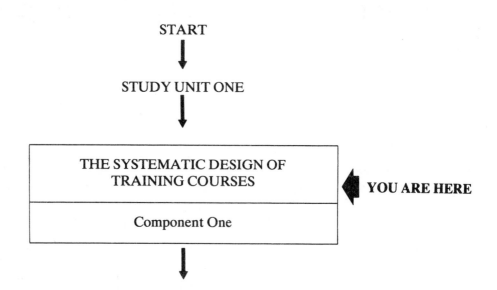

Step 1

Needs Analysis
Setting the Scene
Component Two

Component 1:

An Overall View of the Design System

Key Words

Systematic approach; design system; 'feedback'; traditional methods; system activities; analysis; synthesis; implementation; assessment; evaluation; improvement; system functions.

The Systematic Approach

In this Package we are providing you with a tool which you can use when designing and implementing your training. This tool is based upon a systematic approach to solving your training problems and to designing training courses. Clearly such an approach must be based upon a design system, indeed this is sometimes called the 'systems approach' and we will show how you can apply this technique to your own work.

BUILDING UP THE DESIGN SYSTEM

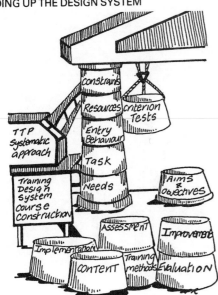

Figure 1

We propose to explain the whole system here and when designing, overhauling or modifying a complete course initially you will find it is best to apply the full systematic approach. When familiar with it you can select appropriate parts of the system or use your own short cuts depending on the training or pieces of training which you are developing. **On completing this Package you will have a blueprint for the systematic design of training courses.**

▰▰▰▰ Checkpoint

Let us start by defining a system. Can you do this? Have a look in the dictionary if you wish.

Does your definition look something like this?

> **'A system is a group of related parts which interact for a purpose'.**

Using this definition it seems that we have to find out about the characteristics and requirements of the training design system by:

● deciding what the parts of the system are and how they relate to each other.
● how these parts interact.
● what is their purpose.

As it is always best to have a sense of purpose or an aim from the outset, let's deal with that now. Just as one aim of training is to prove the efficiency and effectiveness of job performance, the purpose of the system and of the systematic approach is to improve the efficiency and effectiveness of training.

Remember that because our approach is systematic we must ensure that the arrangement of the parts is orderly, i.e. they follow a sensible sequence and that they are methodically arranged. We should follow this sequence step-by-step.

Let's get on with identifying parts of our design system with a diagram. Can you draw a diagram which shows a training system very simply?

How does this look to you?

Figure 2

In the above diagram where would you add the process of 'training design' to this system? Training design is what you do when you **design, organise and construct your training courses.**

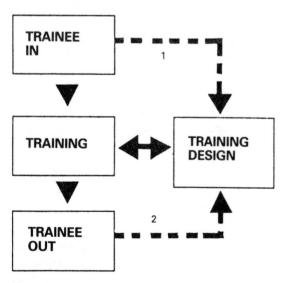

Figure 3

What do the two pecked lines (1 and 2) represent in our second diagram?

They show 'feedback'; this is information which you gain from the learners like their comments on the course and which you use to modify the system, i.e. the design of the training in this case. Pecked line 1 is really called 'feedforward' for obvious reasons and is fed into the design system from information gained before the learners start the course — more about this later.

What is the definition of a system?

Check your answer with our definition on the previous page.

We have now begun the construction of our system. Throughout this Package we shall be showing you how the systematic design of training is superior to 'traditional' methods. Bear this in mind and when a difference between the systematic approach and the traditional ways occurs to you, jot it down on a sheet of paper. In Package Two we shall make a comparison of these two methods and it will be interesting to see how your observations compare with ours. We will start this comparison off with Figure 4 shown below:

TRADITIONAL TRAINING DESIGNERS AT WORK

Figure 4

▰▱▰

- What fundamental problem in course planning is featured in the cartoon in Figure 4?
- What fundamental principle in course planning should be followed in order to minimise the problems illustrated?

- *Lack of a system of construction, or design.*
- *You must follow a systematic, orderly and methodical approach to training course design.*

▰▱▰

Continuing with identifying the parts of our system, you will know that whether designing a course systematically or traditionally, many questions of design arise and the answers which we give lend shape to the training itself. Make a list of those questions which have occurred to you previously when constructing courses.

Spend some time making your list as this is an important exercise in this Study Unit.

Now see if you can place your questions into groups which contain queries of a similar nature. To each group give a name which reflects the general nature and activities of the group, i.e. if some of your questions are concerned with making your training better then that could be called the 'improvement' group.

Figure 5 below shows your questions may be placed together into five groups, each single group representing one type of major activity:

GROUPING QUESTIONS

Figure 5

It seems that providing the answers to questions about training course design involves **five major activities: analysis, synthesis, implementation, asessment/ evaluation and improvement.** These activities are basic to our system of designing training courses and we can now extend Figure 3 to include them, so extending our simple system.

BASIC ACTIVITIES IN THE TRAINING DESIGN SYSTEM

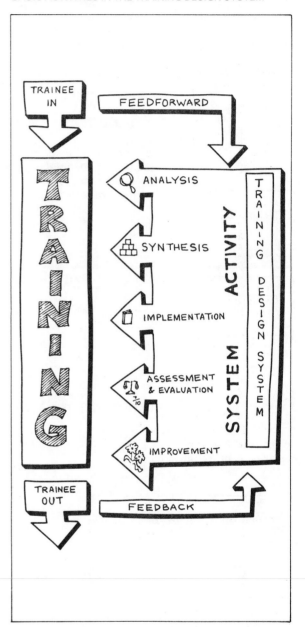

Figure 6

▰▱▰

We now need to know what goes on and what questions are asked within each of these basic System Activities. Write down your own ideas before reading the blocks which follow overleaf.

1

SYSTEM ACTIVITY: ANALYSIS

includes 'breaking down' questions and operations which help you decide what you are trying to do; if this is the solving of a training problem, then analysis defines and shows the parts of the problem. At the beginning of course design, analytical questions and activities identify the needs which have arisen, the parts of the task which face you as well as possible alternative solutions. Analysis defines and then takes apart the training problem.

2

SYSTEM ACTIVITY: SYNTHESIS

'building up' questions which help you decide how to build onto the parts identified by the analysis activities into the course required to solve your training problem, or meet your training need. Synthesis puts together the solution to the training problem.

3

SYSTEM ACTIVITY: IMPLEMENTATION OF THE TRAINING

this activity is the carrying out of the training. Implementation puts the solution into practice.

4

SYSTEM ACTIVITY: ASSESSMENT AND EVALUATION

questions which ask how the trainees on your course are doing, combined with activities which are designed to check their progress, so providing evidence which allows you to question and evaluate the effectiveness of your training. Evaluation is the measuring of the effectiveness of the parts of your solution to the training problem.

5

SYSTEM ACTIVITY: IMPROVEMENT

questions which ask how you are going to improve the effectiveness of your training, especially those parts which evaluation has identified as needing revision.

Figure 7

If you glance at Figure 6 and 7 again and at the definitions of a system which we made at the beginning of this Study Unit, you can see that the five major System Activities which we have identified must also represent the five basic parts of our system of course design.

However, if you study your own lists of training design queries you will realise that many of your questions require more detailed types of answers and of activities. So each of the parts of training design shown in Figure 7 illustrating the basic **activities** of our design system **must contain further, more specific activities or functions.** Shown as a diagram these relationships could look like this, using the activity of analysis as an example:

ANALYSIS: FROM QUESTIONS TO FUNCTIONS

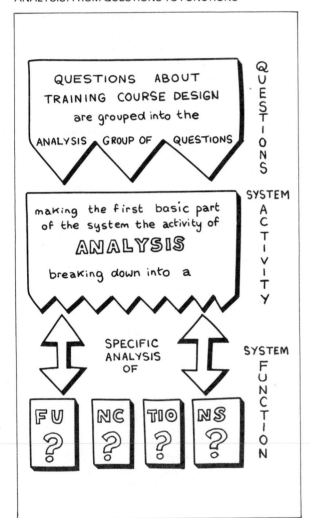

Figure 8

We have placed a question mark under the Functions because we haven't decided what these Functions are yet. Any ideas about how to find out? Perhaps we could try the same method we used for identifying the system activities. Try this layout.

YOUR TRAINING DESIGN QUESTIONS	SYSTEM ACTIVITY	SYSTEM FUNCTION
1 Column One	Column Two	Column Three
2		
3		
etc.		

Figure 9

What you do to fill in this layout:

Step One

List your training design questions, placing your questions in Column One of the layout shown above.

Step Two

Decide which of the basic **System Activities** (analysis, synthesis, implementation, assessment/evaluation and improvement) the question represents and fill in Column Two.

Step Three

Decide what your question is asking about in detail; for example if the System Activity is, say, analysis fill in Column Three by deciding exactly what it is you are trying to analyse when asking your question. Thus you define your **System Function.**

Here is an example of how this works:

Step One
TRAINING DESIGN QUESTION
'Why am I doing this training?'

Step Two
SYSTEM ACTIVITY-ANALYSIS
Your question is asking you to analyse your reasons for offering training.

Step Three
SYSTEM FUNCTION
Your question is also asking for a specific reason or reasons. If you are offering training you must be meeting a need which has been expressed, therefore this is an analysis of needs. Our system must now define which need, or needs, more closely by NEEDS ANALYSIS

Check your questions in this way then look overleaf at our table, Figure 10.

TRAINING DESIGN QUESTIONS	SYSTEM ACTIVITIES	SYSTEM FUNCTIONS
Why am I doing this training? What do the trainees want?	ANALYSIS	1 Analyse the need for training ie 'NEEDS ANALYSIS'
What's the job for which I'm doing the training? How does this job break down?	ANALYSIS	2 Analyse the job or task, ie 'TASK ANALYSIS'
Who am I training? What do they know?	ANALYSIS	3 Analyse the trainees joining the course, ie 'ENTERING BEHAVIOUR ANALYSIS'
What equipment, personnel, money, space do I have?	ANALYSIS	4 Analyse the resources available, ie 'RESOURCE ANALYSIS'
What training restrictions face me?	ANALYSIS	5 Analyse the restrictions ie 'CONSTRAINTS ANALYSIS'
How do I know where we are going? Where is the training going?	ANALYSIS	6 Analyse the training aims and objectives, ie 'AIMS & OBJECTIVES ANALYSIS'
How will I know if we're moving? or what yardstick will I measure progress by?	SYNTHESIS	7 Synthesise tests which show progress, ie 'CRITERION TESTS SYNTHESIS'
Upon which knowledge/skills do I build my training? Do I have a syllabus and how valid is it?	SYNTHESIS	8 Synthesise a syllabus, ie 'CONTENT SYNTHESIS'
How will I get this knowledge, these skills and attitudes across?	SYNTHESIS	9 Synthesise an array of appropriate teaching techniques ie 'TRAINING METHODS SYNTHESIS'
What's the best way of structuring my lessons? What media will I select?	IMPLEMENTAITON	10 Synthesise a training approach for your lessons, ie put together the 'IMPLEMENTATION OF THE TRAINING''
How do I know the trainees are learning? What are they learning?	ASSESSMENT	11 Assess the learners work, ie 'ASSESSMENT OF THE TRAINEES'
If we're here, did we come the best way? Which parts of the training went best/worst? Surely there must be a better way?	EVALUATION	12 Evaluate assessment results and trainee comments ie 'EVALUATION OF THE COURSE'
Are things getting better as we go along?	IMPROVEMENT	13 Strengthen your training weaknesses 'IMPROVEMENT OF THE TRAINING COURSE'

Figure 10

Each System Function represents a step to be taken when following the systematic design of training courses. "You are here" diagrams at the beginning of every Component in this Package show you which of the 13 steps (functions) you are undertaking in each Component.

8

Can you now describe the differences between System Activities and System Functions and say what each does?

A System Activity is a basic part of the process of designing training courses and shows the major activities which you carry out when following the system in an orderly and methodical fashion.

The System Activities of analysis and synthesis have several System Functions each of which fines down and focuses the activity onto parts of the systematic approach. In the case of the System Activities of assessment, evaluation and improvement the System Function is really a more specific indication of what you actually do when undertaking the broader System Activity itself.

By examining the boxes under System Functions you can see that we have now identified 13 such Functions. Each Function is a step to be taken in our design system.

Figure 11

In this Component we have described what each function is about very briefly and most of the remaining Components in the Study Units of this Package will examine the operation of each System Function in detail.

It is much easier to envisage all of these Functions if they are drawn as a diagram. Try doing this now, then compare your diagram with ours shown below in Figure 12 and on page 22.

THE SYSTEMATIC DESIGN OF TRAINING COURSES

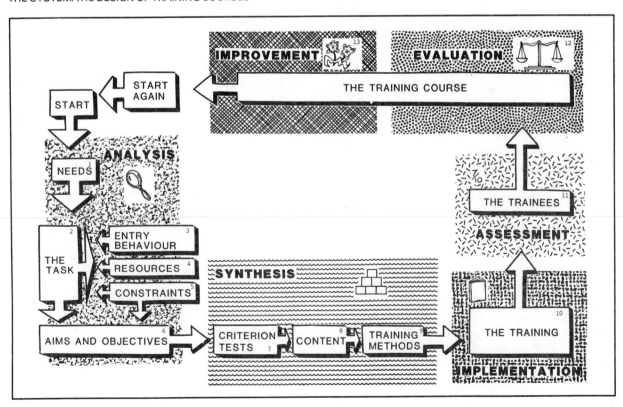

Figure 12

After viewing Figure 12 see if you can recollect the important characteristics of a simple training system. Does the system which we have outlined meet the requirement of our original definition?

- *Has it parts related to each other?*
  YES: these are five System Activities and 13 System Functions.
- *Do these parts interact?*
  YES: interaction is shown by arrows in the diagram. There are many more interactions than those shown and we shall develop this as we look at the System in detail.
- *Do the parts of the System, forming the systematic approach, have a purpose?*
  YES: to improve the efficiency and effectiveness of training.
- *Is the arrangement of the parts orderly?*
  YES: They follow a logical order.
- *Is the arrangement of the parts methodical?*
  YES: following the sequence step-by-step gives a blueprint for structuring and organising your training.

We shall now work our way through this design system step-by-step. At this stage decide on a course to which you would like to apply the systematic approach to training design and prepare the materials simultaneously with our discussions. You may wish to select either a new course yet to be offered or current training which you want to re-organise.

Alternatively you can apply the systematic approach to part of a course where the design needs to be improved e.g. you may not be satisfied with the objectives which you have written for a current course and wish to rework them after reading the relevant Component of this Package.

Summary

The design system has five System Activities and thirteen System Functions. By following through the steps of the System and carrying out the successive Activities and Functions in an orderly and methodical way, the trainer can approach the design and implementation of training courses in a systematic, orderly and methodical way.

Now for some work for you to do. With an actual course of training in mind, review the material which you would consider under each of the five System Activities and make a summary of your review.

A
ANALYSIS

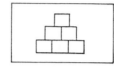
S
SYNTHESIS

I
IMPLEMENTATION

A
ASSESSMENT/
EVALUATION

I
IMPROVEMENT

Figure 13

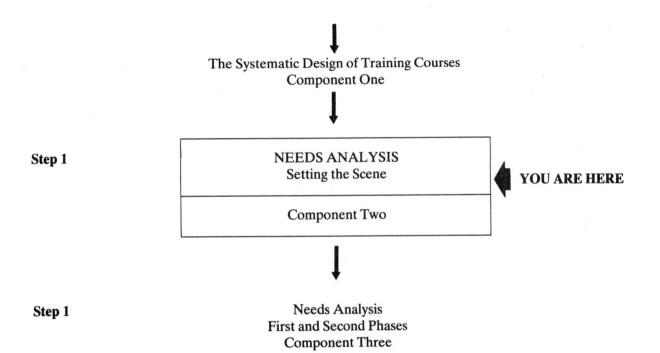

The Systematic Design of Training Courses
Component One

Step 1

NEEDS ANALYSIS
Setting the Scene

YOU ARE HERE

Component Two

Step 1

Needs Analysis
First and Second Phases
Component Three

Component 2:

Needs Analysis: Setting the Scene for a Needs Analysis

Key Words

Needs analysis; 'what is' and 'what ought to be'; discrepancy and performance deficiency symptoms; overtraining; determining goals; ordering the goals; measuring needs; deciding on priorities (the four elements of needs analysis); advantages of needs analysis; goals versus aims.

Considered in this Component
System Activity: Analysis
System Function: Needs Analysis

Our procedure for the remainder of this Package is to follow through the systematic approach described in Component One. This means that we examine each of the System Activities and System Functions shown in Figures 10 and 12.

As you will remember, there are 13 System Functions.

▓▓▓ Checkpoint

Can you recollect what they are and the order in which they appear?

You should set yourself the task of remembering all the Functions, so why don't your write out the list now and stick it up in the kitchen at home or in your office or somewhere else where you will see it regularly. Carry it with you if you like; in a couple of weeks you will know it off by heart.

Each Function represents one Step in our systematic approach. So if we start with Step One we have to analyse the need for training by a **Needs Analysis.** You may be saying to yourself, 'Examine the need for training? Of course there's a need!' Let's have a look at the situation.

First of all, what is a need? You can say, 'I need a new pair of shoes.' So what does that mean in terms which we can apply to training? Well, there's a **discrepancy** isn't there? Between what you have and what you want. Presuming that your need is a reasonable one, we can say that a need is some sort of discrepancy or **deficiency** and express it in this way:

'A Need is a discrepancy or deficiency between what is and what ought to be'

As trainers, we should bear in mind that the 'ought to be', can usually only be achieved after training. Improvement reaching towards an 'ideal' state of 'ought to be', can usually only be realised after a careful programme of training and this emphasises the fundamental and central part of training in the progress and development of any organisation. As if you didn't know!

Using the definition on the previous page, how would you express a need related to job performance?

Your thinking could go like this:
'If there's a need there must be some sort of discrepancy or deficiency in the job performance. So the operator must be deficient in some way, or the equipment inadequate'.

Does the following 'equation' express this clearly?

PERFORMANCE DEFICIENCIES AND NEEDS: AN EQUATION

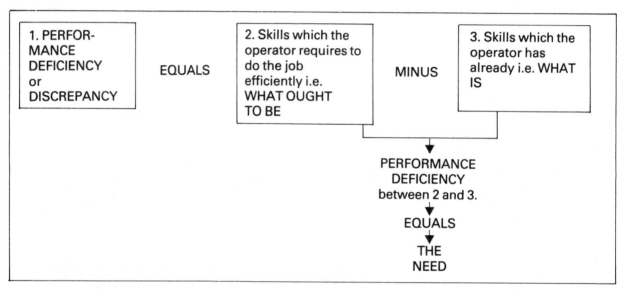

| 1. PERFOR-MANCE DEFICIENCY or DISCREPANCY | EQUALS | 2. Skills which the operator requires to do the job efficiently i.e. WHAT OUGHT TO BE | MINUS | 3. Skills which the operator has already i.e. WHAT IS |

PERFORMANCE DEFICIENCY between 2 and 3.

EQUALS

THE NEED

Figure 14

Yes, but we haven't mentioned equipment (and working conditions etc.) deficiencies and this must be remembered; we'll look at this later.

DISCREPANCY IN PERFORMANCE

Figure 15

■▨▨

Now, how do you as a trainer and your firm or organisation become alert to performance deficiency?

Well, there must be evidence of this in the form of symptoms.

■▨▨

Like what? Write down your own list of symptoms of performance deficiency which are possible in your organisation, then check it with ours in the next column.

- *Profitability has declined*
- *Labour turnover is high*
- *Equipment is always breaking*

- *Frequent strikes*
- *There are a lot of accidents*
- *Machinery down-time is high*
- *Relationships between staff and management are poor*
- *Scrap rates are high*
- *A lot of grievance procedures are arising*
- *Accident rates are high*
- *Firm has bad reports for unsafe working practices*
- *Cycle times are excessive*
- *Firm's products have an increasing reputation for poor quality and unreliability*
- *Nobody shows much initiative and motivation is low*
- *Shops are untidy and goods are poorly displayed*
- *Frequent customer complaints about unco-operative staff attitudes*
- *Frequent customer complaints about staff inefficiency and slowness*

SPRIGG'S CANNONBALL FACTORY

Figure 16

■▨▨

Our Figure 16 shows that Sprigg's Cannonball Factory isn't working too well these days. Amidst faulty machinery and reject cannonballs, two trainers are having a look at the situation. Does anything strike you as odd about what they are doing?

Well, whilst one trainer is examining the operator, the other is checking the machinery, which is unusual for a trainer. The message of the picture is that you must make sure that the deficiency in job performance is an **operator deficiency,** *which can be cured by training, rather than a* **deficiency in the tools** *which the operator has to use or the unsuitable environment in which the operator has to work.*

So the problem of deficiency in job performance can be tackled either by doing something about the operator or about the job (or both, if the situation is serious) i.e.

FITTING THE PERSON TO THE JOB

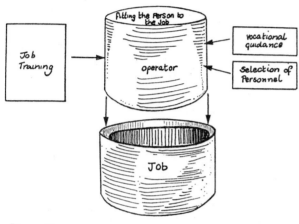

Figure 17

FITTING THE JOB TO THE PERSON

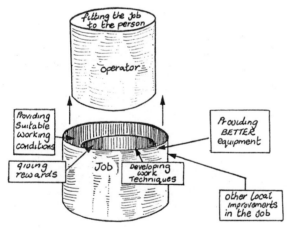

Figure 18

You should talk to as many people as possible in your organisation to decide whether improving job performance is a matter of training, i.e. fitting the operator to the job (Figure 17) or the other way around (Figure 18). Some solutions are shown in both Figures and you can see where **job training** is applied in Figure 17; of course, this is the activity which concerns us most directly.

However, we must be careful to keep a proper sense of perspective and not overdo the solution by overtraining.

Can you suggest what may result from too much training?

Here are some bad results:
- *More and longer courses organised than are necessary*
- *More money is spent on instructors, accommodation and equipment than the job requires*
- *Operators may be overtrained for higher calibre jobs than they have a hope of doing and dissatisfaction results*
- *Training becomes an end in itself with courses sometimes becoming too theoretical and high level. So overtraining can be very costly*

However, with the safeguard of ensuring that training is really necessary always in mind, let us now get back to analysing closely the actual need for training.

Review what we said before about discrepancies and deficiencies, needs and 'what is' compared with 'what ought to be'. Can you summarise this in a couple of diagrams?

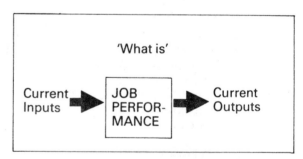

Figure 19

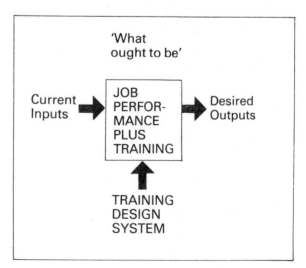

Figure 20

By glancing at Figure 12 again, you will recollect that we are concerned with the System Activity of Analysis and the System Function of Needs Analysis.

THE FOUR ELEMENTS OF NEEDS ANALYSIS

```
TRAINING COURSE DESIGN SYSTEM.
SYSTEM ACTIVITY: ANALYSIS
SYSTEM FUNCTION: NEEDS ANALYSIS



DESIGN SYSTEM
START
     ↓
'NEEDS              System Function
ANALYSIS'
```

Figure 21

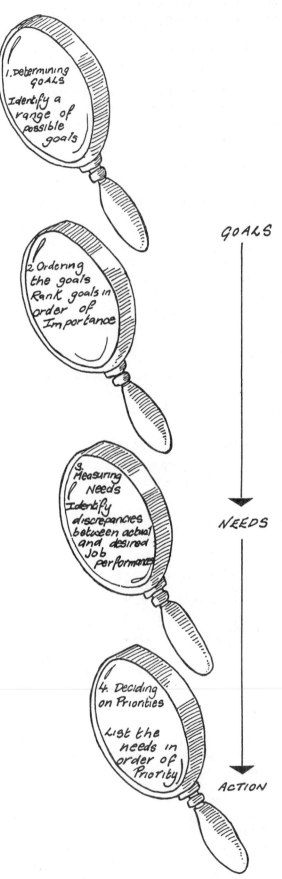

■▨▨■

'A need is a .... between ....
and ....'.

Answer: 'discrepancy' or 'deficiency'; 'what is' and 'what ought to be'

First, we must define just what needs analysis is. In determining what ought to be and how to remedy deficiencies we are stating our **goals.** As it is unlikely that all of our Goals are of equal significance, we ought to know how important each of the Goals really is and how they compare with each other in degree, i.e. **order of importance.**

Next, we have to know if the difference between the **actual performance** ('what is') and the **desired performance** ('what ought to be') is significant; you will remember that if there is a significant discrepancy or deficiency, then we have established a **need.** Lastly, it would seem sensible to decide on **priorities** between needs, so that we can decide on the **action** which we have to take.

Can you now put all of this information together into a definition?

Our definition is:

'Needs Analysis is a systematic process of determining and ordering **Goals,** measuring **Needs** and deciding on **Priorities** for **Action'.**

If you examine this definition closely, you will see that there are four main elements to the analysis.

Figure 22

So far so good. But have you asked yourself in detail what a Goal is yet? What do you think it is?

Goals are statements of your intentions: they say in broad terms what you are trying to do in achieving the 'ought to be' condition. Let's take some examples of Goals from outside training. One Goal everybody has is 'to be happy'. Another is to 'take a holiday'. Yet another is 'to stay healthy'. Each can be broken down into more detail, of course. Take the 'stay healthy' one.

How would you break it down?

STAYING HEALTHY

GOAL - 'TO STAY HEALTHY' (the 'ought to be' state)

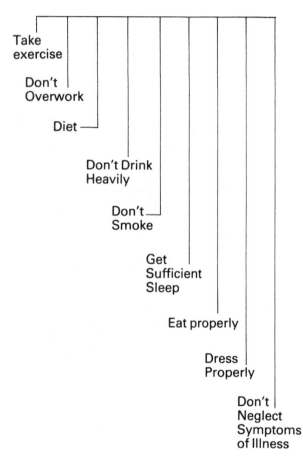

Figure 23

The Goal, 'to stay healthy' could hardly be more general, could it? The 'breakdown' is more specific.

Now think of some examples of Goals from your training. Here are some examples:

- The course shows how to work a lathe.
- The training is to help develop an understanding of customers' attitudes.
- The trainee will become aware of the principles of good interviewing.
- The trainees will know the role of a stewardess.
- The course is intended to fulfil trainees' vocations/ needs.
- It is the intention to develop trainees' understanding of packing processes.
- The trainees will be able to demonstrate efficiently the operation of a cash-out till.
- At the end of training, the students will be able to list the objectives of the course accurately.

In the next Component, we shall follow through the steps of an actual Needs Analysis. Before we do that let us consider the **advantages** of carrying out a Needs Analysis.

On a separate piece of paper, write down what you think are the **benefits** of making a Needs Analysis.

Do you agree with these?
- *Needs analysis shows which are the most important needs and draws the focus of the training designers to them.*
- *By establishing priorities, the most efficient utilisation of resources is effected.*
- *Establishing needs and priorities facilitates course design and other training decisions.*
- *A large number of opinions are sought, in addition to those of trainers, about training Goals and Needs and a consensus is arrived at, to which everyone involved can work.*
- *As many members of the organisation are included in the process of Needs Analysis, they have a stake in ensuring success and are motivated to offer support for training.*
- *Trainers have a logical and detailed document which gives supporting evidence for training proposals and can be used as a part of the presentations outlining training schemes in discussion with management and other staff.*
- *Training sections benefit from the high profile these activities have in their firms. At least a lot of people know and are involved in what the trainers are doing.*

Figure 24

Summary

(Try writing out your own summary first and then compare it with ours).

The initial step of the systematic approach to training, the course design system, is to undertake the first System Function, which is Needs Analysis.

A Need is a discrepancy, or deficiency, between 'what is' and 'what ought to be'. Discrepancies in job performance are shown by the difference between which skills an operator has and the skills which he or she ought to have.

There are numerous symptoms of deficiencies in job performance and we are concerned with fitting the person to the job through training, although it should be remembered that overtraining can be an expensive hazard.

Training Goals seek to state how to remedy deficiencies in job performance by training and are statements of general intentions.

Needs Analysis, which identifies measures and prioritises needs has four main elements:
● Determining Goals.
● Ordering the Goals.
● Measuring Needs.
● Deciding on priorities for action.
Needs Analysis involves discussions with interested parties, especially those who do the job and numerous advantages come from being able to present a documented case which specifies needs as a basis for training and course design.

 Try this exercise now.

1. You have decided to design a new training course for your organisation. Using the information which you have received in this Component, make a short outline Needs Analysis, using our guideline questions shown below, if you wish.

2. Examine one job in your firm in which you consider that there may be a deficiency in performance. Describe the deficiency and how you identified it, in general terms.

Here are some guideline questions to help you:

For 1.
● What are your goals?
● How did you decide what they were?
● Did you decide which are the more important and which are the less important goals?
● How did you identify your training Needs?
● Did you try to measure the size of the Needs?
● Are there any Needs priorities decided?
● Have you organised a clear format to show the results of your Needs Analysis?

For 2.
● Did you identify clearly the job in which there is a deficiency?
● Did you identify the deficiency, or deficiencies, in terms of job skills, knowledge, and what were the symptons of the deficiencies?
● What sources of information did you draw upon to determine the discrepancy in performance between 'what is' and 'what ought to be'?
● Did you try to measure the deficiency?

For revisionary purposes try drawing Figure 12 so that the design system is held firmly in your memory. You can simplify the diagram as we have below. This diagram does not show feedback lines, for simplicity. They could have been drawn in to interconnect all of the boxes.

Each box represents a function, or step to be taken, in our design system.

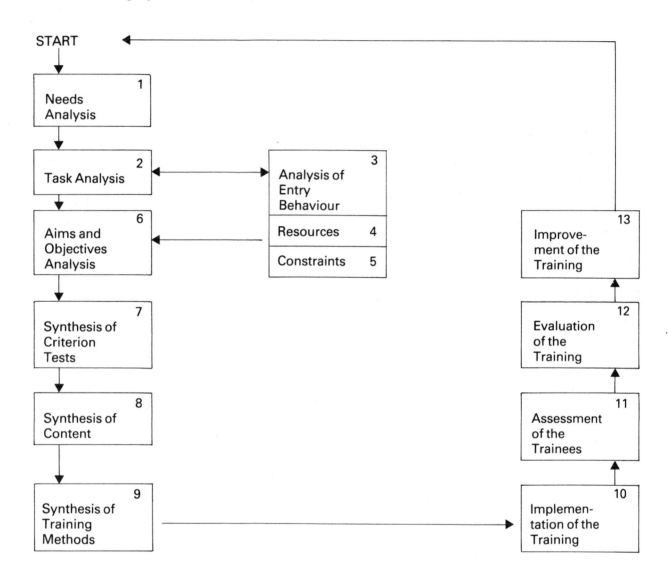

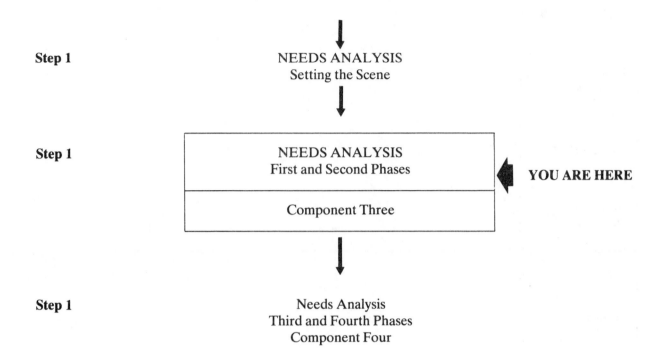

Step 1   NEEDS ANALYSIS
Setting the Scene

Step 1   NEEDS ANALYSIS
First and Second Phases   **YOU ARE HERE**

Component Three

Step 1   Needs Analysis
Third and Fourth Phases
Component Four

Component 3:

Carrying Out the Needs Analysis: First and Second Phases

Key Words

Determining goals; sources of information; working party; all the other interested parties (A.O.P.'s). Surveys: preset; open; delphi; 'in-a-hurry'; task analysis; performance analysis and indicators; rating survey; rating scales; card sort; Q sort; paired weighting procedure; rank order; points and weightings.

Considered in this Component **System Activity: Analysis** **System Function:** **Needs Analysis**

We will now examine and explain the techniques for carrying out a Needs Analysis. The four phases of which it consists are:
● Determining Goals.
● Ordering the Goals.
● Measuring the Needs.
● Deciding on priorities.
At the end of the last Component you had a chance to think over how you would set about this task and that activity should have given you a general idea of the problems raised by this type of analysis.

Within each phase, we will describe the techniques of Needs Analysis under the headings:
● **Purpose**
● **Input**
● **Staff Involved**
● **Methods**
● **Output**
Figure 54, at the end of Component 4, provides you with a plan of the Phases of Needs Analysis. Refer to it as you work through the next couple of Components.

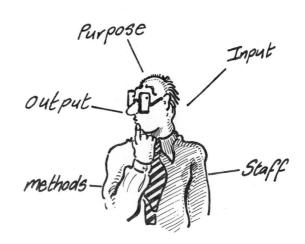

▨▨▨ Checkpoint

What do you think is the very first thing which you have to do when starting a Needs Analysis?

Initially you must identify the job and the job performance for which you are designing training and making your Needs Analysis. So start with

NEEDS ANALYSIS OF JOB: (Name of job)
Then carry out the First Phase

Important: throughout this description of how to analyse needs, always relate what is being said to your own training situation by selecting an actual job with which you are concerned and where a job deficiency is likely. Make your own outline Needs Analysis as you go along following the procedures described.

DEFICIENCIES IN THE JOB

Figure 25

First Phase:
How to Determine the Goals

Purpose

To identify a wide range of possible and relevant training Goals related to the named job, or to a group of core skills, or training geared to a special context. At this stage the emphasis is on **quantity,** rather than quality, i.e. getting as many Goals as reasonable rather than deciding on their value, practicability or usefulness. For each Goal you should also be prepared to make a brief indication of how performance is deficient. In this Phase you are finding out 'what ought to be', in general terms.

Input

You need to draw your information and ideas from as many people and places as possible. So inputs must be explored and documented fully from the following **sources**:-

1. Syllabuses from previous courses of a similar nature.
2. The experience and opinions of other trainers, both within your organisation and without.
3. Award requirements if awards are to be given, especially the regulations of external examining bodies.
4. Course materials from similar courses.
5. Information available on resources ready for use and obstacles to operation of the course.
6. Relevant literature, especially where up-dating courses are being designed and recent research is important.
7. Present skill levels of entering trainees.
8. Entering Behaviour of the trainees, what they know, their skills and attitudes.
9. Views and opinions of senior management, foremen, departmental heads, and skilled operators.
10. Views of previous trainees on past courses.
11. Needs Analyses made previously.
12. The observations of administrative and finance departments.

Figure 26 shows this information diagrammatically.

SOURCES OF INFORMATION FOR NEEDS ANALYSIS FIRST PHASE

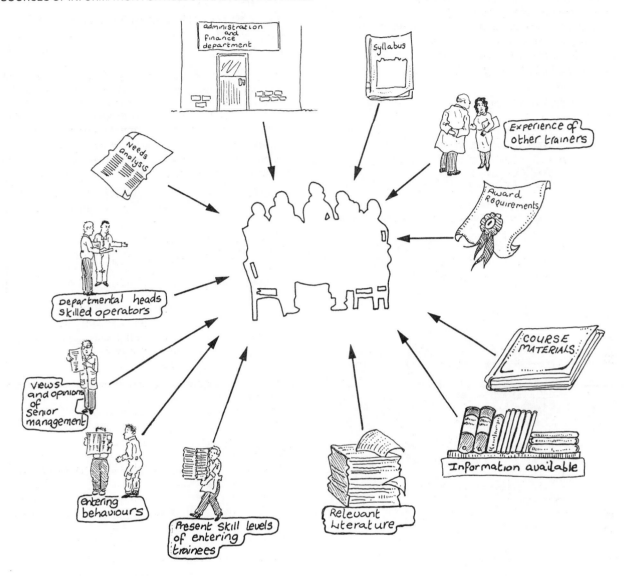

Figure 26

Note that three of these sources in Figure 26 are examined more fully in our systematic approach, should you require detailed information. Which are they?

After reflection, you should find that you may wish to undertake further examination of Input numbers 5, 7, and 8, all of which are represented by Steps in our System of design.

Staff Involved

The staff involved in operating the Needs Analysis will vary widely in character and composition according to the job being considered and between different organisations. Your selection of staff has the objective of providing a small Working Party who will carry out the operation of the Needs Analysis under your direction. In a very small firm this Working Party may only consist of two or three people, but do try to get as wide a range of experience as possible, wherever you are employed.

Who would you invite to join such a Working Party in your organisation?

Composition of this Working Party could be drawn typically from the following:

1. All those involved **directly** *in making the Needs Analysis, e.g.*
- *Yourself as Director.*
- *Anybody helping such as an assessment and evaluation expert.*
- *Someone who has taught the course before.*
- *A secretary.*

2. Several of the following, according to availability and the size of your organisation:
- *A trainer who is to instruct on the course.*
- *A skilled employee who does the job.*
- *A trainee who is likely to join the course.*
- *Any trainers who teach related courses, e.g. preparatory courses or subsequent, more advanced training.*
- *Any management and administrative staff who are closely involved or interested (especially those with supportive attitudes!).*

THE WORKING PARTY

Figure 27

Methods

METHOD STEP ONE
Form your Working Party by selecting from the above and include all staff working on the analysis.

METHOD STEP TWO
Collect all inputs, document and organise them properly and present them to your Working Party for review. This will give a uniform and informed perspective and background to your Needs Analysis.

METHOD STEP THREE
Produce a set of likely Goals by discussion or 'Brainstorming' (see Package Two). Your Working Party is trying to produce a range of Goals rather than making judgements on the value of each one now. We are after quantity not quality, so don't bother about expressing Goals precisely. There are several techniques which you can use to generate your set of Goals.

Technique One: Preset Survey
Your Working Party is identifying 'what ought to be', the desired performance and then developing Goals. Your Working Party should be suitably composed to be able to ask the necessary, pertinent questions.

Remembering to name the Needs Analysis job, let's have a look at some examples of one way of developing Goals.

Job:	Selling
Desired Performance:	Proficiency in selling techniques
Goal:	Sales staff are to acquire proficiency in selling techniques
Job:	Garment machining
Desired Performance:	Perfect garments, without wastage
Goal:	Machinists should have the skills necessary to produce perfect garments without wastage

Figure 28

Think of some more examples from your own firm, but extend the procedure by producing several Goals. Incidentally, more than just the one Goal indicated can be developed from the two examples given already.

WORKING PARTY LIST OF GOALS

Job:	Training Skills
Desired Performance:	Trainers should have a wide range of training knowledge and be proficient in a range of training skills.
Goal 1:	Trainers should understand learning theory.
Goal 2:	Trainers should be able to operate a wide range of audio visual (a-v) equipment.
Goal 3:	Trainers should know how to use computers.
Goal 4:	Trainers should understand the techniques of course design.

Figure 29

There are other ways of finding Goals which we can look at later, but the point is that your Working Party must establish a list of likely Goals one way or another; this is called the **pre-set list**, i.e., shaped (set) before (pre) use by other people.

Now you must circulate this list to **'all other parties'** (AOP's) who have an interest, skill and expertise in the job operation with which you are concerned, e.g. trainers, operators, management at all levels, administrators, clients, trainees past and future and anyone else who is involved in the training which you are organising. Ask them to comment on your list and to add any other Goals they believe are relevant. AOP's then return your list and your Working Party collate the information. In this way you benefit from receiving a wide variety of opinions and different perspectives.

Some Goals which OAP's add will be about conditions, rather than performance; usually this sort of Goal is not one which you can do anything about by training, so consolidate them into a separate report which you then send to management.

Returning to our Job, **Training Skills,** you ought to find comments on all four of the Goals which you circulated, **plus additional ones,** say,

Goal 5: Trainers should have a good grounding in methods of training and learning.

Goal 6: Trainers should be able to use Graphic and Reprographic techniques.

Goal 7: Trainers should understand the context of training.

You now have seven Goals under **Training Skills.** Do they remind you of anything?

Well, they correspond roughly to the Packages of this Training Technology Programme. They would, wouldn't they?

PRESET SURVEY : HOW IT WORKS

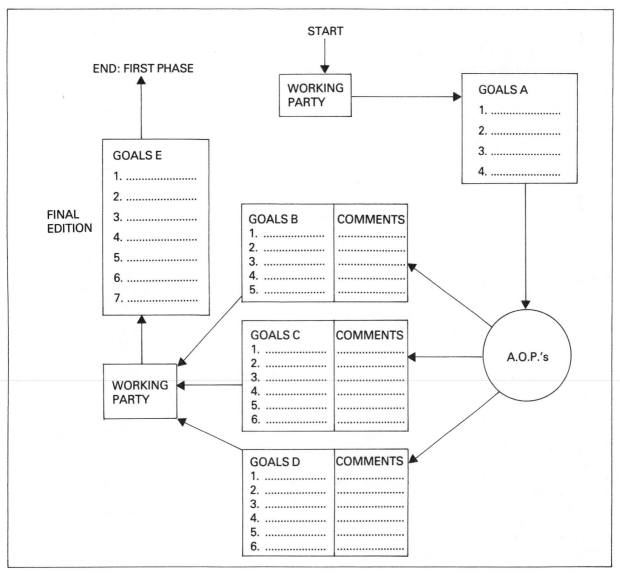

Figure 30

Technique Two: Open Survey

Just give your Needs Analysis job and the Desired Performance, **with no other information**, to all other interested parties (AOP's) and ask them to return their list of Goals related to the performance in question. You then consolidate a list of Goals.

OPEN SURVEY : HOW IT WORKS

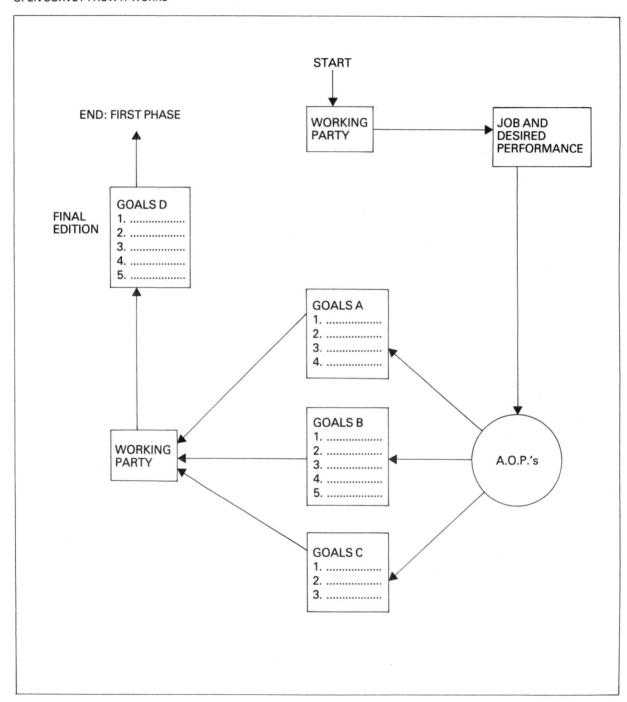

Figure 31

Technique Three: Delphi Technique

This technique has two distinct stages, each of which represents a single, complete circulation of material from the Working Party around the AOP's.

Stage One: 1. Circulate a preset list of Goals produced by your Working Party to AOP's and ask them to respond by commenting on the list. The AOP's can add more Goals if they want to.

            2. Collect this first set of responses and document them into a single list of Goals with AOP's comments attached. You may have to summarise comments.

StageTwo: 3. Circulate your consolidated list of new Goals and comments and ask for a second set of replies. AOP's are not required to comment on Goals which they have observed previously, but they should remark on Goals which they have not seen before. They may add more Goals, if they wish.

            4. Collect the second set of responses and Goals and consolidate as your final list of Goals.

Note:

This is a well-known technique and has the advantage of obtaining a consensus whilst recognising dissent. All justifications are welcome and as AOP's do not know who has written what, they feel no pressure to conform. This anonymity is useful in firms with strong hierarchies, as opinion leaders' and bosses' comments don't count any more than anyone else's.

Draw a couple of diagrams, in the style of Figures 30 and 31, to show the operation of the Delphi Technique. Then compare with our diagram, identifying differences.

THE DELPHI TECHNIQUE : HOW IT WORKS

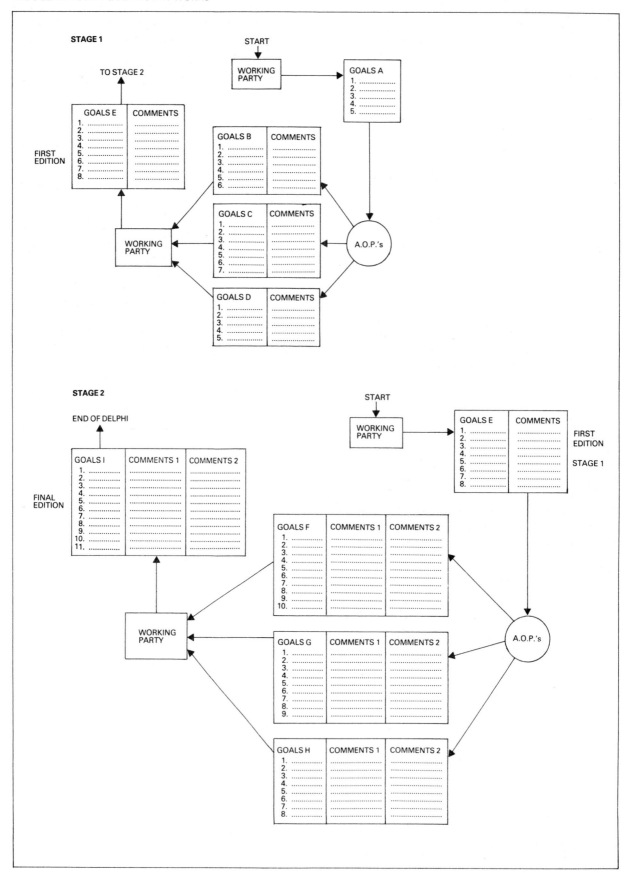

Figure 32

By examining Figure 32, say which Goals and which comments come from AOP's and which from the Working Party.

Stage One
Goals *1, 2, 3, 4, 5,*	*from Working Party*
Goals *6, 7, 8*	*from AOP's*
All comments	*from AOP's*

Stage Two
Goals *1 - 8*	*from Working Party. (Consolidated from Stage One)*
Goals *9, 10, 11*	*from AOP's.*
All comments	*from AOP's*

Finally, all Goals all Comments - Consolidated by Working Party into Final Edition.

Technique Four: 'In a Hurry'

If you feel you haven't time for a full survey, just use the list of Goals which your Working Party produced by 'brainstorming' or discussion. Although quick, this is the least effective method because it doesn't take a wide range of opinions.

Technique Five: Task Analysis

As you know, task analysis is one of the major steps in our design system, i.e. a System Function. However, it has many uses and it can be employed in different stages of the systematic approach. Used here, task analysis could help you provide an initial list of Goals for your Working Party to discuss, or even act as an alternative to Needs Analysis, where the full design system is not required.

However, you can only decide this when you have studied the technique and as this occurs in later Components, we'll leave it, presently.

Now on to Step Four of our Method: check back to where Step Three was, before the survey techniques.

METHOD STEP FOUR

Having obtained an extensive list of Goals, your Working Party does some sorting by removing irrelevant ones; simplifying complex ones; making sure you don't have any hidden 'solutions' disguised as Goals; deleting Goals which cannot be achieved by training.

METHOD STEP FIVE

Your Working Party agrees, by consensus, on a final list of Goals.

METHOD STEP SIX

You now have to carry out a further performance analysis of your Goals. What you are getting at here is to define your Goals by indicators of performance or by measurable terms, so you should try to identify what sort of job performance you expect to be achieved when each Goal is fulfilled at the desired level of performance. In other words you are trying to state your Goals, 'what ought to be', in broad performance terms so that you can later sort out the difference between 'what ought to be' and 'what is', i.e. the Need.

However, don't be too specific, otherwise you are moving into the area of writing performance objectives and that is for a later stage.

How would you set about making a performance analysis of your Goals?

Here are some simple stages for a **Performance Analysis** *of your Goals:*
1. *Write down your Goals individually.*
2. *Write next to each Goal the performance indicators which would show you that the Goal has been achieved, without duplication or irrelevancies.*
3. *Personally check that these performance indicators show the nature, quality and level of the desired performance involved. Use* **General Terms Only***; more detail is in the next phase.*
4. *Next, check with your Working Party that your indicators describe the desired performance accurately, although generally.*
5. *Finally, check that you have deleted all Goals which are non-instructional, eg. say about working conditions.*

Output

This is your list of Goals, tabulated something like this:

GOALS AND PERFORMANCE INDICATORS FIRST PHASE (What Ought to be)

Goal	Source/s	Performance Indicators
Write your Goal here, i.e. 'what ought to be', e.g.	Who suggested the Goal?, e.g.	Write the performance indicators here, ie indicators of 'what ought to be', e.g.
Goal 2: 'Trainers should be able to operate a wide range of a-v equipment'	**'Training Staff Management'**	**'Each trainer be able to operate common a-v equipment efficiently for effective use in the classroom'.**

Figure 33

Second Phase:
How to order the Goals

Purpose

To rank the Goals in order of importance by attaching ranks or weights to each. This phase also deals specially with 'what ought to be' and gives you a perspective.

Inputs

Your list of Goals from the First Phase (Figure 33).

Staff Involved

As for the first phase.

Method

METHOD STEP ONE
Call together your Working Party and a selection of those whom you involved in the First Phase, i.e. AOP's.

METHOD STEP TWO
Now choose a technique for rating and then ranking your list of Goals from the First Phase.

Can you suggest any techniques suitable for this procedure?

Some techniques follow.

Technique One: Rating Survey

● Carry out a survey of your Working Party and selected AOP's either by telephone, face-to-face or a mailed questionnaire. We use a 'Likert Scale' here, asking respondents to rate First Phase Goals on a five point scale thus:

RATING SCALE

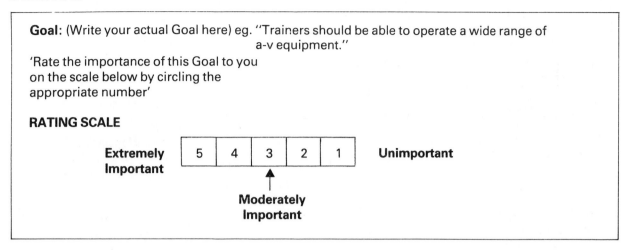

Goal: (Write your actual Goal here) eg. "Trainers should be able to operate a wide range of a-v equipment."

'Rate the importance of this Goal to you on the scale below by circling the appropriate number'

RATING SCALE

Extremely Important | 5 | 4 | 3 | 2 | 1 | **Unimportant**

↑ Moderately Important

Figure 34

- Rate each Goal in this fashion.
- When responders have completed and returned their scales to you, simply add up the points awarded to each Goal. The Goals with the greatest total number of points are the most important, as the more important the Goal the more points it will have gained. You then rank the Goals according to the order of the points received, most at the top.

Technique Two: Card Sort

Write each Goal on a card. As this is a variety of the Likert Scale each responder is asked to sort the cards into piles or place them in envelopes for you. Each pile corresponds to the five-point scale of Technique One. As for Technique One, 'points equal importance'. You then add up points for each Goal and rank order them.

Technique Three: Q Sort

Same method as for Card Sort, but the responders must place a certain number of cards only into each 'important' category. The numbers correspond to a curve of normal distribution, so that the 'moderate importance' category (3 points on the 5 point scale) will have the most cards.

You will need to tell your responders how many cards to put into each box, i.e. category.

Technique Four: Budget Allocation

This is a 'forced-choice' method of deciding Goal importance, so that responders cannot rate all Goals as being of equal or major importance, which can occur with the simple rating scales described already.

Each responder, or rater, allocates a number of points (or pounds if you want to change the perspective) amongst your set of Goals. Usually, there are twice as many points as there are Goals; with, say, 15 Goals you would give 30 points for allocation. Each responder allocates points to each goal on a five point scale until all of the points are used up. Sum up the points (or pounds) and rank order as before.

Technique Five: Paired Weighting Procedure

Another forced choice method: each Goal is compared with every other Goal and a single point allocated to the Goal considered to be the most important. Only one decision is made for each pair. Points are summed for each Goal across all responders and then rank-ordered by 'weight' (total number of points which each Goal attracts, compared).

Q SORT

Important   moderate   unimportant
                   Importance

Figure 35

WHO'S A LUCKY GOAL?

Figure 36

RANK ORDER AND WEIGHT OF GOALS: SECOND PHASE

METHOD STEP THREE
Analyse the responses and determine the ranking for each Goal

Output
List of Goals in rank order, i.e. order of importance.

RANK ORDER	GOAL	WEIGHTING
1.	Trainers should be able to operate a wide range of a-v equipment.	Write down the number of points scored here, i.e. 'What ought to be' given a rating e.g. 60 points, 36 points
2.	Trainers should be able to write effective training materials	

Figure 37

Summary
- We have now completed the First and Second Phases of Step One of our design system, Needs Analysis.
- We have examined sources of information for determining Goals, the composition of our Working Party, likely other interested parties (AOP's), how to survey 'what ought to be' and arrive at performance indicators.
- We then went on to order our Goals, considered further methods of survey for doing this and finally rank-ordered our Goals by their weighting scores in points.
- In the next Component we shall complete the method of Needs Analysis, but before we do that you should mentally compare the relative advantages and disadvantages of the Needs Analysis techniques which we have considered so far, deciding which is best for your use.

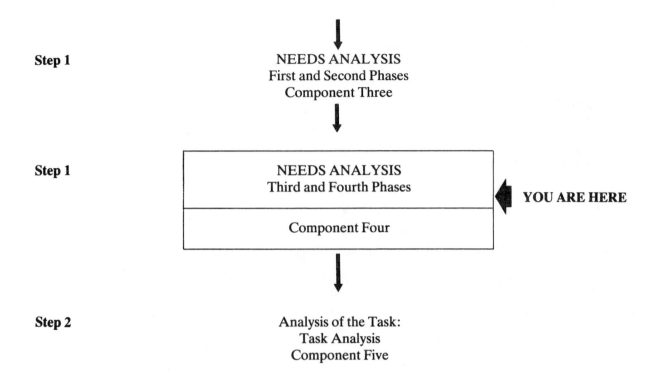

Step 1
NEEDS ANALYSIS
First and Second Phases
Component Three

Step 1
NEEDS ANALYSIS
Third and Fourth Phases

Component Four

◀ **YOU ARE HERE**

Step 2
Analysis of the Task:
Task Analysis
Component Five

Component 4:

Carrying Out the Needs Analysis: Third and Fourth Phases

Key Words

Measuring the needs ; perception and data discrepancy surveys; performance statements; paired scales; needs index; performance criteria; establishing needs; deciding on priorities for action.

Considered in this Component
System Activity: Analysis
System Function: Needs Analysis

We are now completing the last two Phases of the Four Phases of our Needs Analysis.

FIRST PHASE: How to determine Goals

SECOND PHASE: How to order the Goals

THIRD PHASE: How to measure the Needs

FOURTH PHASE: How to decide on Priorities

Third Phase:
How to Measure the Needs

Purpose

To measure the **discrepancies**, or **deficiencies**, between the actual and the **desired job performance**, i.e. the difference between 'what is' and 'what ought to be' and to express these as statements of Needs which will respond to training.

There are two themes underlying this Phase:
● Determining the current levels of actual job performance for each of the Second Phase Goals, Figure 37, i.e. finding out 'what is'.
● Comparing this actual job performance with the desired performance of the First Phase, i.e. 'what ought to be', Figures 33 and 37.

ACTUAL VERSUS DESIRED PERFORMANCE

ACTUAL

DESIRED

Figure 38

Inputs

Goals listed in Rank Order of importance from Second Phase (Figure 37).

Staff Involvement

As for previous Phases. You may want to call in an assessment specialist, or someone who has completed Package 6. However, the techniques explained here will be completely adequate by themselves.

Methods

Remembering that you are now collecting information which shows 'what is', i.e. current and actual job performance and making a comparison with 'what ought to be'. You are making a **discrepancy, or deficiency survey**. There are two main types:

A. Perception Discrepancy Survey
B. Data Discrepancy Survey

A. PERCEPTION DISCREPANCY SURVEY

We are concerned here with finding out the perceptions of AOP's about our Goals and Needs and about conditions as they exist now. How do the staff of our organisation perceive performances in the firm and to what degree do they believe improvement is needed?

▰▰▰ Checkpoint

In what areas of an organisation's activities do you consider the use of this type of survey to be suitable?

Perception surveys are used especially where relations between people are important, for example, when you are trying to improve the way in which:
- *Shop floor staff deal with customers.*
- *Receptionists and telephonists greet clients.*
- *Complaints by customers are dealt with.*

- *Salesmen deal with prospects.*
- *Management and operators get along.*

Technique One: Perception Survey
METHOD STEP ONE
First, you devise a questionnaire which makes statements about performances related to each of the training Goals identified in the First and Second Phases, Figure 37.

METHOD STEP TWO
These are called **Performance Statements** and you usually find that your general Goals may have to be broken down into several Performance Statements, each of which covers one of the operations embodied in each Goal. We will give you more examples of this later, but one example of the structure of a Performance Statement is, 'Our sales staff have very good customer relations with very few complaints made against them'.

METHOD STEP THREE
You now circulate these questionnaires to AOP's who individually rate each of the Performance Statements on two matching five-point scales; these are called **Paired Scales**.

- One scale shows their perception of 'what is', i.e. the condition as it actually exists now, or the actual performance; this is Scale 2 in Figure 40.
- The second scale shows their perception of 'what ought to be', i.e. the level or condition of the desired performance as it should exist; this is Scale 1 in Figure 40.

SKILLS AND KNOWLEDGE: AN IMBALANCE

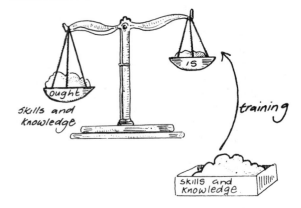

Figure 39

What do you think this Figure illustrates?

An imbalance between an operator's present skills and knowledge and what the operator should have, to do the job efficiently and effectively. Training can improve the balance of this situation.

Now let's put all of this together into an example of a questionnaire you would circulate (Figure 40) which uses a Goal identified before, i.e. 'Trainers should be able to operate a wide range of a-v equipment'. The Performance Statement of Figure 40 is derived from this Goal.

PERCEPTION SURVEY: PAIRED SCALES

Performance Statement: 'Our trainers can operate a wide range of audio-visual equipment efficiently'

Circle the Number which you think shows the appropriate degree of truthfulness for this Performance Statement

Scale 1:   This condition **should** exist

TRUE | ⑤ | 4 | 3 | 2 | 1 | **UNTRUE**

NEED INDEX:
(Leave this box blank)

Scale 2:   This condition exists **now**

TRUE | 5 | 4 | 3 | ② | 1 | **UNTRUE**

Performance statement ....

Figure 40

After the questionnaire is completed, you fill in the Need Index Box. In this case you write 3, which is the Need Index, ie $5 - 2 = 3$.

The Need Index of 3 shows that a Need has been established, as far as this responder is concerned.

The box shown in Figure 40 is part of the actual questionnaire which you would circulate to AOP's. The remainder of the questionnaire would consist of other Performance Statements and their associated paired Scales and Need Indexes (see overleaf).

METHOD STEP FOUR

The overall discrepancy, or deficiency, for each Need is established by **adding together all of the Need Indexes indicated by responders in their replies to each Performance Statement.** So if there are, say, 20 responders to the Performance Statement in Figure 40 and each averaged, say, a Need Index of 3 when completing their Paired Scales, the overall Need Index when added up would be 60. Quite a substantial need is indicated!

What are Performance Statements?

A description of Performance related to and derived from each Goal in the First and Second Phases of the Needs Analysis. Remember that a Goal is NOT a Need. Let's give you an example of this. One of the goals of Bill Bloggs' life has been to make a great deal of money. However, as he has become a multi-millionaire he feels little need to achieve this goal. So Bill's goal, making money, is not the same as his need.

We can only establish Needs by examining Performance and each Goal will probably contain several performances which must be examined. The general performance indicators of the First Phase (Figure 33) should be consulted when writing your Performance Statements; they will be very helpful.

Questionnaires circulated to AOP's are made up of a series of Performance Statements and Paired Scales. The Performance Statements are derived from their related Goals. Each questionnaire could contain Performance Statements related to one, or two or three Goals. The actual Goals are not written into the questionnaire, of course; the responders see only the Performance Statements and the Paired Scales associated with each Performance Statement. A questionnaire could look like this:

QUESTIONNAIRE SHOWING PERFORMANCE STATEMENTS

Performance Statement One: ....

Circle the Number which you think shows the appropriate degree of truthfulness for this Performance Statement

Scale 1:   This condition **should** exist

TRUE | 5 | 4 | 3 | 2 | 1 | **UNTRUE**

Scale 2:   This condition exists **now**

TRUE | 5 | 4 | 3 | 2 | 1 | **UNTRUE**

> **NEED INDEX:**
> **(Leave this box blank)**

Performance Statement Two: ....

Circle the Number which you think shows the appropriate degree of truthfulness for this Performance Statement

Scale 1:   This condition **should** exist

TRUE | 5 | 4 | 3 | 2 | 1 | **UNTRUE**

Scale 2:   This condition exists **now**

TRUE | 5 | 4 | 3 | 2 | 1 | **UNTRUE**

> **NEED INDEX:**
> **(Leave this box blank)**

Performance Statement Three ....

Figure 41

What is a Need Index?

An indication of the degree to which a Need exists. *The size of the Need is shown by adding up the individual Need Indexes. The greater the total the greater the Need.*

METHOD STEP FIVE

You'll recollect that we said that your general Goals can usually be broken down into several Performance Statements and that the questionnaire which you construct during the first step of this Perception Survey Technique should contain several Performance Statements related to the Goal shown in Figure 40 – see next Checkpoint.

GOAL: 'Trainers should be able to operate a wide range of a-v equipment'. Write down some examples of Performance Statements which can be derived from this Goal.

Here are our examples. No doubt you can add to the list.

- *'Our trainers can use video equipment efficiently'.*
- *'Our trainers can use 35mm projectors efficiently'.*
- *'Our trainers can make an effective audio tape'.*
- *'Our trainers can operate 16mm projectors efficiently'.*
- *'Our trainers can operate an OHP efficiently'.*
- *'Our trainers can write effective distance-learning material'.*
- *'Our trainers can write effective training materials'.*

Let's take two of these as examples and see how a typical responder may have replied.

QUESTIONNAIRE SHOWING SCALES (completed by trainee) AND NEED INDEX (completed by trainer)

PERFORMANCE STATEMENT: 'Our trainers can write effective distance-learning material'.

Circle the number which you think shows the appropriate degree of truthfulness for the Performance Statement

Scale 1:　This condition **should** exist

TRUE　| 5 | 4 | 3 | 2 | ①　**UNTRUE**

> **NEED INDEX:**
> **(Leave this box**
> **blank)**　0

Scale 2:　This condition exists **now**

TRUE　| 5 | 4 | 3 | 2 | ①　**UNTRUE**

PERFORMANCE STATEMENT: 'Our trainers can operate an OHP efficiently'.

Circle the number which you think shows the appropriate degree of truthfulness for this Performance Statement

Scale 1:　This condition **should** exist

TRUE　| ⑤ | 4 | 3 | 2 | 1　**UNTRUE**

> **NEED INDEX:**
> **(Leave this box**
> **blank)**　1

Scale 2:　This condition exists **now**

TRUE　| 5 | ④ | 3 | 2 | 1　**UNTRUE**

Figure 42

In the case of Figure 42, no Need is established for this responder who believes that the trainers cannot write distance learning materials, nor is there any requirement for them to do so.

Also, the responder thinks that everyone should be able to operate an OHP effectively, but that most of them are good at it anyway. A small Need is established, perhaps for a revisionary exercise, demonstrating more advanced OHP techniques.

When you have added up the scores for each Need Index for each Performance Statement shown in the last Checkpoint, let us imagine that the overall totals of the Needs Indexes came out as follows:-

PERFORMANCE STATEMENTS (Shortened)	OVERALL NEED INDEX
● Video	71
● 35mm Projector	39
● Audio	–6
● 16mm Projector	56
● OHP	8
● Distance-learning material	0
● Training materials	36

Remember to add up the Need Indexes for each Performance Statement, one at a time. After totalling the first Performance Statement Need Indexes then move on to the second Performance Statement and so on.

What do these figures mean to you?

Well, strong Needs are established for training in video and 16mm projector operation. Also use of 35mm projector and writing training materials (but not such strong ones). Nobody sees a Need to improve performance for OHP operation and distance-learning writing. Trainers are now actually better at making audio tapes than your organisation presently needs! Remember that you can vary your Performance Statements to get at the information which you wish to know.

METHOD STEP SIX

All you need to do now is to tabulate the Performance Statements and the overall Need Indexes for each one and state whether or not a **need** has been established.

PERCEPTION SURVEY: ESTABLISHING NEEDS

GOAL	PERFORMANCE STATEMENT	OVERALL NEED INDEX	NEED ESTAB-LISHED
Trainers should be able to operate a wide range of a-v equipment.	● Our trainers can operate a wide range of a-v equipment efficiently	60	Yes
	● Our trainers can operate video equipment efficiently.	71	Yes
	● Our trainers can use 35mm projectors efficiently.	39	Yes
	● Our trainers can make an effective audio tape.	−6	No
	● Our trainers can operate 16mm projectors efficiently.	56	Yes
	● Our trainers can operate an OHP efficiently	8	No
	● Our trainers can write effective distance-learning material	0	No
	● Our trainers can write effective training materials.	36	Yes

Figure 43

ESTABLISHING NEEDS

NEED

NO NEED

Figure 44

SOURCES OF DATA

- Rating of Performances based on observing the job.
- Skills Test Results.
- Return Goods Figures.
- Sales Figures.
- Reject Rates.
- Output per Operator.
- Quality Control Results.
- Materials Wastage.
- Accident Rates.
- Breakdown Figures.
- Machinery Downtime Figures.
- Tool Breakage Rates.
- Cycle Times.
- Data produced by your own tests and methods.

So we are involved here with the **numerical assessment** of deficiencies, rather than with the **opinions** of the perception survey.

Technique Two: Data Discrepancy Survey
METHOD STEP ONE
With your Working Party, decide on what sort of data you want and where to get it, i.e. what source you will use. You have to collect data for each of your Goals in order to assess how things are ('what is'). If your organisation has this information available already then your job is made that much easier.

INFORMAL SURVEY

Figure 45

B. DATA DISCREPANCY SURVEYS
Here we are concerned with collecting data in order to **assess the way things are.** Instead of determining the perceptions of AOP's, we are using statistical materials to decide on levels of performance skills and knowledge. You will get your statistics from all sorts of sources and you may wish to develop your own test instruments (many are described in Package 6) which will provide the data. It all depends on which performance you are focussing.

Can you suggest some sources of data within your organisation?

We give some possible sources here, but they are only examples, as sources will vary greatly from firm to firm, depending on what your differing organisations do.

METHOD STEP TWO

If the information is not available readily, then you and your Working Party have to decide how to get it and what methods or records you have to develop to provide the required data about the actual job performance. Try to ensure that your methods are quick and not too elaborate. **As examples, you can arrange for skills tests of operators, or if knowledge of a process is required, then a multiple choice question paper would determine what the operator knows about the process.** Obviously, where operators or trainees are projected to join your training course, you concentrate on them, including those who are scheduled to pass examinations for a qualification. Results from your Entering Behaviour Analysis (Component Seven) our System Step Three, will be useful here.

METHOD STEP THREE

From information available already, or from your own tests or whatever method you have elected to use, you now know the current, actual job performance.

METHOD STEP FOUR

The next step is for your Working Party and selected AOP's to determine, or find out, what is an acceptable level of performance for a competent operator for each of your Goals. How much skill or knowledge does the operator who has reached the desired level of skill or knowledge have to achieve? What criteria do you judge by? These standards are stated statistically, (you will find your general performance indicators from Figure 33 useful here) and are called **Performance Criteria.**

METHOD STEP FIVE

If there is a difference, or discrepancy, between the actual job performance and the Performance Criteria and the difference is positive, then you have established a Need. There may be only one **Performance Criterion.**

▰▰▰

Consider several jobs in your organisation for which you know the current, actual job performance and the Performance Criteria. Can you establish any training Needs?

Here are some examples; again answers and examples will vary widely because of the huge range of job performances in industry, commerce and the service industries, so let's begin with our familiar Sprigg's Cannonball Factory.

- *In Sprigg's, each cannonball is required to be made to 1/200 inch tolerance. This is the Performance Criterion. However, tolerances on the actual job are to 1/100 inch. A Need for training is established, presuming that the cannonball making machinery is OK.*
- *In a garment factory, the wastage rate in the job is 22%; management wants it to be 8% only (the Performance Criterion). Output is 30 garments per*

shift and the Performance Criterion is also 30. In the case of the first of the Performance Criteria, a Need is established, in the case of the second, no Need is established.

METHOD STEP SIX

You now tabulate your findings. As we are all from different jobs we'll use Sprigg's again as a sort of common ground.

DATA DISCREPANCY SURVEY: ESTABLISHING NEEDS

JOB	ACTUAL JOB PERFOR-MANCE	PERFOR-MANCE CRIT-ERION	DEFICI-ENCY IN PERFOR-MANCE	NEED ESTAB-LISHED
Tolerance of size of cannonballs	1/100 inch	1/200 inch	1/100 inch	Yes
Weight of cannonball	4.5 kg	4 kg	0.5 kg	Yes
Sphericity of cannonball	Perfect Sphere	Perfect Sphere	Nil	No
Reject Rate	15%	2%	13%	Yes
Wastage Rate, Iron	21%	5%	16%	Yes
Output per shift	101 Cannon-balls	100 Cannon-balls	Nil	No
Cooling time per ball	16 minutes	25 minutes	9 minutes	Yes
Cannonball hardness (according to C.H. Scale)	Scale 4	Scale 5	Scale 1	Yes
Surface smoothness	95% Smooth	100% Smooth	5%	Yes
Bounce Factor	1 Bounce/foot	1 bounce/foot	Nil	No

Figure 46

1/100 INCH CAN MAKE ALL THE DIFFERENCE

Figure 47

Output

Finally, prepare a list of Need Statements for each of the Needs which you have identified.

However, make sure that you delete non-training Needs first. For example, in the case of Spriggs it has been found that the equipment used for cooling the cannonballs (a water spray) is ineffective. As this is not an operator deficiency which can be improved by training you do not accept it as a training Need.

TRAINING IMPROVES OPERATORS, NOT EQUIPMENT

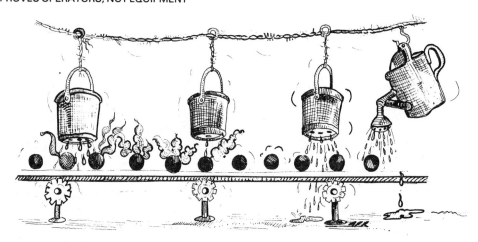

Figure 48

You base your Need Statements upon identified Needs for which you can offer training and for which there is a high Need Index (Perception Survey) or a Need established by a significant statistical etc Performance Deficiency (Data Survey).

NEED STATEMENTS

NEEDS - showing training required	NEED INDEX	DEFICIENCY IN PERFOR- MANCE	TARGET POPU- LATION
1. Operation of a-v equipment general	60	–	Trainers
2. Operation of video equipment	71	–	Trainers
3. Operation of 35mm Projector	39	–	Trainers
4. Operation of 16mm Projector	56	–	Trainers
5. Writing Training Materials	36	–	Trainers

NEEDS - Sprigg's Cannonballs			
1. Achieving smaller tolerances on cannonballs	–	1/100 inch	Cannonball Operatives
2. Pouring the pig iron to correct weights	–	0.5 kg	Pourers
3. Reducing reject rates	–	13%	Operatives
4. Reducing wastage rate, iron	–	16%	Operatives
5. Cannonball hardening process	–	Scale 1	Hardeners
6. Improving moulding process for surface smoothness	–	5%	Moulders and Finishers

Figure 49

Two of the Need Statements shown in Figure 49 are only generally indicative of the type of training needed. Which are they?

They are Need Statements Number 1 for Trainers and Number 3 for Cannonball Operatives. Number 1 shows a general need for training only, although the other statements define the Needs more closely, once you have been alerted to the overall Need. Number 3 Need Statement will be improved when training is given for the remaining needs, where overall greater efficiency will reduce the reject rates automatically. Probably the only training required for Number 3 will be a lecture - presentation, highlighting the importance of reducing reject rates and the factors which can contribute to such a reduction.

Fourth Phase: How to decide on Priorities

Purpose

To list the Needs in order of priority for action. For those Needs which have a Need Index, the job has been done for you already. For the others, you'll have to make a subjective decision. To help you to do this you should certainly take advice from your Working Party and as many AOP's as possible.

Inputs

List of Need Statements from the Third Phase, (Figure 49).

Staff Involved

As for the previous Phase, but the Working Party may play an even bigger part.

Methods

You may have to give each Need Statement a rating, so that they can be listed in order of priority.

NEEDS: LISTING YOUR PRIORITIES

Figure 50

Read through Components Two, Three and Four and consider ways of prioritising Needs. What methods do you believe would be useful?

Here is our selection of methods:
1. First you have to select which information you will use to decide on your order of priorities. This means that you are rating the Needs according to various criteria.
These could be as follows:-
● *Rate Need Statements according to Need Indexes from your Perception Survey (Figure 49).*
● *Use the rank of the corresponding Goal from which the Need was derived originally. So you arrange your Needs priority according to the rank order of the Goals in the Second Phase output (Figure 37). Do remember that a Goal is not a Need, so this method is not completely accurate.*
● *Find out for how long the Need has existed. The longer the Need, the higher the priority.*

A LONG EXISTING NEED

Figure 51

As a trainer, how do you view the Need demonstrated by the Tower of Pisa?
Although the Need is long existing, it is a building (environmental) Need and certainly can't be improved by training so it doesn't concern you. However, the original builders of the Tower could have done with a little more training.
● *Determine how many trainees or operators are affected by each Need and give highest priority to the Need with the greatest Number.*
● *By discussion with your Working Party and the management element of your AOP's, decide on*
  ● *the cost of meeting the Need, compared with the cost of ignoring it, and for*
  ● *the impact that reducing the Need by training would have on the Company operation.*
Biggest differences in cost and greatest impact are Needs with the highest priority.
2. Now list your Need Statements in rank order of priority.
3. With the consensus of your Working Party, AOP's and management set actual target dates for the resolution of the Needs.

NEED STATEMENTS IN ORDER OF PRIORITY OF ACTION

NEED STATEMENT IN ORDER OF PRIORITY: Training required in:	TARGET POPULATION	TRAINING BEGINS/ENDS	TYPE OF TRAINING
Operation of video equipment	Trainers	1 March 21 March	Full-time intensive, groups of 3
Operation of 16mm Projectors	Trainers	23 March 28 March	4 x 1 hour Workshop
Operation of 35mm Projectors	Trainers	2 April 2 April	1 x 2 hour Workshop
Writing training materials	Trainers	10 May 1 August	1 x 2 hour sessions weekly
Sprigg's Cannonballs			
Achieving smaller tolerances on cannonballs	Selected cannonball operatives	1 March 24 March	Full-time Workshops, 2 days; 10 groups of 12
Improving moulding process for surface smoothness	Selected Moulders and Finishers	10 March 20 March	3 x 2 hour sessions; 3 groups of 6
Pouring pig iron to correct weights	Selected Pourers	23 March 23 March	2 x 3 hour sessions; 2 groups of 8
Cannonball hardening process	Hardeners	2 April 4 April	4 x 2 hour sessions; 4 groups of 4
Reducing wastage rate, iron	All Operatives	10 May 14 June	1 day, full time; Workshops; 20 groups of 7
Reducing Reject Rates	All Operatives	May - August	1 hour lecture presentations; groups vary

Figure 52

Conclusion

You now have a complete list of Need Statements showing what training is required, who is to be trained and when. You may wish to get management confirmation of your proposals before embarking on the next step or Function of your design system, that of Task Analysis.

SKILLS AND KNOWLEDGE: A BALANCE

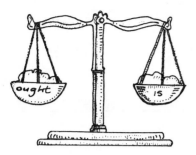

Figure 53

Summary of Components Three and Four

We will make our summary of the last two Components in diagrammatic form covering the whole of Step One in our System of Design (See Figure 54).

Finally, you may wish to carry out your own Needs Analysis. Contact your tutor if you have any problems.

Start	NEEDS ANALYSIS System Step One

FIRST PHASE:	**DETERMINING THE GOALS**
INPUT	Sources
METHODS:	Preset Survey; Open Survey; Delphi Technique; In-a-hurry; Task Analysis; Performance Analysis
OUTPUT:	List of Goals and general performance indicators

SECOND PHASE:	**ORDERING THE GOALS**
INPUT:	List of Goals from First Phase
METHODS	Rating Survey; Card Sort; Q Sort; Budget Allocation; Paired Weighting Procedures
OUTPUT:	List of Goals in rank order of importance and weightings

THIRD PHASE	**MEASURING THE NEEDS**
INPUT:	List of Goals in rank order from Second Phase
METHODS:	Perception Discrepancy Survey; Data Discrepancy Survey
OUTPUT:	List of Need Statements, Need Indexes and Deficiencies in Performance

FOURTH PHASE	**DECIDING ON PRIORITIES**
INPUT:	List of Need Statements from Third Phase
METHODS:	Need Index; Rank of Goal; Length of Need (time); Size of Target Population; Cost; Impact
OUTPUT:	List of Need Statements in order of priority for action, target population, details of training proposed

	END

SYSTEM STEP TWO
TASK ANALYSIS

Figure 54

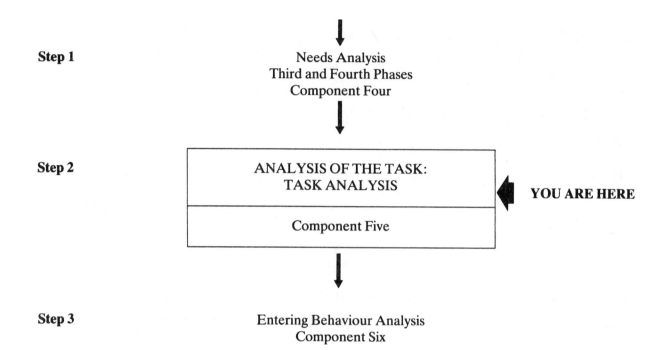

Step 1

Needs Analysis
Third and Fourth Phases
Component Four

Step 2

ANALYSIS OF THE TASK:
TASK ANALYSIS

Component Five

YOU ARE HERE

Step 3

Entering Behaviour Analysis
Component Six

Component 5:

Task Analysis

Key Words

 Job, topic and skill analysis, levels of analysis; unit of analysis; duties; tasks; task elements; rules; acts; cues; sequencing and style.

Considered in this Component
System Activity: Analysis
System Function: Task Analysis

Use of the term 'Task Analysis' varies a great deal between users and occupations; very little is standard. As far as possible, we will avoid the use of too many of these differing terms, so avoiding confusion. We'll concentrate on what you do when you make an analysis.

Obviously, we are analysing a task here and in training this usually means a job or a topic or a skill. We know already that when analysing we are breaking the subject of analysis into smaller parts, or **units of analysis**, and we have seen examples of this in previous Components. This process of analysis can be repeated several times, with the products of the first analysis being examined again in greater detail and then again and again, if necessary. Each breakdown represents a **Level of Analysis.**

▨▨▨ Checkpoint

Attempt a definition of 'task analysis' yourself.

Here is our definition:

TASK ANALYSIS: A DEFINITION

'Task analysis is the process of breaking down, or analysing, a task into smaller and more detailed constituent units and of then sequencing these units of analysis in an order of priority based on their importance in the learning.'

Figure 55

Whether we are concerned with analysis of a Job or a Topic or a Skill the process of task analysis is the same, i.e. a

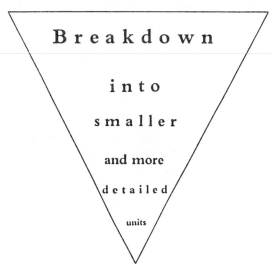

Draw a simple diagram to show the process of task analysis.

TASK ANALYSIS: BREAKDOWN INTO UNITS OF ANALYSIS

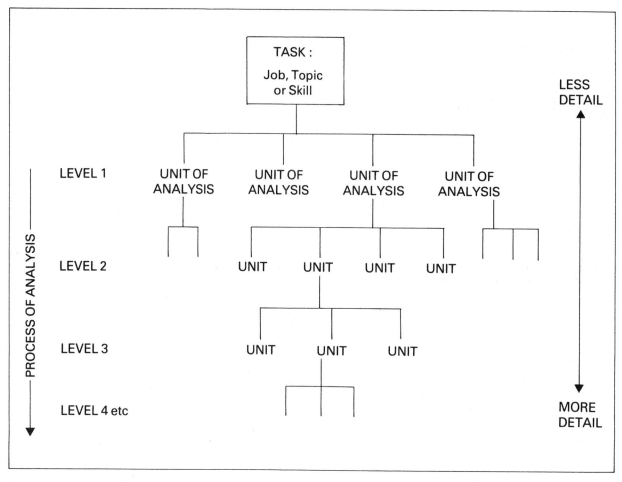

Figure 56

As you can see from Figure 56, there are always several Levels of Analysis and each succeeding level produces **greater detail** *than the one before.*

Let's take a topic with which we are all equally familiar, the external appearance of the human body and make a Task (Topic) Analysis of that.

Using the systems which we have described, draw your Topic Analysis in the way we have in Figure 56; number the Levels of Analysis.

Our diagram is shown on the next page.

TASK (TOPIC) ANALYSIS: THE HUMAN BODY, EXTERNAL APPEARANCE

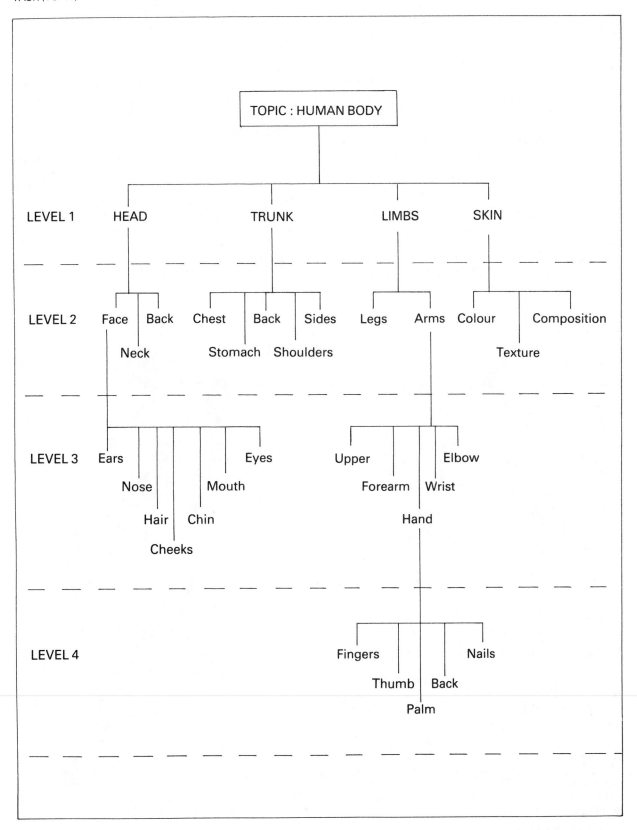

Figure 57

It is quite surprising what detail you can get into, isn't it, when you make a Task Analysis of a topic which appears quite simple and familiar on the surface? Because of shortage of space and a degree of delicacy, we have not developed many of the Levels of Analysis as extensively as we could have in Figure 57, but the diagram does show the Task Analysis principles of Levels of Analysis and increasing detail and how each Level follows **progressively and logically** from the one before it.

You can analyse anything, of course: jobs, skills, topics, primarily, but think of the variety under each of those. Obviously, we are concerned with jobs, skills and topics which have a training connotation, but you can analyse equipment design, working conditions, union rules or whatever, if you want to.

Below we show some units of analysis which we could call components or elements and which make up a piece of architecture. Can you guess what the architectural feature is of which they form units?

COMPONENTS OF ?

Figure 58

We have put these units or components together into an easily recognisable piece of architecture in the next diagram. We are trying to show here that Task Analysis helps organise your thinking in an orderly way and that **unrelated** thoughts, as units or components of anything are meaningless.

Now that we have defined Task Analysis, and shown how you go about it, we had better take stock and decide more closely how Task Analysis fits into our design system.

Where and when would you use Task Analysis?

Well, the somewhat evasive answer is 'Anywhere it is useful'. After all, it is really only a tool for helping you to think logically, so you can apply it where necessary.

However, there are some parts of our design system where it is particularly appropriate. We recommended it as a technique in Needs Analysis, if you remember: Technique Five in the First Phase. It will help us to analyse in detail the Need Statements of the Fourth Phase of Needs Analysis, Figure 52. Let's now examine these two uses in greater detail, beginning with Technique Five, First Phase, where we suggested that Task Analysis could provide us with a list of Goals for our Preset Survey. The job we were considering then, you'll remember, was 'Training Skills'. Have a try at working out your own Task Analysis before you compare it with ours, shown in Figure 59.

THEY ARE COMPONENTS OF NELSON'S COLUMN

Figure 58 (Assembled)

TASK ANALYSIS: 'TRAINING SKILLS'

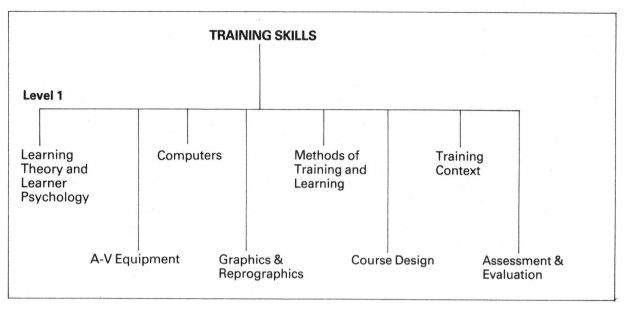

Figure 59

Naturally, when making your first Level of Analysis, you will take the advice of other trainers and experts in your own organisation (Working Party and AOP's) especially when the job is one which you personally don't know a great deal about. Now let's see what we can do with one of the Need Statements from Phase Four of Needs Analysis, Figure 52. 'Writing Training Materials'. Below is our first Level of Analysis:

TASK ANALYSIS: WRITING TRAINING MATERIALS

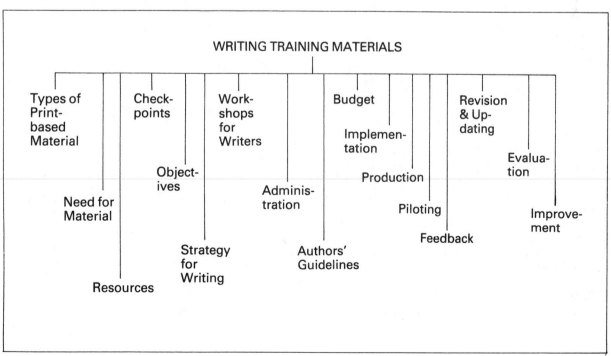

Figure 60

As you can see, making a Task Analysis of each of your Need Statements is the next essential step in our design system. Before we can proceed with designing our training systematically, we must carry out Task Analyses, so that we know what training we have to do and what areas we have to cover in detail. It is unlikely that we can decide on the length of training required, for example (shown in the fourth column of our final output from Needs Analysis, i.e. 'Need Statements in Order of Priority for Action', Figure 52) until we have completed the appropriate number of Task Analyses.

When Task Analysis is completed, we shall know what skills, knowledge and attitudes we have to deal with in training. We can then carry on with our systematic approach, by deciding on our objectives. So we have a sound basis for the content and key features of our training programme.

What are the principles of Task Analysis?

The principles are that:
- *Task analysis is accomplished by making succeeding Levels of Analysis.*
- *Each Level of Analysis produces its own Units of Analysis.*
- *Each succeeding Level of Analysis is more detailed than the one before it from which it derives.*
- *Units of Analysis focus increasingly closely on the task or job, and are more detailed than those previous to them.*
- *Each Level of Analysis and associated Units of Analysis follow logically and progressively from those which precede them.*

Can you illustrate these principles by a diagram?

TASK ANALYSIS: LEVELS AND UNITS OF ANALYSIS

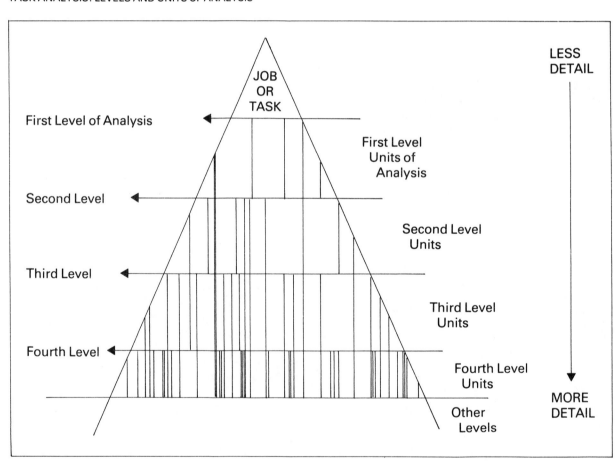

Figure 61

Now that we have established the principles of how to proceed when making a Task Analysis, we can carry on beyond the first Level of Analysis which we made in Figures 59 and 60 following the lines of Figures 56 and 57.

As space is limited, to begin with we shall develop only a couple of the first Level of Analysis units shown in Figure 59: 'A-V equipment materials' and 'Course Design'. Once again, before you look at our diagram try to follow through this Task Analysis, or part of it, yourself.

TASK ANALYSIS: TRAINING SKILLS

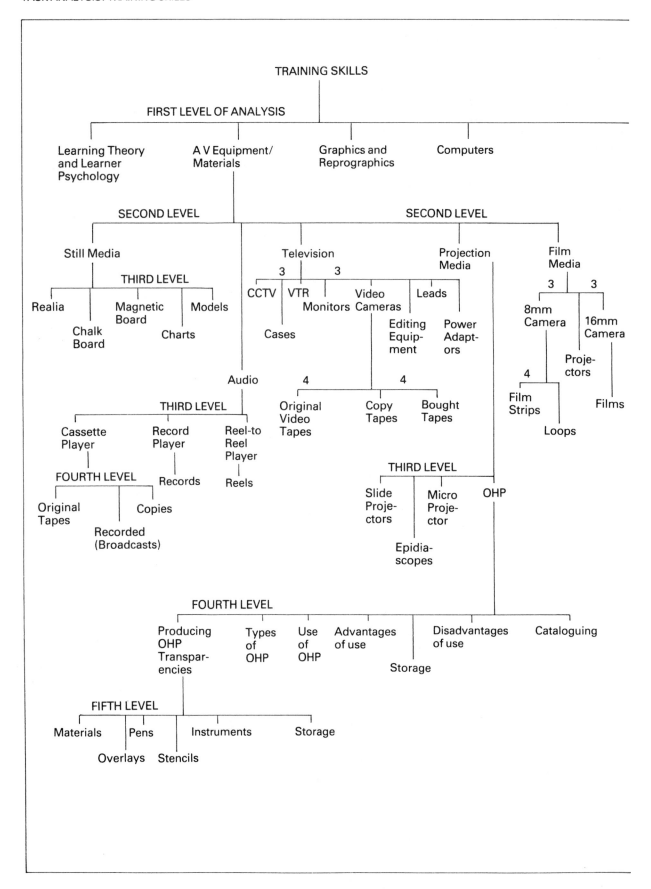

Figure 62

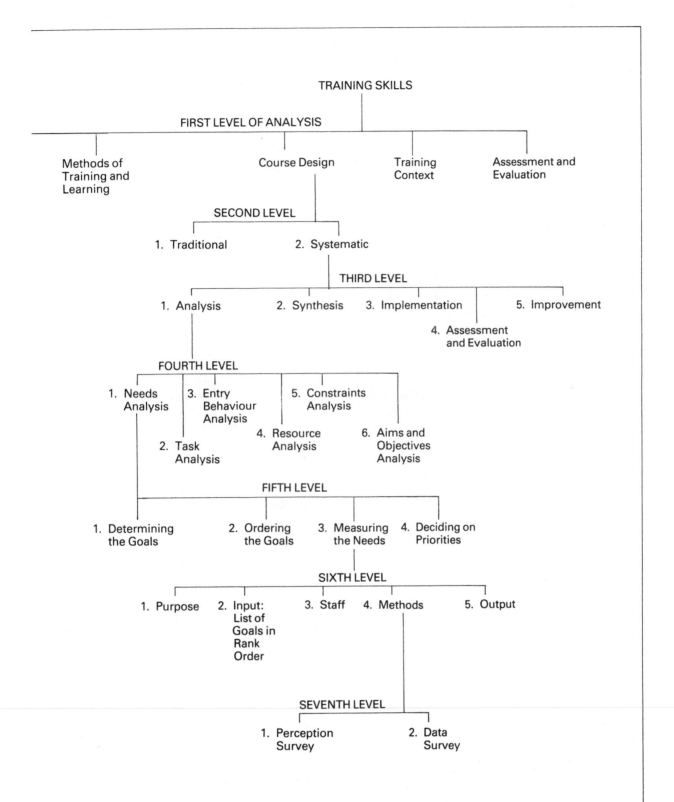

As you can see, Figure 62 is not exhaustive and we have selected only certain of the Units of Analysis for further examination at each Level of Analysis.

Figure 63 illustrates one question which you may wish to ask at this stage. What question does the Figure suggest to you?

'HOW LONG IS A PIECE OF STRING?'

Figure 63

Well, your question should have been, 'How many Levels of Analysis do I carry out?' You would be really asking the 'how long is a piece of string question' here, because you **analyse until you have the sort of detail which you want, or until your task or job operations are covered completely.**

Sometimes the Levels of Analysis which we have described are given names and the next Figure shows those which are commonly used. We are not enthusiastic about naming the Levels because this seems to suggest that you carry out the analysis a certain number of times only, i.e. according to the number of names which you have available; this is an unnecessary restriction. However, there are some names which you will meet commonly when reading.

NAMING THE LEVELS OF TASK ANALYSIS

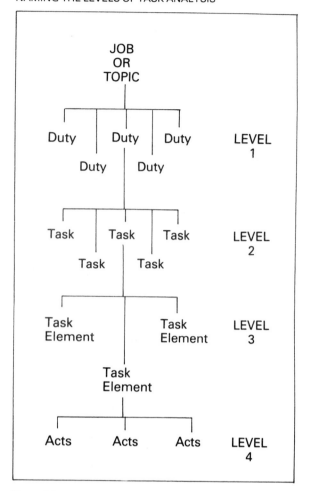

Figure 64

The names shown in Figure 64 do help by providing a structure upon which to base your thinking. When considering a task analysis you can ask yourself initially:

● What duties does doing this job entail?
● What tasks are performed in each duty?
● What are the elements of each task?
● What are the acts (actions) which go to make up each element?

These names refer to a Task (**Job**) Analysis; when making a Task (**Topic**) Analysis, we call the Task Elements by another name: **Rules.** There are other differences and points of emphasis between Job, Topic and Skills analysis and we will now look at these in detail.

TOPIC ANALYSIS

When you are getting down to the last Levels of Analysis, you will be considering the writing of the Rules. There are several important questions to ask yourself when Rule writing for a topic.

What do you think these questions are?

Well, in order to identify the Rules clearly and to make sure that they are understandable to everybody else, ask yourself these questions:

● *What do I expect the trainee to do to show that he or she has learned the topic?*
● *What questions will I ask the trainee?*
● *What level of performance or knowledge do I expect the trainee to attain when following procedures, undertaking tasks and carrying out techniques?*
● *How will I observe and measure successful performance by the trainee?*

Can you think of anything else to consider when making Rules?

There are two factors which you have to consider: the style in which Rules should be written and the sequencing of Rules.

When you **sequence** Rules you are showing the order in which your training will probably tackle them. Incidentally, sequencing all parts of your Task Analysis with a view to ordering your training is sensible and if you glance at Figure 62 again you'll see that we have sequenced the Course Design aspect of the Training Skills Analysis, carefully. You will also have realised that this section of the Task Analysis is part of the blueprint which we followed when constructing this Package.

Here are our rules for sequencing when you are writing your Rules as part of your planning.

RULES FOR SEQUENCING RULES

```
PROCEED FROM

1. Known to the unknown.
2. Concrete to the abstract.
3. Observation to reasoning.
4. Simple to the complex.
5. The whole view to the detailed view (as in
   Task Analysis itself).
6. Follow the correct chronological order,
   i.e. first things first.   Then:
   Number the rules accordingly.
   Keep the Rules in a sensible, logical
   sequence.
   Finally, ask yourself; 'Is this Rule which I
   am writing essential to the trainee's
   understanding of the Topic?' If in doubt
   leave it out!
```

Figure 65

How has the sequencing in Figure 62 been done?

The sequence always begins on the left. Start there for the first action of any sequence, then move to the right for succeeding actions.

WRONG SEQUENCING

Figure 66

Now what about the **style** of writing Rules? Here are our suggestions:

STYLE: 'RULES' FOR WRITING RULES

```
THE RULES SHOULD

1. Be stated simply and clearly.
2. Contain one fact, or idea.
3. Have one doing or active verb.
4. Be essential to the job.
5. Say what has to be done, not what
   hasn't.
6. Be all written at the same level.
7. Be short.
```

Figure 67

As an example of sequencing and writing we use part of a Task Analysis on Black and White film processing:

WRITING RULES: SEQUENCE AND STYLE

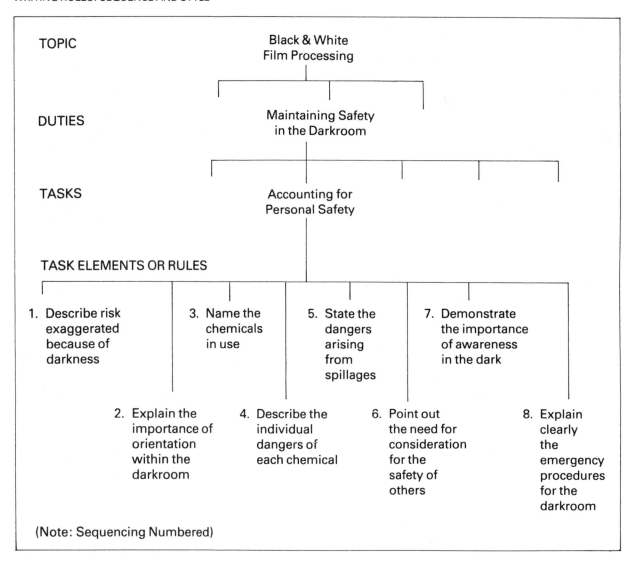

TOPIC — Black & White Film Processing

DUTIES — Maintaining Safety in the Darkroom

TASKS — Accounting for Personal Safety

TASK ELEMENTS OR RULES

1. Describe risk exaggerated because of darkness

2. Explain the importance of orientation within the darkroom

3. Name the chemicals in use

4. Describe the individual dangers of each chemical

5. State the dangers arising from spillages

6. Point out the need for consideration for the safety of others

7. Demonstrate the importance of awareness in the dark

8. Explain clearly the emergency procedures for the darkroom

(Note: Sequencing Numbered)

Figure 68

What advantages can you see in carrying out a Task Analysis of the type shown in Figure 68?

Help is given through your analysis in deciding what resources you need, in the training time required to cover the Topic, in the sequencing of your training objectives and in ensuring that you have a good preview of the training content and processes which you have to consider.

'SO YOU KNOW YOUR WAY AROUND IN THE DARK'

Figure 69

JOB ANALYSIS

The same procedure of undertaking Levels of Analysis is followed so that the job is placed in context, clearly defined and isolated.

The main difference between Topic and Job Analyses is in the writing of the Task Elements. In Job Analysis you will certainly find yourself on the shop floor watching a master performer or an experienced worker actually doing the job, preferably at a speed at which you can make notes. You are asking yourself, 'What does the experienced worker do?' and as he or she performs each one of the elements of the Task you write them down on an analysis sheet. When writing a Topic Analysis you would probably refer more to text books and manuals, as well as real-life situations; it's a question of emphasis.

The writing of the Task Elements follows the same procedure as the writing of Rules, but you'll also have to watch out for Cues which signal a required and/or different course of action on the part of the operator. Take care that you pick up and note down special tips, difficulties, hints or operating standards.

Cues are particulary important and we illustrate the main types here:

THE FOUR MAIN TYPES OF CUE

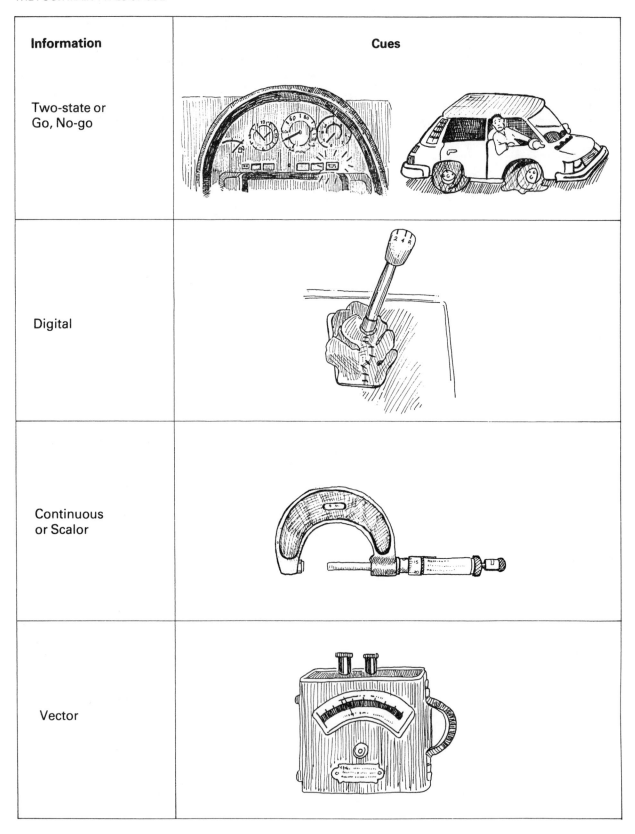

Information	Cues
Two-state or Go, No-go	
Digital	
Continuous or Scalor	
Vector	

Figure 70

Finally, you tabulate the Job Analysis information

We have given a simple example of a job which we all know — stopping a car and opening the bonnet:

JOB ANALYSIS: WRITING DOWN THE TASK ELEMENTS

TASK ELEMENT	CUE	SPECIAL CARE FACTORS
Foot off accelerator. Decelerate by applying brakes.		Until stationary
Depress clutch pedal	Feel Clutch losing 'bite' (1)	Depress slowly
Gear stick to neutral. Foot off clutch pedal.		Move to check in neutral
Apply handbrake.	Handbrake Warning Light on (2)	Safety Requirement
Switch off ignition.	Ignition Warning Light on (3)	
Depress clutch pedal.		
Gear stick to low gear. Foot off clutch pedal.		Safety Requirement
Pull Bonnet release.		Ensure fully released
Leave car.		
Release bonnet safety catch.		
Raise bonnet.		
Secure bonnet.		Safety Requirement

Figure 71

What types of cue are shown in this last Figure?

Physical — (1).
Two-state (go, no-go) — (2) and (3).

We have picked an example in Figure 71 with which we are all familiar, for obvious reasons. However, even though training roles vary greatly from one firm to the next, you will find that your job analysis is so comprehensive and detailed that it can often be used as an actual job aid which can help job performance immediately.

When the Job Analysis is completed you will have a very clear idea of the extent and type of training required. Always check your analysis for accuracy with the operator and then with the supervisor; you may then wish to observe the job being performed again, as a final check.

SKILLS ANALYSIS

Generally speaking, a job analysis will be sufficient for training purposes. Where a job is complex, unusual, requires very skilled movements or decision making, then you may have to make a Skills Analysis. Briefly, you have to break down each Task Element into the Acts which each operator does when performing a job. Therefore, Skills Analysis is an extension of Job Analysis: the procedure is the same, except it has at least one more Level of Analysis, giving greater detail.

Most of our Figures illustrating Task Analysis have been straight line diagrams. This is because the Levels of Analysis produce a hierarchy of Analysis Units as shown in Figure 68. As a method of revision, try to show the process of Task Analysis diagrammatically but not by using straight lines. Our attempt is shown in Figure 72.

TASK ANALYSIS: A DIFFERENT VIEWPOINT

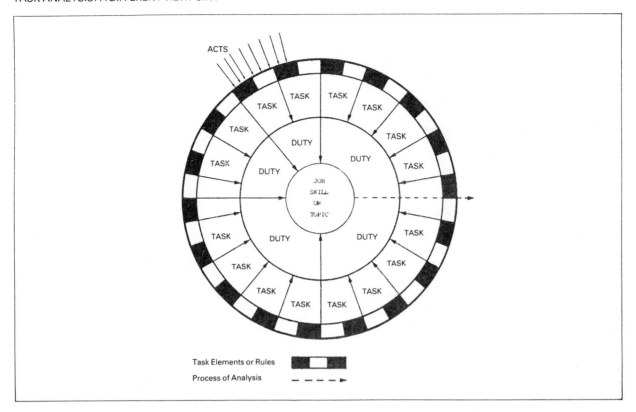

Now compare this with our straight line diagram shown below, which shows the same information in a different form.

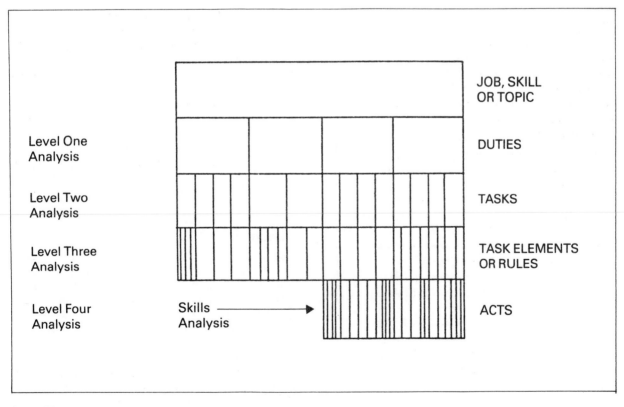

Figure 72

Because trainers are not required to carry out a Skills Analysis frequently, we'll give you a single example in Figure 73, so that the procedure is clear to you. By comparing Figure 72 and 73 you will see that Skills Analysis follows the same early procedures as Job Analysis, but adds another level of analysis to produce further and more detailed Units of Analysis called Acts. So, when making a Skills Analysis, carry out all of the stages for Job Analysis, then continue with stating Acts to complete the Skills Analysis.

SKILLS ANALYSIS CARRIES ON WHERE JOB ANALYSIS ENDS

TASK ELEMENT: Replace Rotor Arm	JOB ANALYSIS ENDS
ACTS Identify rotor arm Identify shaft Identify fingers and hand employed Position rotor arm to locate keyway Seat rotor arm securely.	SKILLS ANALYSIS CONTINUES

Figure 73

Whatever type of Task Analysis you are making, when you have completed your last Level of Analysis, there are several questions which you should ask yourself, whether your last Units of Analysis are Rules, Task Elements, Acts, or Units to which you have not given a name. We tabulate these questions as follows:

QUESTIONS WHICH YOU SHOULD ASK YOURSELF WHEN WRITING THE FINAL UNITS OF ANALYSIS

- What has the trainee to do to show that she or he has learned the Unit?
- When I ask the trainee questions about the Unit, will he or she be able to answer them with the training explanations, descriptions and demonstrations which I have arranged for him or her?
- Do the Units cover all of the fundamental parts of the job, topic, or skill?
- What changes is my training going to bring about in the attitudes of the trainee?
- Am I sure that my organisation wants these attitudinal changes, anyway?
- A last question, covering all of those above: 'If not, why not?'

Figure 74

Apart from the obvious advantages of asking yourself these questions, can you see any other benefits?

Benefits which we consider valuable are:
- *Helping you design your training lessons.*
- *Making sure that you have covered all that the trainee needs to know.*
- *Giving a basis for setting test questions and test procedures where skills are involved.*
- *Helping you formulate your objectives.*
- *These answers to these questions give a summary of the shape of your training.*

The questions shown in Figure 74 do help you to identify the final Units of Analysis accurately. You'll know you are on the right lines in the planning of your training if you can answer these questions affirmatively.

Summary

Task Analysis is the process of carrying out an 'Audit' or making an 'Inventory' of the knowledge, skills and sometimes the attitudes associated with performing a job, considering a training topic or examining a Need Statement.

There are three main types of Task Analysis:
Job, Topic and Skill.

In each case the fundamental process of analysis is carried out by breaking down the topic, or job, or skill into increasingly detailed components called Units of Analysis. Each 'breakdown' is called a Level of Analysis.

You may now wish to carry out a complete Task Analysis yourself, based on an activity in your place of work, but before you do so, let's revise how far we have got with our design system.

First, we completed a Needs Analysis and the product of that process was a list of Need Statements in order of priority for action (Column 1, Figure 52). Before you go on to complete the Need Statements table, Figure 52, you will find it helpful to gain an accurate perspective on length and type of training required by carrying out a Task Analysis for each Need Statement.

Subsequently, in our systematic approach, we will translate the information from Needs and Task Analysis into detailed objectives for our Training.

However, before we do that, we should take account of those other factors which affect our training before we move into the detailed planning of the training. These factors involve three main areas: the entry behaviour of our trainees; the resources which we have available; the constraints under which we work.

All of these factors affect our task and give a background to Task Analysis. So our next Components will undertake a study of these three main areas into which we grouped our factors and how they can affect our Task Analysis. We show this diagrammatically below.

DESIGN SYSTEM: STEPS ONE TO SIX

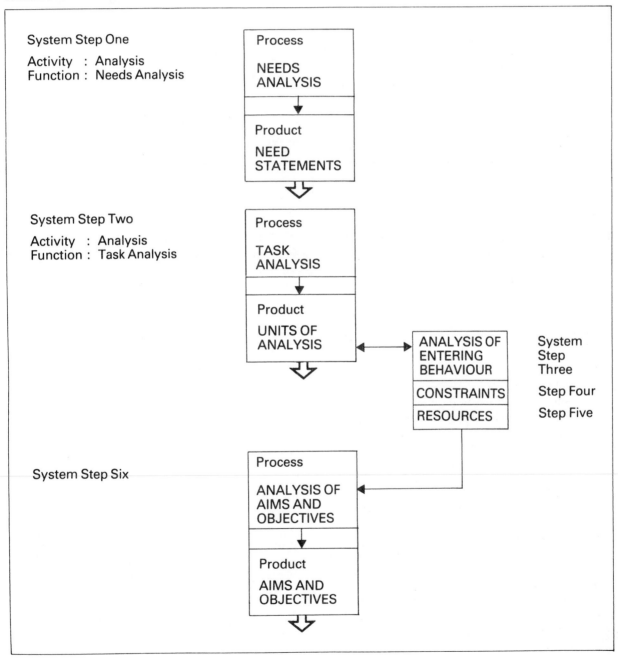

Figure 75

71

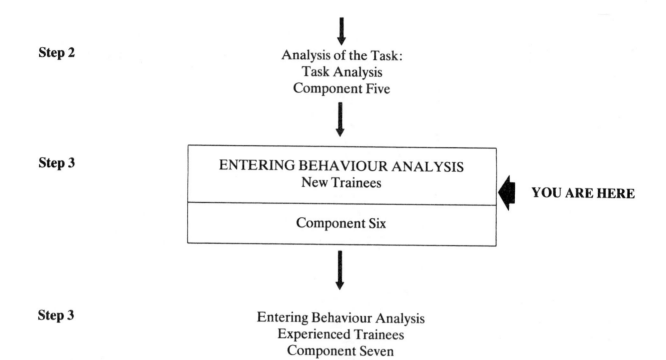

Step 2   Analysis of the Task:
Task Analysis
Component Five

Step 3   ENTERING BEHAVIOUR ANALYSIS
New Trainees   **YOU ARE HERE**

Component Six

Step 3   Entering Behaviour Analysis
Experienced Trainees
Component Seven

Component 6:

Analysis of the Entering Behaviour of the 'New' Trainees

Key Words

 Target population; entering behaviour; 'new' and more experienced trainees; aims of entering behaviour analysis; analysis of knowledge and mental skills; of motor skills; of attitudes; recorded and research information; pre-tests; pre-requisites; sources.

Considered in this Component
System Activity: Analysis
System Function:
Entering Behaviour Analysis

'Entering Behaviour: The behaviour, that is knowledge, skills and attitudes, which the trainees have when entering training'.

In this and the next Component we are examining the Entering Behaviour of trainees. We are going to find out what they know, what skills they have and what their attitudes are when they begin their training. This places the training on a firm footing and gives us important information on how the trainees themselves expect to gain. Knowledge about where the trainees are at the beginning of training also helps us to gauge how much they improve during the course. We can compare how far they have moved from their individual starting points, with where they have got to at the end of training. Consequently, we have a measure of the progress of each trainee.

Initially, when considering this System Function, there are two terms which we must define: 'Entering Behaviour' and 'Target Population'. Our definitions are shown as follows:

'Target Population: Those trainees at whom the training is aimed and for whom it is organised'.

▨▨▨ Checkpoint

In the literature on training you will see other terms used synonymously with Entering Behaviour and Target Population. Which of these terms have you come across before?

Some terms which are commonly used include:
Entry Behaviour; Target Audience; Target Group;
Entering Characteristics; Entering Knowledge.

In a way, looking at the Entering Behaviour of trainees is like launching a ship. When a ship (the trainee) enters the water (the training) it does certain things and these have to be calculated by the shipyard staff (the trainers). For example, the shipyard personnel have to calculate length of slipway and angle of launch, depth of water for launch, times of deep water, width of river into which the launch is made, the number and placement of retaining chocks and chains related to the weight and length of the vessel and the number of men needed for the job.

All this information has to be known and calculated to make the launch successful. Similarly, the trainer has to have a great deal of information before he launches his trainees into training . Failure to collect this information can result in training just as disasterous and misdirected as a bad launch. Cases have been known when a launched vessel has proceeded straight across the water and into the riverbank opposite!

MISCALCULATING THE LAUNCH

Figure 76

We are proposing to consider Steps Three, Four, and Five of our design system in Components Six, Seven and Eight, so that we can gather information which will help us to launch the training successfully.

We now have some idea of why we make our next three Steps of the systematic approach. We would also like to know when we carry them out and what we do in each case.

From Figure 12 shown in Component One, you can see that Steps Three, Four and Five appear to be executed simultaneously with the System Function of Task Analysis, Step Two. This is a suitable timing, but in practice we can make the analysis of Entering Behaviour, Resources and Constraints at any time during the carrying out of the System Activity of Analysis. During Needs Analysis we may find slack periods, for example, when waiting for our survey questionnaires to be returned, when we can set about analysis of Entering Behaviour.

During Step Two, we will find that Task Analysis information will help in providing a structure within which to work and will also be improved itself by information from other sources such as knowing more about the incoming trainees, the resources which we have available and the constraints which we work under.

So the most suitable time to carry out the System Functions of Steps Three, Four and Five of our design system is really when it suits you best as the training designer.

What you have to know are the methods of making these further system analyses and let's set about doing this now.

▨▨▨

Before beginning our analysis of Entering Behaviour, we have to recognise that the trainees fall into two broad groups and Figure 77 shows them. Can you put a name to each group?

Figure 77

This Figure shows that there are two goups of trainees which have such differing training requirements that we must consider them separately because their entering behaviours vary considerably. These two groups are:

● *'New' trainees*
● *More experienced trainees and experienced trainees*

You have some idea of the 'why' of making an analysis of Entering Behaviour of these two groups. Can you translate your general idea into something more formal, i.e. the Aims of this analysis?

Our Aims are shown in Figure 78.

ANALYSIS OF ENTERING BEHAVIOUR: AIMS

● To analyse the trainee's ability to cope with the training.
● To shape the training methods to suit the trainees.
● To develop an understanding of the trainee's potential.
● To provide information which will act as a background to the planning of the training and selection of the curriculum.
● To provide information with gives a depth of perspective on Needs and Task Analysis.
● To give an accurate perspective on the individual differences between trainees.

Figure 78

New Trainees

These are the trainees who are entering your firm directly from school or joining you for the first time. In Figure 78 we established our general Aims, but we now need to know in more detail just what we are trying to find out about these trainees.

WHAT ARE YOU TRYING TO FIND OUT ABOUT THE TRAINEES?

Figure 79

We think that Sherlock Holmes, whether he is a member of your Training Department or not, would be able to group his findings into three main areas:
● Trainee's Knowledge and Mental Skills
● Trainee's Physical or Motor Skills
● Trainee's Attitudes

Let's deal with these in order. The next three Figures do show the detail which you may need to find out, but the detail will vary according to the organisation which employs you, of course. We begin with trainee's knowledge and mental skills.

ENTERING BEHAVIOUR: KNOWLEDGE AND MENTAL SKILLS

● What does the trainee know about the job already?
● What is the trainee's standard of literacy?
● What is the trainee's standard of numeracy?
● What are the trainee's particular mental aptitudes and skills?
● What previous experience has the trainee had in the mental skills required by the training (and the job for which training is a preparation)?
● What do the trainee's records say about his or her potential for training in mental skills?
● What has the trainee achieved already in previous training tests and examinations in this area?
● CONCLUSION: Does the trainee appear to have the knowledge and mental skills necessary to undertake and complete training and the job for which the training is a preparation?

Figure 80

We have used the term 'mental skills' frequently, in Figure 80. What does it mean?

Mental skills cover a wide range of processes. Included amongst these are creativity; deductive capacity (arguing from generalisations to specific examples); inductive capacity (arguing from specific examples to generalisations); logical thinking; problem-solving capacity; word and number skills, e.g. report writing, articulateness, mathematical and accounting skills or just simple adding up, depending on the job the trainee is entering.

In Figure 80, the final point is a concluding question, to which the answer is 'Yes/No' or 'Maybe'. If 'No' or 'Maybe' then the trainee will require remedial training before entering full training.

Finally, it is up to you, as the trainer with specialist knowledge of the training and the job, to make sure that you establish accurately the level of knowledge and mental skills required of the trainee.

MENTAL SKILLS VARY GREATLY IN LEVEL

Figure 81

We will now turn to Physical or Manual Skills. These are usually termed Motor or Psychomotor Skills and are shown in Figure 82.

ENTERING BEHAVIOUR: MOTOR SKILLS

- What manual dexterity does the trainee have?
- What specific motor skills does the trainee have?
- What previous jobs has the trainee had which required the use of these skills?
- What previous training has the trainee had in the use of these motor skills?
- CONCLUSION: Does the trainee have the motor skills necessary to undertake training and do the job?

Figure 82

Obviously, for both mental skills and knowledge and for motor skills, you must have a clear idea of what knowledge and which skills are required by the job for which you are training. Task Analysis help here. You don't want to be finding out about skills which aren't required.

Finally we consider the trainee's attitudes and this is a much less well-defined area. After all, there is a huge variety of attitudes to everything in life, not just work and training and not all of these attitudes are expressed in physical terms which make them easy to identify.

ATTITUDES WHICH HAVE A PHYSICAL EXPRESSION

Figure 83

Having a 'good' attitude to work, i.e. being enthusiastic, diligent, and co-operative is important in all employment, but in some jobs, e.g. a receptionist, or where dealing with people is an important part of the work, it is vital that trainees show the ability to form good relationships with customers as well. With this in mind, let's have a look at some of the aspects of attitudes which we will want to know about.

ENTERING BEHAVIOUR: ATTITUDES

- ● How did the trainee get on with people (peers, staff, customers etc.) in previous employment or at school?
- ● Is the trainee diligent? Enthusiastic? Co-operative? Motivated?
- ● Does the trainee react well to correction?
- ● How does the trainee respond to advice?
- ● How does the trainee view the training?
- ● What are the trainee's expectations of the training?
- ● CONCLUSION: How trainable is the trainee?

Figure 84

We have touched on only a few aspects of attitudes. Make out a list of any others which apply to your work situation.

▨▨▨

Remember that we are considering what you do when making an analysis of Entering Behaviour. So far we have identified three main areas of information about trainees which we would like to know about. What are these areas?

We require information on trainee's knowledge and mental skills; their motor skills; their attitudes.

So far, so good, but we must tackle the question of finding out where this information comes from.

▨▨▨

What sources will provide us with the information we require?

There are two main sources; these are:
- ● **Information which is available already,** *i.e. recorded information.*
- ● **Information which you have to find out for yourself by research,** *i.e. research information.*

FINDING INFORMATION WHICH IS RECORDED

Figure 85

As Figure 85 shows, **Recorded Information** can be substantial in volume. We know the sort of information which the trainer in the Figure is looking for, but what sources is he consulting? Perhaps these sources can best be shown diagrammatically as illustrated in Figure 86.

ENTERING BEHAVIOUR ANALYSIS: SOURCES OF RECORDED INFORMATION ABOUT A NEW TRAINEE WHO **IS** A SCHOOL LEAVER

Figure 86

A TRAINEE WHO IS **NOT** A SCHOOL LEAVER

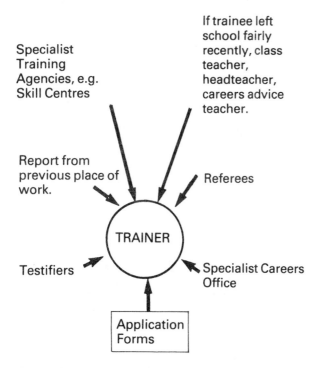

Figure 87

So much for recorded information. You may wish to support this by finding out for yourself, i.e. by developing your own sources which will provide **Research Information.** We will show these diagrammatically once more.

ENTERING BEHAVIOUR ANALYSIS: SOURCES OF RESEARCH INFORMATION ABOUT A NEW TRAINEE

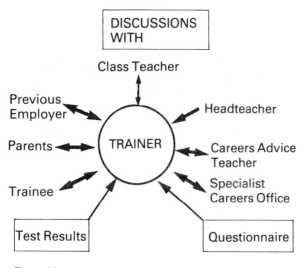

Figure 88

As you can see from Figures 86 - 88 most of the material for Recorded Information comes in the shape of reports, whilst you gain your Research Information by interviews and discussing the trainee with those who have the necessary knowledge. Two important new sources are shown in Figure 88 and they are **Test Results and Questionnaires.**

RESEARCH INFORMATION

Figure 89

Questionnaires

If Recorded Information is not available and it is difficult to arrange interviews, you may have to rely on distributing a questionnaire to informed people, rather like the Surveys of Needs Analysis. In any case, your interviews should be structured so that you obtain the proper information and your questionnaire will elicit the same material.

▰▰▰

What sort of material is this? Where is it shown in this Component?

The information which you require is shown in Figures 80, 82 and 84. If the Reports which you receive do not show it, then you will have to send out questionnaires anyway, to find out that information which you consider to be vital.

Test Results

As an alternative, or in addition, to reports, discussions and questionnaires, you may decide to **test** your incoming trainees. As they will be starting a job for the first time, you will want to know how far they measure up to it and you'll wish to identify those parts of the job where training is most needed.

You already have the structure of the task which faces the trainees in your Task Analysis and if you have begun to formulate your Objectives (described in detail in the next Study Unit) you will have a clear view of the direction of your training.

Tests given at this stage of training are known as **Pre-Tests** and they play an important part in the whole process of training assessment, in addition to helping you identify the strengths and weaknesses of your new trainees, see Figure 90.

PRE-TEST: FUNCTIONS

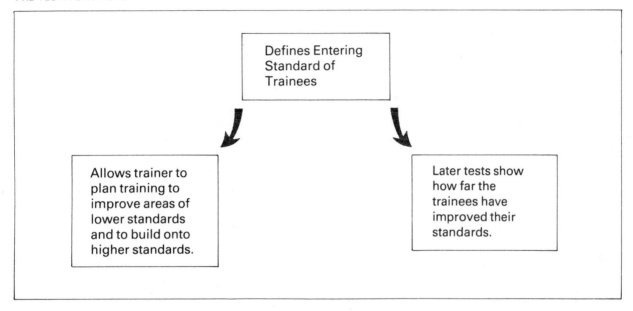

Figure 90

Frequently, trainees must have acquired certain skills and knowledge before they begin training. These 'need-to-know-before-training' requirements are known as **Pre-Requisites** and if a trainee does not know them, then preliminary, remedial training is needed before the trainee can embark on the normal course. Admittedly, this is less likely for new trainees who are school leavers than for more experienced personnel, but it is essential that trainers always consider this aspect of entering behaviour, making sure that the pre-requisites are identified correctly and tested.

So it is a question of bringing the right kit (the pre-requisites) so that you can play the training game.

Whether you are pre-testing knowledge and mental skills, or motor skills or attitudes, make sure that you test each piece of knowledge and skills which your training contains.

Remember, you are not setting a test which precludes entry to the training, unless the necessary pre-requisites are missing. Some trainees may know little or nothing about many of the test items. This is O.K.: you now know what to concentrate on in the training. Sometimes, it is said that the best result for a trainee is that he or she knows nothing about anything in the pre-test; improvement after training is then certain!

We can show these ideas diagrammatically in Figure 92.

PRE-REQUISITES: HAVE YOU BROUGHT THE RIGHT KIT WITH YOU?

Figure 91

RELATIONSHIPS BETWEEN PRE-TESTING AND THE LIKELY AMOUNT OF TRAINING REQUIRED

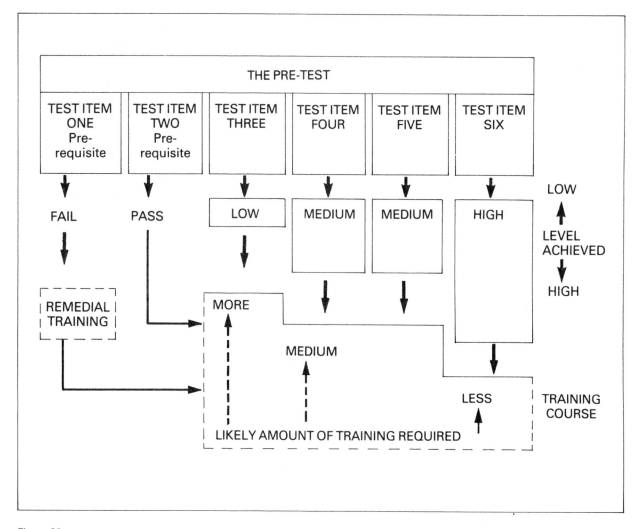

Figure 92

Describe in your own words, what you think Figure 92 shows.

A six-item Pre-test, two items of which are pre-requisites, one of which the trainee fails and has to take remedial training before joining the training proper. In Test Item Three, the trainee achieves a lower level of competence and consequently needs more training; in Item Six the trainee has a high level of achievement and requires less training; Items Four and Five are 'average' for both achievement and degree of training.

Figure 92 is very over-simplified, of course, but it does show the relationship between pre-test achievement and the planning of training, in a crude way. After a fashion, the pre-test helps you to 'foretell' the degree of training required.

FORETELLING THE TRAINING

Figure 93

We may not be able to provide you with a crystal ball in the Training Technology Programme, but our systematic approach ought to give you a good shot at prophesying the shape of your training by following the design system blueprint. You read the lines of the blueprint rather than the lines of your palm!

We have indicated in general terms that the analysis of entering behaviour of new trainees provides information which helps you plan your training. In the next Component, we will examine the entering behaviour of more experienced, or experienced trainees.

Finally, we will look in more detail at the way in which the **analysis information gained here may be used to plan training.** We offer a few examples of how this can work, in Figure 94. One example shows a new aspect: the fact that Entering Behaviour Analysis may help choose trainees, if **selection** is required.

TYPE OF TRAINING	TRAINEES	ACTION BY TRAINER
Well-established training: no changes anticipated.	Type of trainee who will benefit from training is known.	Select trainees from Entering Behaviour Analysis information which shows those trainees who fit required pattern most closely.
Established training: changes anticipated.	Entering Behaviour Analysis shows trainees have a different ability (wider, narrower, lower, higher) from previous entries.	Modify the emphasis of training to meet the requirements shown by Entering Behaviour Analysis.
Training not yet established: planning in progress	Entering Behaviour Analysis shows the profile of trainee's requirements.	Plan training accordingly

Figure 94

Don't forget that Entering Behaviour Analysis is supportive of both Needs and Task Analysis. We have shown them as separate System Functions and therefore steps in our Design System, but in practice they are interwoven and each provides different yet complementary information which helps the planning of training.

Summary

Entering Behaviour Analysis helps define the knowledge, skills and attitudes of the target population.

This analysis gives information which helps the trainer design the training by providing a profile of the learners, whether they are 'new' or more experienced trainees.

The analysis of Entering Behaviour is developed from sources of both Recorded and Research Information, by means of reports, interviews and discussions, questionnaires and Pre-Tests.

This type of analysis helps launch the trainees into training which is right for them.

Before you begin the next Component, consider carefully how the analysis of the Entering Behaviour of experienced trainees may differ from that of 'new' trainees.

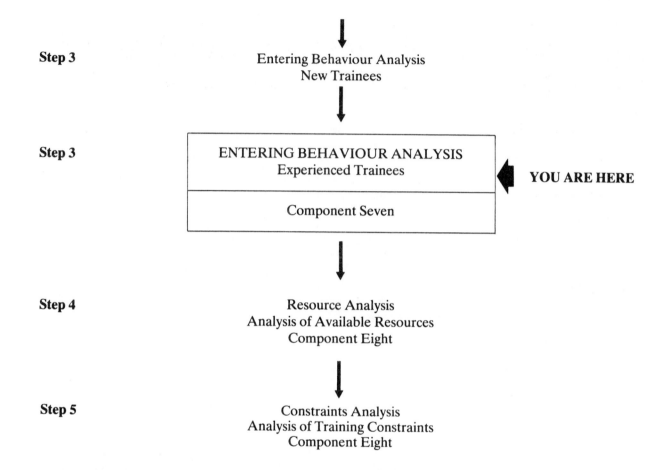

Step 3   Entering Behaviour Analysis
New Trainees

Step 3   ENTERING BEHAVIOUR ANALYSIS
Experienced Trainees   **YOU ARE HERE**

Component Seven

Step 4   Resource Analysis
Analysis of Available Resources
Component Eight

Step 5   Constraints Analysis
Analysis of Training Constraints
Component Eight

Component 7:

Analysis of the Entering Behaviour of More Experienced and Experienced Trainees

Key Words

Aims; knowledge; mental skills; motor skills; attitudes; recorded and research information; pre-course expectations; general expectations; detailed expectations; adjective rating scale; semantic differential; pre and post-tests; acquirement and accomplishment; planning and modifying training through entering behaviour analysis.

Considered in this Component
System Activity: Analysis
System Function:
Entering Behaviour
Analysis

In the last Component we considered the analysis of the Entering Behaviour of 'new' Trainees. We now turn to the Entering Behaviour of **more experienced and experienced trainees.** Mostly, there will be operatives who are employed already by your organisation and there will usually be some information available about them already.

In itself the term 'more experienced and experienced' trainees covers a wide range of employees; some might be young and have recently completed mastery of what they do in the firm. There will be all ages and all levels of skills and knowledge and some will be so experienced as to be hardly regarded as trainees at all. Similarly, the levels of your organisation from which they come will vary from tea boy to director!

WHAT! ARE ALL THESE TRAINEES?

Figure 95

Time for a little revision now. Have a look at Component Six again, to make sure that you have the structure of it firmly in your mind. We will follow the same structure in the first part of this Component, but will abbreviate our descriptions because you know some of the background already.

▰▰▰ Checkpoint

What are the Aims of Entering Behaviour Analysis?

See Figure 78, Component Six.

▰▰▰

What are you trying to find out about the trainee, whether new or more experienced?

Broadly, much the same things for both experienced and for new trainees. We can show this by an illustration.

WHAT DO WE WANT TO KNOW ABOUT THE TRAINEE?

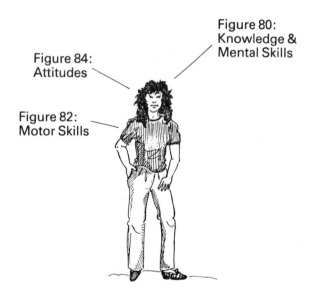

Figure 84:
Attitudes

Figure 80:
Knowledge &
Mental Skills

Figure 82:
Motor Skills

Figure 96

Now, what about the **sources** of information? Here we have differences between our new and our more experienced (let's just call them 'experienced' in future; you know what we mean!) trainees. We will deal with recorded and research information as before. Check with Figures 86, 87 and 88 before reading on. Let's begin with **Recorded** information.

ENTERING BEHAVIOUR ANALYSIS: SOURCES OF RECORDED INFORMATION ABOUT EXPERIENCED TRAINEES

REPORTS FROM

Previous Training
and Trainers

Organisation's
Employee Files

TRAINER

Employee Progress
Reports

Previous Entering
Behaviour Analysis

Supervisors

Management

Company Training
Policy Statements

Figure 97

The item shown in Figure 97, 'Company Training Policy Statements' is a general one and in it you would attempt to identify just where the trainee fits into the Company's training scheme and especially where he or she is on the ladder of training and promotion, e.g. what promotion is the person being fitted for and what is the next training they can expect after this course?

TRAINING CAN HELP YOU CLIMB THE LADDER

Figure 98

Turning now to **Research** information, you will already have material available from both your Needs and Task Analysis. You should recollect that our Needs Analysis furnished us with a list of Need Statements in order of priority for action, target population and some details of the training proposed (see Figure 52).

Our Task Analysis gave us a series of Units of Analysis which defined closely the detail of the knowledge and skill required to form a framework of training (various Figures in Component Five). So we already have a clear picture of who needs training and what that training is. Our analysis of Entering Behaviour will firm up the information available as it applies to each individual trainee. This is important; fitting the training to the person (sometimes called 'personalising' or 'individualising' the instruction) as far as possible is always worthwhile.

Obviously, the Needs and Task Analysis information can also be applied to new trainees, equally well, so you can now add these additional dimensions to the blueprint in Component Six.

We will now show diagrammatically the **Research** information which we can develop about experienced trainees.

ENTERING BEHAVIOUR ANALYSIS:
SOURCES OF RESEARCH INFORMATION ABOUT
EXPERIENCED TRAINEES

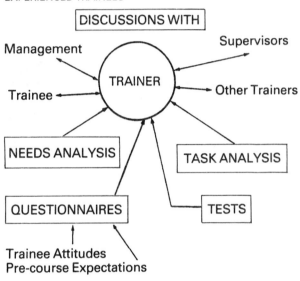

Figure 99

Remembering that our Needs and Task Analyses offered detailed information, but not about individual trainees, to help train each person better we should research each one individually with questionnaires and tests with a view to personalising the instruction, as we suggested above. All of this takes time, of course. Just how far you go in Entering Behaviour Analysis might well be limited by the time which you have available.

TIME WAITS FOR NO TRAINER

Figure 100

Let's examine the use of questionnaires and tests (pre-tests) more closely. Revise the appropriate sections of Component Six which describe the use of questionnaires and test results before you read on.

Questionnaires

As we suggested for new trainees, you may well wish to support your discussions and interviews with your sources of research information (Figures 99 and 88) by the use of questionnaires which give you information in writing. Such material is easier to record, store and analyse than that which comes from interviews, for example. Your questionnaires will find out about trainees' knowledge, skills and attitudes and help to build up your picture of each trainee. When added to and compared with information from your Needs and Task Analyses, you will find that the shape of the training required is beginning to build up in your mind.

THE SHAPE OF THE TRAINING

Figure 101

Formulate your questionnaires so that you are asking specific questions about the jobs and job performance of each trainee.

Questionnaires are especially useful in finding out about the attitudes of trainees; each trainee answers your questionnaires personally, of course. An important area here is finding out what the trainee thinks about the training which he or she is to undertake and what the likely benefits will be. These are called **Pre-course Expectations.**

TRAINING QUESTIONNAIRES: PRE-COURSE EXPECTATIONS

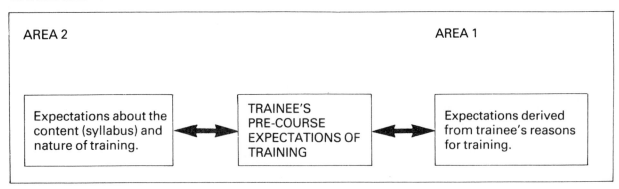

Figure 102

We now have to decide what sort of questionnaires are to be answered by every trainee for each of the two Areas shown in Figure 102.

We shall begin with Area 1.

Questionnaire about Area 1, Figure 102: Expectations derived from trainee's reasons for joining.

QUESTIONNAIRE, AREA 1:
PRE-COURSE EXPECTATIONS DERIVED FROM A TRAINEE'S REASONS FOR TRAINING

Answer very carefully on the sheets of writing paper attached, each of the following questions which apply to you. Don't worry if some of your answers seem to overlap each other.

1. What is your main reason for joining this Course?

2. Did you volunteer, or were you selected?

3. If you were selected, who selected you? Management, a Supervisor or some other person?

4. What did Management/a Supervisor tell you to expect this training would do for you?

5. Is this training to prepare you for another job?

6. If it is, which job?

7. Do you hope for promotion after this training?

8. Do you expect to receive a pay rise after the Course?

9. Are you hopeful that training will generally equip you better for the future, even if immediate promotion is not likely?

10. Do you anticipate that this training will increase your satisfaction with your present job?

11. Do you expect this Course to prepare you for further training?

12. Would you expect such training to happen soon, or later?

13. If you do expect further training, what sort of Course do you hope to take?

14. Can you write down how you expect this training to improve your efficiency?

15. What and when was the last training which you did?

16. Any training before that? When and where and what?

17. Do you think you need any help in how to study?

18. Is there any other information which you would like to add?

NAME IN BLOCK CAPITALS .... SIGNATURE ....

Figure 103

These are only examples of the questions which you might ask. You'll have to jiggle them around perhaps deleting some and thinking of new ones which may be more pertinent to your training and your organisation. Mix general with specific questions and remember that what trainees write down first is the most important, i.e. these are the most salient considerations in their minds. You'll find some interesting answers!

THE VOLUNTEERS

Figure 104

Questionnaires about Area 2, Figure 102: Expectations about the content (syllabus) and Nature of the Training

Turning to the second area shown in Figure 102, how do you find out what the trainee's expectations are about the forthcoming training itself? This is an important area; the attitudes of the trainees will have a significant influence on what they learn. Certainly, if they are hostile to the training they are unlikely to learn much, or to learn it well. There are two areas for consideration as shown in the next Figure and we shall show questionnaires on each.

QUESTIONNAIRES, AREA 2:
TRAINEE EXPECTATIONS ABOUT THE CONTENT (SYLLABUS) AND NATURE OF TRAINING

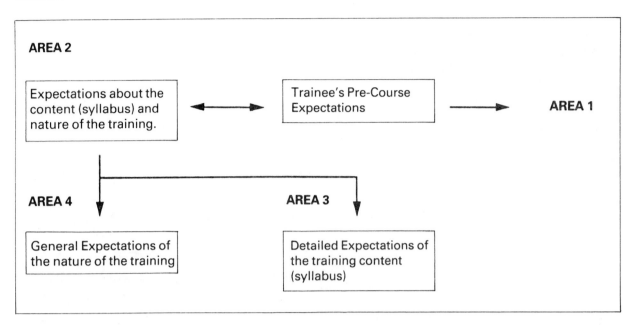

AREA 2

Expectations about the content (syllabus) and nature of the training.

⟷

Trainee's Pre-Course Expectations

⟶

AREA 1

AREA 4

General Expectations of the nature of the training

AREA 3

Detailed Expectations of the training content (syllabus)

Figure 105

Questionnaires about Area 3, Figure 105: Detailed Expectations of the Training Content

Under this heading you must examine how the trainees view the content of the course, whether or not they have developed positive or negative attitudes to all or parts of the training, so encouraging or impeding learning; where their values lie in relation to the various elements of the training; which parts they consider likely to be most useful; whether they would prefer the balance to be changed by reducing certain elements or introducing new ones; any options they would consider valuable; whether they are satisfied with the look of the proposed training as it is, or if they really don't mind.

Quite a lot to think about there! Of course, modifying an established course, or your plans for a new one, is usually restricted by lack of time, resources and even energy, but at least you will know what your students want.

A TRAINER UNDERTAKING CAREFUL MODIFICATIONS OF A TRAINING SYLLABUS

Figure 106

Now what about a questionnaire covering the trainee's detailed expectations of the training content? In the example shown next we have omitted detail of the topics under the training content, so that you can fill in your own topic details according to your course. Your Needs and especially your Task Analysis will offer valuable guidance here; if you are planning new training you could fill in the blanks in Figure 107 with Tasks or Task Elements, (depending on the detail you will want). If the training which you are considering is established, then you will have a syllabus available already. (Later you might use your training objectives when we have considered that part of the systematic approach). Here is our questionnaire.

The Systematic Design of Training Courses

TITLE OF COURSE ....

Fill in the questionnaire by ticking (✓) each scale on the right hand side of the form.
Place only one tick in each scale.

COURSE CONTENT   **SCALE**

DO YOU CONSIDER THIS TOPIC TO BE

TOPIC 1   **IMPORTANT TO YOU?**
(Describe the
details of one
topic of your

Very Important	Important	Fairly Important	Not very Important	Un-important	Don't know
course content
here)

INTERESTING TO YOU?

Very Interesting	Interesting	Fairly Interesting	Not very Interesting	Uninter-esting	Don't know

TOPIC 2   **IMPORTANT TO YOU?**

INTERESTING TO YOU?

TOPIC 3   etc, etc

Now add any topics which you would like to see included in this Course, and include your own
scales. You may add as many as you like.

Your Topic 1   **IMPORTANT TO YOU?**

INTERESTING TO YOU?

Your Topic 2   etc, etc

Have you any other comments on the Training?

NAME IN BLOCK CAPITALS..**SIGNATURE**............................

Figure 107

We have shown only three Topics, but your questionnaires will include all of the major topics in the content of your training. Consequently the questionnaire could extend to several pages in length.

You can vary what you ask in the scales, and how you ask it of course. You might want to enquire about what is 'useful' rather than what is 'important' or you may ask 'Does this item worry you?' or simply query 'How exciting is this item to you? It all depends on what you want to know and that depends on what job you are training for and the type of training which you and your firm offer.

This type of questionnaire uses the technique known as **Semantic** ('signifying' or 'meaning') **Differential.** Here **bi-polar** adjectives (i.e. describing opposite extremes of the same thing, e.g. 'interesting' at one extreme and 'uninteresting' at the other) are used to represent the dimensions of a course. Each trainee is asked to respond by indicating his or her position on each scale with reference to a specific dimension, e.g. the dimension of being 'interesting'. We first came across this type of questionnaire in the Rating Scales of the Needs Analysis (Figures 34, 40, 41, 42 etc). You can use this technique as an alternative, or in addition to the scales which we are going to explain soon. They can be applied to new or experienced trainees.

Continuing with our examination of trainees' expectations about the content (syllabus) and nature of training (Area 2, Figures 102 and 105) and particularly about trainees' **Detailed Expectations** of the training content (Area 3, Figure 105) we will now give you an alternative to the questionnaire used in Figure 107; this alternative is shown on the next page; once again we will leave blank the actual topics of the course content so that you can fill in your own materials.

POLES APART

Interesting pole

uninteresting pole

THE TRAINEE'S VIEWS AND DETAILED EXPECTATIONS OF THE TRAINING CONTENT (part completed).

What do you expect from the Training which you are starting now?

TITLE OF COURSE ....

Here are the six topics which we will cover on your Course:

Topic 1
Topic 2
Topic 3
Topic 4
Topic 5
Topic 6

In the boxes shown below, for each of the Topics shown above, place the number of the Topic in the box which shows how you feel now about your forthcoming course.

Interesting	5	1	3 4	6	2	Uninteresting
Useful	4 6		1	2 5	3	Useless
Practical	4 6	1	5	2	3	Impractical
General	3 5	2		1 4	6	Detailed
Difficult	1 2	6	4	5	3	Easy
Important	6	1 4	2	5	3	Unimportant

Figure 108

On your actual questionnaire you will require much more space for writing your Topics. Nevertheless, you should get the whole questionnaire easily onto one A4 page. This format is a space saver.

This style of questionnaire is similar to that shown in Figure 107; whilst it offers more information, it is also more difficult to interpret.

This completes our examination of questionnaires for Area 3, Figure 105.

Questionnaires about Area 4, Figure 105: General Expectations of the Nature of the Training

Let's have a look now at the **general expectations** of trainees who are entering training. We will use two methods: the **Semantic Differential** which you have met and the **Adjective Rating Scale.** When you examine Figure 109, you will find this questionnaire technique explains itself. On the next page is our **Adjective Rating Scale.**

QUESTIONNAIRE AREA 4: GENERAL EXPECTATIONS OF THE NATURE OF THE TRAINING

What do you expect from the training which you are starting now?

To give us an idea of what you expect of your training let us know how you feel about it by putting a letter in each of the boxes below against those adjectives which describe what you think about the course now. Use the following code:

A - Extremely   B - Very   C - Slightly   D - Not at all

I expect to find the Course in .... to be:

Interesting		Relevant	
Useful		Demanding	
Boring		Dull	
Practical		Irrelevant	
Challenging		Rewarding	
Good		Enjoyable	
General		A Waste	
Informative		Different	
Necessary		Worthwhile	
Provocative		Valuable	
Exciting		Stimulating	
Enlightening		Difficult	

NAME IN BLOCK CAPITALS.. SIGNATURE............................

Figure 109

There are several ways in which you can use these letter answers; one method is to make a simple comparison of 'good' (positive) and 'bad' (negative) responses, but one of the best techniques is to 'collapse' the four-point scale (A, B, C, D,) into a two-point scale (A & B; C & D) and to use the same questionnaire again at the end of the training, comparing the answers as follows.

HOW DID YOUR TRAINING GO? RESPONSES FOR 100 TRAINEES

		Extremely or Very		Slightly or Not at all
INTERESTING	Pre	80		20
	Post	85		15
USELESS	Pre	36		64
	Post	15		85
DIFFERENT	Pre	50		50
	Post	89		11
PRACTICAL	Pre	70		30
	Post	40		60
CHALLENGING	Pre	86		14
	Post	30		70
				(100 trainees)

Figure 110

You check for each adjective (we have shown five only) and you will then have a good idea of how your training went. You can refine the results by selecting the half-dozen adjectives which show the greatest difference between the pre and post-tests, which helps you focus on the main changes in expectations.

Describe in your own words what Figure 110 tells you about your training.

Generally, trainees expected to find the course interesting and challenging. A majority expected the training to be practical and useful, but really didn't know if it would be different or not.

After training, the course was proved to be interesting, and more useful than anticipated but less practical and easier than expected. Trainees certainly found it different!

You have an example of adjective rating scales in Figure 109; we will now use a **semantic differential scale** to check on trainees' general expectations about the content and nature of training, Area 4, Figure 105.

From what you know already, can you work out a semantic differential scale which suits your training for Area 4?

Ours is shown in Figure 111.

QUESTIONNAIRE, AREA 4, FIGURE 105: A TRAINEE'S GENERAL EXPECTATIONS OF TRAINING

'For each of the pairs of words below, fill in ONE box with a tick which shows your general feelings now about your forthcoming Course'.

I expect to find the training in .... to be:

Interesting											Uninteresting
Useful											Useless
Exciting											Dull
Practical											Impractical
Challenging											Unchallenging
General											Detailed
Informative											Uninformative
Necessary											Unnecessary
Provocative											Unprovocative
Enlightening											Unenlightening
Relevant											Irrelevant
Demanding											Undemanding
Rewarding											Unrewarding
Enjoyable											Unenjoyable
Different											Not Different
Worthwhile											Not Worthwhile
Stimulating											Unstimulating
Difficult											Easy

If you fill in this box it means that you expect to find the training to be neither one thing nor the other, neither 'interesting' nor 'uninteresting' but exactly in between the two, so you have a middle view.

Figure 111

Naturally, for all of these questionnaires, you just don't throw the questionnaires at the trainees and tell them to get on with it; you'll need to explain to them what its all about and demonstrate some examples to them of how to fill in the forms.

TRAINER DEMONSTRATES HOW NOT TO DEAL WITH QUESTIONNAIRES

Figure 112

Now for some revision. You will remember that we began our discussion of the use of questionnaires with Figure 99. Have a look at that Figure and follow the text through again from the section entitled Questionnaires, paying particular attention to Figures 102, 103, 105, 107, 108, 109 and 111. Now, draw a line diagram which shows how these questionnaires all fit together to provide information about Pre-Course Expectations of Training. Figure 102 is a good starting point; use our Figure numbers as a sort of shorthand if you want to.

Our line diagram is shown in the next Figure.

TRAINEE'S PRE-COURSE EXPECTATIONS: QUESTIONNAIRES

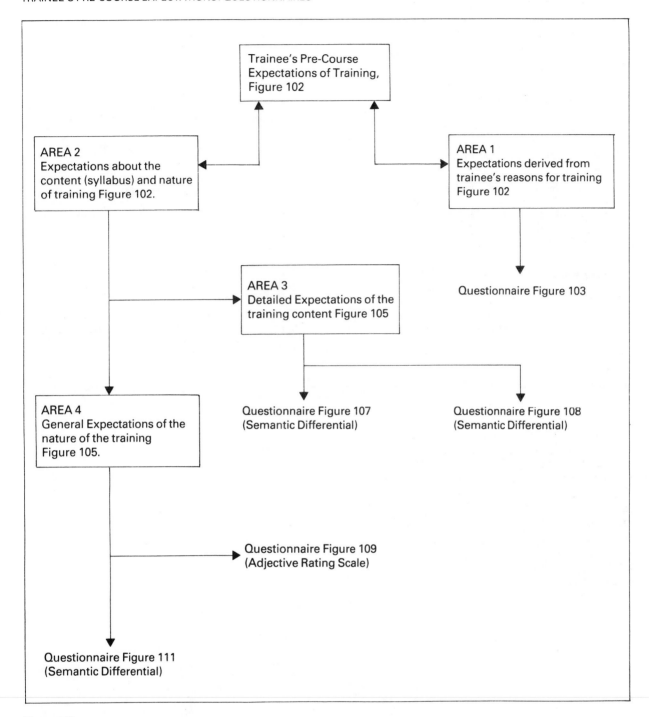

Figure 113

This ends our examination of questionnaires used as sources in determining trainee attitudes and pre-course expectations. We must now consider the use of **Tests** as sources of research information in the entering behaviour of experienced trainees (see Figure 99; revise text of Component Six and Figures 90 and 92).

What sort of tests are we using and what information are we seeking?

*We are using **Pre-Tests** and we are looking for **facts.** That is, facts of how much trainees already know about the forthcoming training content in the areas of knowledge, skills and pre-requisites. Shall we examine each of these in turn?*

KNOWLEDGE AND MENTAL SKILLS TESTING:
PROCEDURES

- Divide the knowledge (course content) in which you are going to train into discrete items (use Task Analysis Units or Objectives from previous courses or information from Needs Analysis).
- Set a suitable test for each item by
  - Problem solving or
  - Multiple-choice questions or
  - Essay questions or
  - Gapped handouts or
  - Questions specific to your subject, e.g. mathematical formulae, office procedure.
- When marked, your results will show the extent of trainees pre-entering knowledge, strengths to be built upon and weaknesses to be remedied.
- **Plan and modify your training accordingly**

Figure 114

SKILLS TESTING

- Use Task Analysis Results to identify skills to be tested. Concentrate on skills defined as most important by Needs Analysis.
- Test each skill by a suitable method, e.g. situational tests or performance on machinery or equipment or following laboratory procedures, following firm's manual of instruction procedures.
- Identify weak and strong skill performances.
- **Train accordingly.**

Figure 115

PRE-REQUISITE TESTING

- Identify pre-requisite knowledge and skills.
- Test, using procedures from Figures 115 and 114.
- For those who have all (or most, say 90% plus) of pre-requisite skills, **Admit to training**.
- For those who do not have adequate pre-requisite skills or knowledge either **Refuse Training** or **Carry out remedial training** and re-test

Figure 116

Obviously, you can include testing for pre-requisites as part of your knowledge and skills pre-testing procedures. Sometimes it helps to have set a pre-requisite test earlier as part of your selection procedure; this gives you time for remedial training.

PRE-REQUISITES: REFUSED ENTRY

Figure 117

One last point about pre-testing. Often the results which we obtain help us to distinguish between two important aspects of performance achievement and performance deficiency in trainees: 'Accomplishment' and 'Acquirement'. Therefore, performance achievement has two main aspects:

Acquirement: What a trainee has learned already, i.e. his or her basic repertoire of knowledge and skills.

Accomplishment: The value of that repertoire.

For example, most of you know many of the operations carried out by a bank teller, but there is no way in which you could do that job successfully, because there are a few operations which we do not know and we'd never balance the books successfully! In terms of what you and the bank teller know about job performance, there's not much difference (i.e. little difference in the basic repertoire of knowledge and skills or acquirement) but in terms of the value of what you know (accomplishment) there is a great gulf.

So a deficiency in performance mainly involves acquirements; if your pre-testing shows some trainees as short of a little knowledge or a very few skills, then they may not need the full training course. Their performance deficiency can be removed with just a short course, instead of the full treatment. Your organisation will be happy if you know the difference between acquirement and accomplishment and can save money for training accordingly.

Accomplishment is important when you are concerned with training, promotion, selection or starting a new job.

A final word about testing. Needs Analysis will be able to offer a lot of material about trainees' performance deficiencies, so don't forget that source of research information which you have completed already.

By now, you know how to gather a great deal of information which tells you about the Entering Behaviour of your incoming trainees. It is worth the work involved, because the information which you acquire will help you make your training more realistic and beneficial to the trainees.

Summary

We are going to summarise Component Seven and Component Six with a line diagram. You may wish to have a shot at drawing your own diagram first.

ACCOMPLISHING - AND NOT ACCOMPLISHING!

Figure 118

The Systematic Design of Training Courses

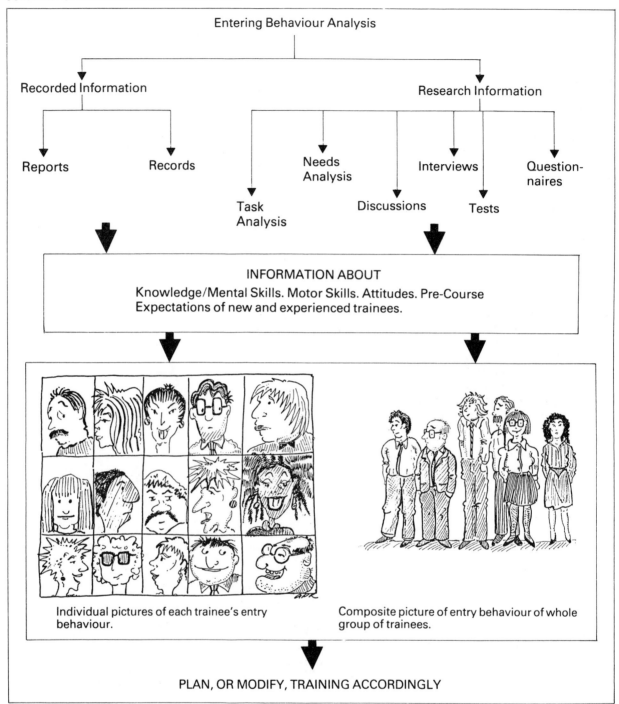

Individual pictures of each trainee's entry behaviour.

Composite picture of entry behaviour of whole group of trainees.

Figure 119

You may now wish to practice by carrying out an **Entering Behaviour Analysis** of some trainees whom Needs Analysis has identified as needing training.

In our next Component we are considering the last two types of Analysis of this Study Unit: Constraints and Resource Analysis. Try to define in your own mind just what these analyses are and what ground they might cover.

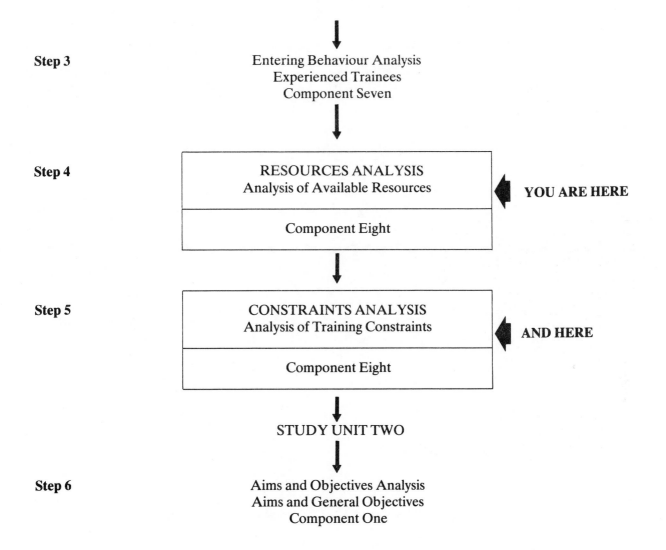

Step 3   Entering Behaviour Analysis
                      Experienced Trainees
                      Component Seven

Step 4   RESOURCES ANALYSIS
                      Analysis of Available Resources   **YOU ARE HERE**

                      Component Eight

Step 5   CONSTRAINTS ANALYSIS
                      Analysis of Training Constraints   **AND HERE**

                      Component Eight

                      STUDY UNIT TWO

Step 6   Aims and Objectives Analysis
                      Aims and General Objectives
                      Component One

Component 8:

Analysis of Resources for and Constraints on Training

Key Words

Resources analysis; on-job and off-job training; internal resources; equipment; personnel; accommodation; time; money; attitudes; learning materials; nellie; resources checklists. Constraints analysis; identifying constraints; moderating or overcoming the constraint; guidelines; modifying inputs; accommodating the constraint; recording constraints.

Considered in this Component
System Activity: Analysis
System Function: Resources Analysis
System Function: Constraints Analysis

In this Component we shall consider the next two steps of our design system: Step four, analysis of the Resources which are available for training and Step five, analysis of the Constraints on your training. Let's begin with

---

SYSTEM ACTIVITY: ANALYSIS
SYSTEM FUNCTION:
RESOURCES ANALYSIS

Resources which are available to any trainer are related to the size of the organisation and the attitude of the management to training. In the U.S.A., Germany and Japan, a large and increasing part of

industrial and commercial wealth is committed to training. In the United Kingdom the picture is very variable. The essentially important part of training in increasing the effectiveness and efficiency of the workforce is gaining recognition at all levels.

SOME TRAINERS HAVE IT ALL

Figure 120

So analysing the resources of any trainer, or training department can vary from the sublimely well equipped to the ridiculously poorly equipped.

▨▨▨ Checkpoint

How would you set about analysing resources?

One useful method is to make a Task Analysis of the topic, 'Resources'. This will give you a further opportunity to practise making a Task Analysis and for us to show you again how the system works.
It would help if you revised Component Five, now.

Our analysis of resources will be fairly comprehensive and you should pick out the information which most applies to you. After reading this Component you will have a clear idea of what is embraced by the term, 'Resources' and we aim to help you organise a checklist of resources for yourself which will assist you in determining what you have available and what you need.

● First, our Task Analysis shows what comprises each of the different areas of resources.
● Second, you decide which areas are relevant to you. You will probably not require to consider all of the resources which we show by Task Analysis, so concentrate on the Units of Analysis which are of most use to you.

Sometimes we will add a few words of explanation to a group of Units of Analysis, but often the process of Task Analysis is self-explanatory and in these cases, we will pass on without comment.

Let's begin the Analyses Task now.

ANALYSIS OF RESOURCE: EQUIPMENT

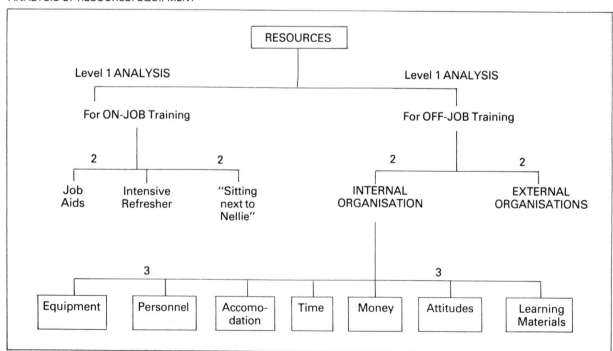

Figure 121

In Figure 121, we have emphasised the most important Units of Analysis by placing them in boxes; we shall proceed to analyse each of these areas in turn. **'Internal'** means training carried on within your organisation and therefore with internal resources.

In the Units of Level Two of analysis for on-job training, you should note that job aids, often derived from Task Analysis of the job, may satisfy the requirement, i.e. if you produce job aids, no further training may be required. Intensive 'refresher' courses often require substitute operatives and you may have to ensure that the department concerned can and will make them available. 'Sitting next to Nellie' is the famous phrase used for learning by sitting next to a skilled operative until you 'know' the job.

NELLIE AS A TRAINER

Figure 122

We will continue by further analysing Level Three Units beginning with Equipment. This (Figures 123 to 133 inclusive) is the most important part of the Task Analysis.

ANALYSIS OF RESOURCE: EQUIPMENT

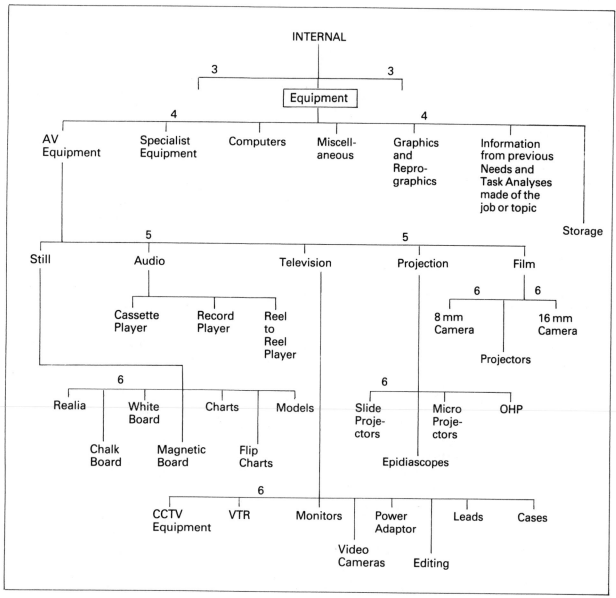

Figure 123

The Figure above shows Level Four analysis in detail, but here examines Levels of Analysis Five and Six for A-V equipment only. We have done it this way for considerations of space only; you are advised that when you make your own Task Analysis, you do so on A3 sheets of paper, which precludes this problem.

At Level Four we have included, 'Information from Needs and Task Analyses made previously for the job or topic' as a Unit of Analysis. Obviously, this is not an equipment resource, but we felt that we ought to include that as a Unit of Analysis to emphasise and draw your attention to the importance of using information from your other Analyses in the material which you are developing through the Task (Topic) Analysis of Resources.

This is an important principle: always interweave the information from all of your Analyses of System Functions into the picture which you are building up of your training through the System Activity of Analysis.

Another important principle to remember when you are reading through this Task Analysis of Resources is that when you arrive at every Unit of Analysis, for all Levels of Analysis, you are saying to yourself, 'Now, what resources do I have available in this area?' Thus, for Level of Analysis Five in Figure 123, you are asking yourself 'What resources do I have in still media, audio, T.V., projectors and film for the training I am planning now?

So the purpose of this Task Analysis of Resources is to indicate to you all those areas in which you ask yourself the right questions about the resources which you have available.

We shall look at the remaining Units of Analysis concerning the resource of Equipment now. You should note that the Unit 'Storage' is a general one and can be a consideration which you can make throughout the analysis of Equipment resources.

ANALYSIS OF RESOURCE: EQUIPMENT (Continued)

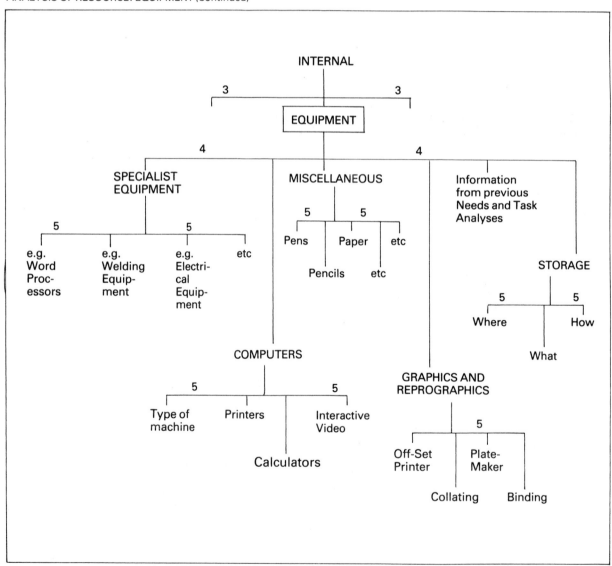

Figure 123a

In Figure 123a we couldn't do much with Specialist Equipment, because only you know what that is. Obviously, this could be one of the most important parts of Task Analysis for you, individually.

MOST TRAINERS AND TRAINEES USE SPECIALIST EQUIPMENT

Figure 124

We will consider Unit of Analysis, Personnel, next.

ANALYSIS OF RESOURCE: PERSONNEL

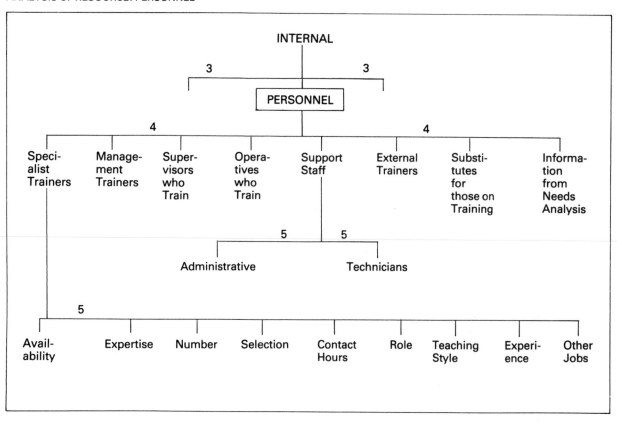

Figure 125

The Systematic Design of Training Courses

In the last Figure, we show that training is carried out not only by 'specialist' trainers but also, as you know, by many others. Specialist, or 'direct' or 'professional trainers' have a specific responsibility for training within their organisations. For the others, training is an integral part of their jobs, whether it is line management, general management or supervision and includes some skilled operatives and technicians; these are sometimes called 'integral' trainers. In all cases, you need the sort of information shown at Level of Analysis Five about each type of trainer.

TRAINING OTHERS: AN INTEGRAL PART OF THE JOB?

Figure 126

All of the information shown at Level of Analysis Five for Specialist trainers also applies to those integral trainers shown at Level Four, of course. This is an example of where we haven't completed all parts of this Task Analysis, mainly to avoid repetition and because of lack of space. So when you read this analysis bear in mind this shortcut which we have made.

External trainers are experts and skilled operators from outside your organisation who can help you with your training because of their special knowledge and skills. Using 'outsiders' will frequently make your training more interesting. If you can't afford it, then try an interchange, you doing something for them on a return basis.

All of this training has to happen somewhere, so next we analyse your **Accommodation** resources.

ANALYSIS OF RESOURCE: ACCOMMODATION

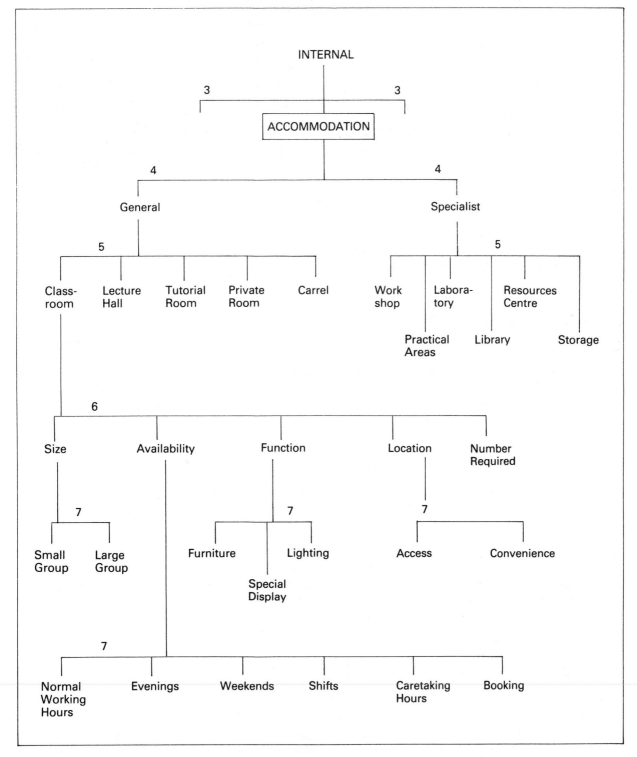

Figure 127

The Figure above speaks for itself in showing you the areas which you should consider when asking yourself the question. 'What resources in accommodation do I have?

To what do the terms, 'Small Group' and 'Large Group' refer in Figure 127?

These are the sizes of group into which you propose to divide your trainees for their course. Obviously, a number of small groups of trainees will require more rooms than one or two larger groups and you must plan accordingly. For courses which are established you should have an accurate idea of group sizes and number of groups at this stage; for training not yet established and still in the planning stage, you may have to wait until you have completed Steps Nine and Ten (Figures 10 and 12) until you decide on group size and number and therefore the number of classroom spaces needed.

CALCULATE THE SIZE OF YOUR GROUPS CAREFULLY!

Figure 128

After the crush shown in Figure 128, we had better move on to our next Resource: **Time,** shown in Figure 129.

ANALYSIS OF RESOURCE: TIME

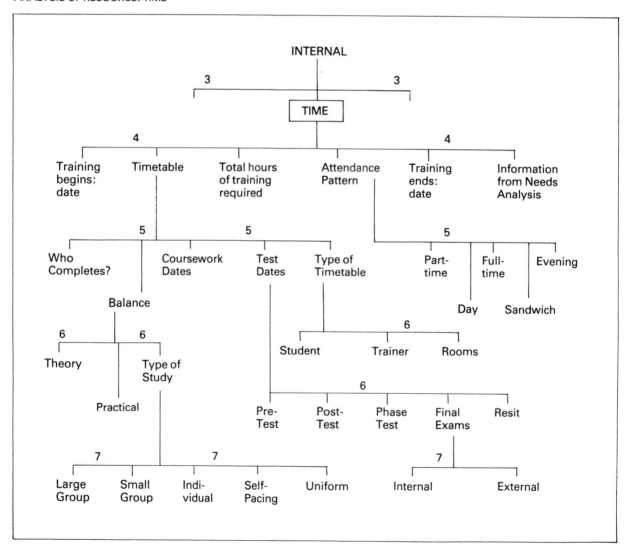

Figure 129

No comments about Figure 129, except for a Checkpoint.

To what do the words 'internal and 'external' in Level of Analysis Seven refer?

The words 'internal' and 'external' refer to whether you are holding final examinations organised by your organisation itself, i.e. internally, or whether the exams are those of some external validating body, e.g. City & Guilds. If the latter you'll have to make sure that your training meets the 'deadlines' of external examining bodies and that you have sufficient time to run the training smoothly into the exam. Finishing your training too early, or too late, has obvious disadvantages.

And what about paying for the training? Our next Unit of Analysis to be examined in detail is **Money.**

ANALYSIS OF RESOURCE: MONEY

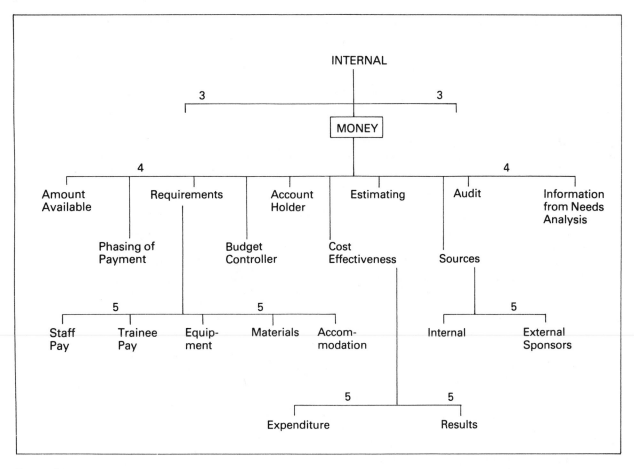

Figure 130

What do the Units of Analysis, 'expenditure' and 'results' indicate at Level of Analysis Five, Figure 130?

Be certain to make sure that your training is cost effective, ie do the results of training justify the expenditure? The ideal is that a course should give good value for money and often training is the cheapest and most effective way of improving job performance, product output and therefore profitability. If you don't ask yourself whether your training is cost-effective or not, somebody else will!

IS YOUR TRAINING COST EFFECTIVE?

Figure 131

Much depends on the views of everyone in your organisation towards training. So our next resource to be viewed concerns **Attitudes**.

ANALYSIS OF RESOURCE: ATTITUDES

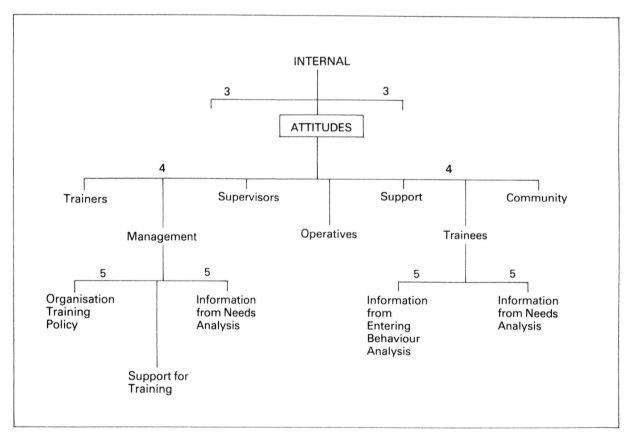

Figure 132

What is your major concern when considering the attitudes of your organisation towards training?

Your major concern is whether attitudes towards training are largely positive, or mainly negative or some point in between, as is often the case.

Clearly, if you have a generally negative attitude to deal with and where you detect negative attitudes in some people, you have a major job to do in attempting to change these attitudes to positive ones; you are 'on the back of a tiger'. You must ensure as supportive an attitude as possible towards training throughout your organisation at all levels for training to be effective. On the other hand, if you do receive a lot of support, then you're 'on the pig's back'.

Incidentally Figure 132 shows that you have a great deal of information about attitudes already from both your Needs and your Entering Behaviour Analysis.

Finally, the last part of our Task (Topic) Analysis deals with **Learning** Materials. This is, of course, an enormous area and your Needs Analysis and your previous Task Analysis of the job or topic should indicate which parts you will wish to concentrate on. In Figure 133, we have written 'Available Externally' as a Unit of Analysis, with no further detail. We mean that you should be aware of all the learning materials which are available for buying, or borrowing, from sources external to your organisation. These materials and this information are along the same lines as that shown under the Unit of Analysis for 'Available Internally' in Figure 133 and the 'list' we show there will serve for both external and internal sources.

ATTITUDES TO TRAINING: 'WHOSE BACK AM I ON ANYWAY?'

Figure 132a

ANALYSIS OF RESOURCE: LEARNING MATERIALS

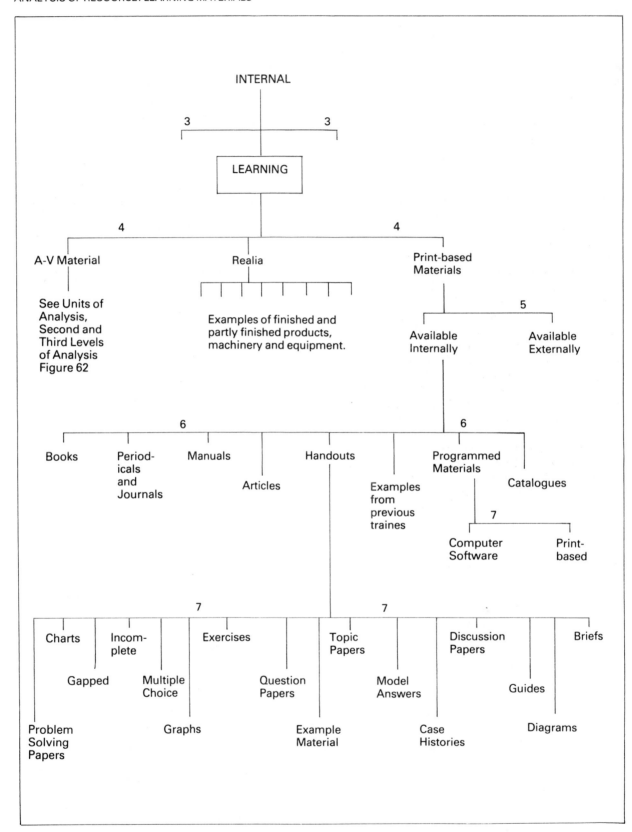

Figure 133

▨▨▨

What do we mean by 'Realia' in Figure 133?

Realia are the 'real things'; you could show examples of finished products in the classroom and of stages in making the finished products of your firm. Realia also includes using specialist equipment, like machinery in your workshops, for example. Here it links with our Task Analysis of Equipment Resources. However, the emphasis is on producing real-life examples of what your training is about in the classroom, workshop or laboratory.

Finally, in our Task Analysis of Resouces we have to examine **'External Organisations'** further when concerned with 'off-job' training, see Figure 121. Here, we mean you asking yourself what bodies external to your firm can help you with your training programme? We have shown some of the organisations which offer training, or help with training, but no doubt you can add others to the next Figure.

REALIA IN THE CLASSROOM

Figure 134

ANALYSIS OF RESOURCE: EXTERNAL ORGANISATIONS

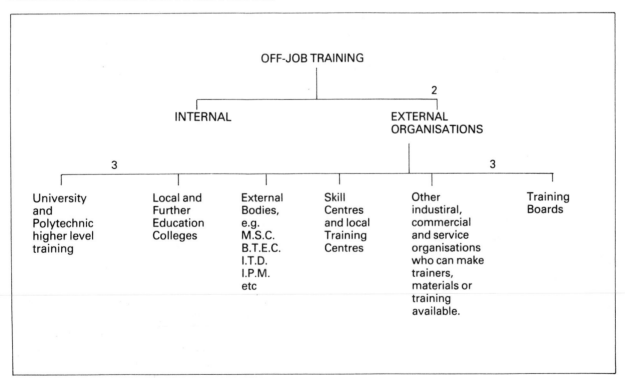

Figure 135

This completes our Task (Topic) Analysis of Resources.

Do you have a full range of the brochures and pamphlets showing which courses are available in institutions which are accessible to your trainees?

If you have, good; if not, then contact your local Divisional Education Office, or the institution directly. If you are not sure that you know all of the local colleges, then use The Educational Authorities Directory and Annual (The School Government Publishing Company Limited) which will give you the sort of detail which you require.

Through our Task Analysis of Resources, we now have a good idea of the range of resources which can be available for training. All we need now are **Checklists** which we can use for each of our courses and which will show what is available quickly and clearly. We give a basic format for one such checklist below; modify it to meet your own requirements.

RESOURCES CHECKLISTS: OPEN FORMAT

TRAINING:	(Give details of course here, including course title, dates of training, attendance pattern, number of trainees etc).			
RESOURCE	**REQUIREMENT**	**AVAILABILITY**	**NEED**	**ACTION**
(Fill in details of resource here).				

Figure 136

You can write in details of your Resources in the blanks under the Resource column or to save writing out such details for each course which you are planning you can have a duplicated list run off with details of most of the Resources which we have shown as Units of Analysis. We show such a duplicated Checklist overleaf completed for A-V equipment; this is derived from Figures 123 and 62.

RESOURCES CHECKLIST: DUPLICATED FORMAT

		TRAINING: 'USE OF AUDIO-VISUAL EQUIPMENT' (Enter other details of course here)			

	RESOURCE	REQUIRE-MENT	AVAIL-ABILITY	NEED	ACTION
	A-V EQUIPMENT				
1	REALIA	Nil			
2	CHALK BOARD	4	4	0	Nil
3	WHITE BOARD	4	4	0	Nil
4	CHARTS	5	2	3	Flip Charts: Buy 3
5	MODELS	Nil			
6	SCREENS	Nil			
7	AUDIO CASSETTE PLAYER	10	6	4	Buy 2; Borrow 2 from Y Dept.
8	RECORD PLAYER	2	2	0	Nil
9	REEL-TO-REEL	1	1	0	Nil
10	VTR	6	5	1	1 to be returned from repair
12	MONITOR	6	4	2	1 from repair; Borrow 1 from X Dept.
13	CAMERA	3 (lxp)	3	0	Nil 'lxp'-portable
14	POWER ADAPTOR	6	6	0	Nil
15	LEADS	6	6	0	Nil. Check Extension blocks and leads
16	CASES	3	3	0	Nil
17	BATTERIES	1	1	0	Check OK for portable camera
18	EDITING SUITE	1	1	0	Nil
19	SLIDE PROJ-ECTOR	4	3	1	?
20	EPIDI-ASCOPES	1	1	0	Nil
21	MICRO-PROJ-ECTOR	2	2	0	Nil
22	OHP	6	5	1	1 to be repaired
23	8mm CAMERA	1	1	0	Nil
24	16mm CAMERA	2	1	1	Replan training
25	PROJ-ECTORS	2	1	1	Borrow from Adminis-tration
26	OTHER				

Figure 137

Is there anything which you could add to Figure 137 to improve its usefulness?

Remember that we have shown a checklist for A-V equipment only; the list would continue by including all other Resources shown by our Task Analysis of Resources. Space precludes us from doing this.

A useful addition could be at the end of the list and would summarise the **Action** *which had to be taken and, more importantly, who is to take it. As you know, jobs often don't get done because it isn't clear whose responsibility it is to undertake them. So we safeguard this by the addition shown in the next Figure.*

Suitable:	Units of Analysis for
	Equipment
	Personnel
	Accommodation
	Learning Materials
Unsuitable:	*Units of Analysis for*
	Time
	Money
	Attitudes

We suggest the following Resources checklist format for the latter; we have filled in part of it for Unit of Analysis, **Money**.

WHOSE RESPONSIBILITY IS IT?

(Last item of checklist would be here eg. 26 on Figure 137)	
ACTION:	RESPONSIBILITY FOR ACTION JOBS ON CHECKLIST:
NAME	CHECKLIST ACTION NUMBER
A. N. Other	4. 11. 12. 17. 28. 46. 52. 60.
A. T. Echnician	7. 15. 21. 23. 32. 61. 62. 81.
R. Wilson	24

Figure 137a

In this Figure A. T. Echnician and A. N. Other are probably technicians; R. Wilson is the trainer in charge of the course and he will have to replan the training to accommodate the fact that he is short of one 16 mm camera (Number 24 on Resources Checklist) – (Additional Items have been added from parts of the Resource Checklist not shown ie. Items numbered over 26).

Clearly, the Resources Checklist shown in Figures 137 and 137a works very well for certain of our Units of Analysis shown in Figure 121 at Level of Analysis Three. It does not fit other Units shown in that Figure. Glance through the preceding Figures of this Component and say:
- For which Units does the Resources Checklist of Figure 137 work well?
- Which Units does it not suit?

RESOURCE CHECKLIST: MONEY

RESOURCE	STATEMENT	ACTION
MONEY		
1. AMOUNT AVAILABLE	£6,000 agreed already	Nil
2. PHASING	£1,000 monthly	Is Carryover possible?
3. REQUIREMENTS	No problems about staff pay, or accommodation, but	
	a. Equipment	Buy 2 audio cassette recorders costing 2 x £28 = £56
	b. Flipcharts	3 needed. Buy 4 pack costing £36
4. BUDGET CONTROLLER	Finance Officer	Check accounting system is agreed
5. ACCOUNT HOLDER	Jack Bloggs	

Figure 138

The style of Resource Checklist shown by Figure 138 is more flexible than that of Figure 137, but you should modify both to suit your own needs more closely.

This completes our System Step Four, **Resources Analysis**; you now have a clear picture of your resource availability and requirement and whose responsibility it is to take any action which is needed. Both availability and action become apparent immediately you have completed your Checklist.

We now move on to the analysis of constraints on your training: **Constraints Analysis**, which is our design system **Step Five**. Before you do so you might wish to complete a Resource Checklist for your organisation, using the material which we have provided but which is incomplete in parts, as a basis.

CHECK YOUR RESOURCES BEFORE YOU START

Figure 139

SYSTEM ACTIVITY: ANALYSIS
SYSTEM FUNCTION:
CONSTRAINTS ANALYSIS

Constraints are restrictions on your training.

You will have done much of the work of Constraints Analysis already when you completed your Resources Analysis and your Entering Behaviour Analysis. How is this?

Taking your Resource Analysis first, you know that this analysis has identified certain needs and problems in your Resource Checklist with some suggestions for suitable remedial or resolving action. Where these actions have failed, your training is restricted, i.e., you have identified a constraint.

If you glance at Figure 121 again, you will see that any of the Units of Analysis of Levels of Analysis Two and Three may throw up a constraint. For example, you may not have enough 'Nellies' to sit your trainees beside; you may have poor links with External Organisations; you may find a need which you cannot meet in your Resource Checklist for Equipment, Personnel, Accommodation, Time, Money, Attitudes or Learning Materials.

Considering Entering Behaviour Analysis, your 'pictures' of your trainees (see Figure 119) may show certain constraints in the knowledge/mental skills, the motor skills, the attitudes or the pre-course expectations of your incoming learners.

ACTING ON CONSTRAINTS

Figure 140

You now have to do something about these constraints.

In broad terms, what would you do?

It seems to us that there are two main types of alleviating action and these are shown in the next Figure.

DEALING WITH CONSTRAINTS

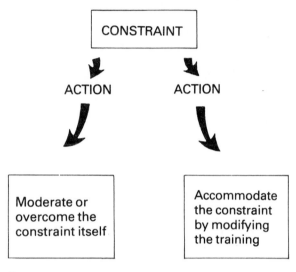

Figure 141

There are a multiplicity of ways of **overcoming** or **moderating** a constraint because their nature varies widely and your alleviating action depends upon your working environment. As your employing organisations vary largely in size and nature, we can only offer general guidelines; these are shown in the next Figure.

GUIDELINES FOR DEALING WITH THE CONSTRAINT ITSELF

- Identify accurately the nature, causes and personnel involved in the constraint. (Use information from your various System Function Analyses).
- Identify the requirements, e.g. expertise, money, skills, equipment or materials, etc., needed. (Use Function Analyses).
- Identify those who can help in fulfilling the requirements.
- Using the information identified, form a plan with those who can help to moderate or overcome the constraint.
- Implement the plan.

Figure 142

Dealing with the other alleviating action shown in Figure 141, how would you accommodate the constraint by modifying the training?

In general terms, you can act as shown in Figure 143.

GUIDELINES FOR DEALING WITH A CONSTRAINT BY MODIFYING THE TRAINING

You have to **modify** your training by
1. changing the training **inputs**, i.e. by
2. changing your **plans** for the appropriate System Functions shown in Figures 10 and 12, viz:

- Aims and Objectives
- Content
- Training Methods
- Implementation

Figure 143

We shall examine an example of changing your training inputs in the series of diagrams shown below.

ACCOMMODATING CONSTRAINTS: MODIFYING INPUTS AND REMOVING CONSTRAINTS

STAGE ONE: ORIGINAL PLAN

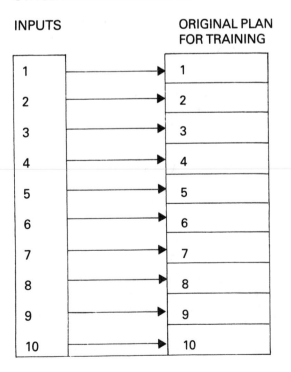

STAGE TWO: CONSTRAINTS IDENTIFIED

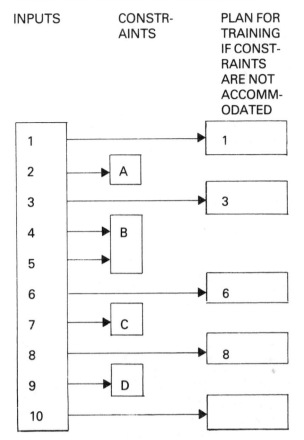

STAGE THREE: CONSTRAINTS ACCOMMODATED

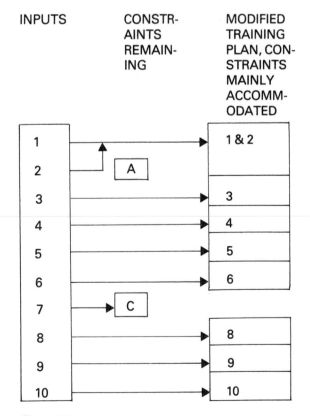

Figure 144

In Stage Three of Figure 144, you succeeded in removing constraints B and D and avoided constraint A by amalgamating inputs 1 and 2; of course this changes your Training Plan, as the diagram shows. Unfortunately, you could not remove constraint C, so that input 7 became impossible; this represents a fairly radical change to your modified training plan and means important changes in one or more elements of your Aims and Objectives, your Content, your Training Methods or your Implementation. This often happens when designing courses, but at least our Stage Three training plan isn't too far away from the original plan intended in Stage One.

However, each constraint which you can't remove means an altered training plan.

REMOVING CONSTRAINTS

Figure 145

We now make an important link with another part of our Design System: Needs Analysis. In this present Component, we have talked about 'inputs'. If you glance back at the Components which dealt with Needs Analysis, especially Component Four, you will realise that your training inputs will be derived from and modelled upon your Need Statement (Figure 52). Each input may represent a Need Statement. So your Constraints may prevent you from fulfilling all of the requirements of your Needs Analysis.

As each constraint which you can't remove means altered inputs, so you have to accommodate these changes in your planning. In Figure 144, this is shown by the difference in the shape of your 'original plan for training', Stage One, compared with your 'modified training plan', Stage Three.

As we are using a systematic approach to the design of training we should systematically record our constraints and our methods of dealing with them. Such a record clarifies our ideas and forms the basis for discussing action with management, trainers and other staff.

Below is our suggested layout, with an example completed.

RECORD OF CONSTRAINTS

CONSTRAINT	IDENTIFIED BY	SUGGESTED ACTION	ACTION BY
1. Main Lecture Hall unavailable through renovation	Resource Analysis see Resources Checklist Item 41	Approach Department Y for use of their classroom, Period 1st to 23 March.	BW
2. etc			

Figure 146

As we mentioned before, much of the material on your Record of Constraints is derived from other analysis, but your Record has the advantage of keeping the information in one easily accessible place.

Summary

★ A Task (Topic) Analysis provides the best method of making a survey of your resources and shows your requirements for both on-job and off-job training. The most important part of the latter comprises a Resource Analysis of your Internal Resources, especially of equipment, personnel, accommodation, time, money, attitudes and learning materials.

★ Resources Checklists pinpoint what you have said and what you need and suggest actions which can overcome deficiencies.

★ Similarly, your Needs Analysis, Resources Analysis and Entering Behaviour Analysis provide information on your Constraints and how you propose to overcome or accommodate them.

★ All of the material generated by the System Activity of Analysis, Steps One, Two, Three, Four and Five (see Figures 10, 12 and 75) is fed into our next System Function, the Analysis of Aims and Objectives. This analysis will be considered in the next Study Unit.

Before you continue with Study Unit Two, you may wish to send your Programme Tutor an analysis, or analyses, which you have completed when working through this first Unit. Ask questions if you wish; your tutor will comment on material and return it to you.

Study Unit 2

The Systematic Design of Training Courses

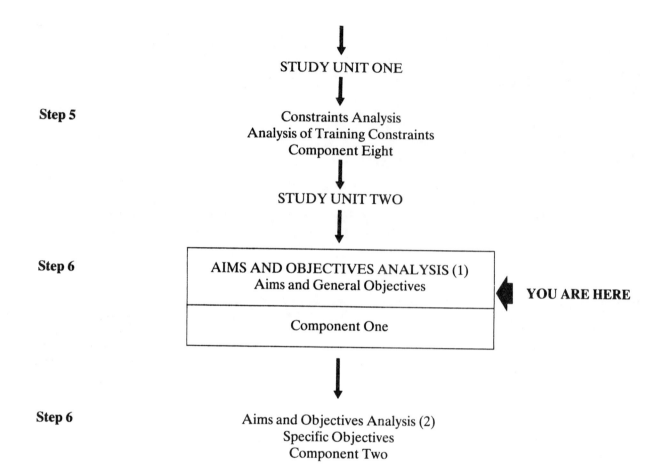

Step 5

STUDY UNIT ONE

Constraints Analysis
Analysis of Training Constraints
Component Eight

STUDY UNIT TWO

Step 6

AIMS AND OBJECTIVES ANALYSIS (1)
Aims and General Objectives

YOU ARE HERE

Component One

Step 6

Aims and Objectives Analysis (2)
Specific Objectives
Component Two

Component 1:

Analysing the Aims and General Objectives of your Training

Key Words

Training aims; general objectives; specific objectives; learning outcomes (end products); trainer intentions; trainees' intentions; trainees' observable behaviour; sources of aims; information from previous system function analysis; principles of writing aims and general objectives; functions; characteristics; principles and procedures for writing aims and general objectives; derivation of general objectives; final checks on writing general objectives.

Introduction

Considered in this Component
System Activity: Analysis
Systems Function:
Aims and Objectives Analysis

Before we take Step 6 of our design system, we will make a revision by means of a diagram of where we have got to so far in our systematic approach. The next Figure is a continuation of Figure 75, Component 5.

DESIGN SYSTEM: SYSTEM ACTIVITY, ANALYSIS, STEPS AND FUNCTIONS ONE TO SEVEN

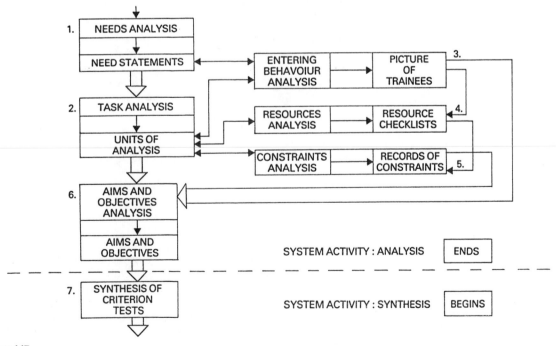

Figure 147

▰▰▰ Checkpoint

Which important aspect of our design system is represented by the arrows in Figure 147?

The large number of arrows, each showing an interaction and a relationship, illustrates how all parts of the system, ie Activities and Functions are connected and how they feed information to each other and how more and more facts become available to the trainer as the systematic approach to the design of training develops.

Whilst all of the System Steps are important, the next, **Aims and Objectives Analysis** is one of the most significant of all. You will recollect that Figure 1 showed a simple training system; here we are concerned more with products and these are the end products of the training system, called **Learning Outcomes.** We illustrate these points in the following Figure.

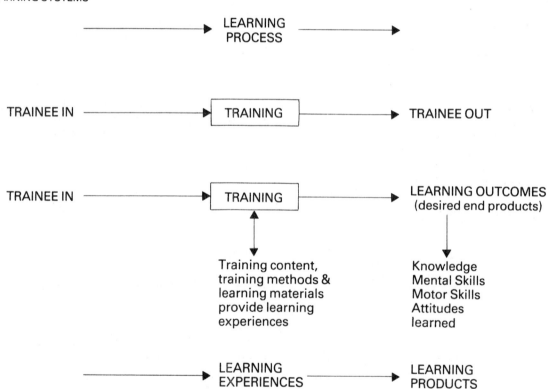

LEARNING SYSTEMS

Figure 148

In the next step of our design system, we are attempting to define the Learning Outcomes as objectives to be fulfilled by the trainees. Clearly, then, our approach to course design is objectives-based and this method is commonly called the **Objectives Model** of training design. A diagram of the Objectives Model looks like this:

THE OBJECTIVES MODEL OF TRAINING

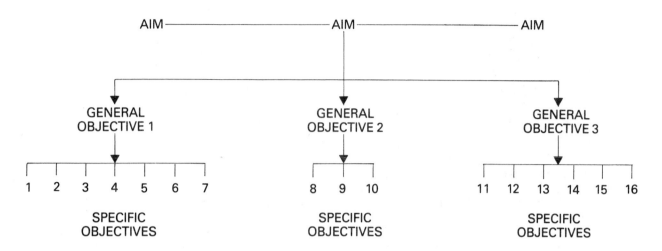

Figure 149

There are other formats for the objectives model and we shall be looking at these in the next Component of this Study Unit. In this Component we shall be examining **Aims and General Objectives** only, but we had better begin with definitions of both Aims and General Objectives, as well as Specific Objectives, so that we have clearly in mind just what we are talking about. .

A DEFINITION OF AIMS

> AIMS are broad, generalised statements of training intent, relating to the whole or a major part of training.

Figure 150

A DEFINITION OF GENERAL OBJECTIVES

> GENERAL OBJECTIVES are summaries of the learning outcomes of training and express the "generalised" behaviour expected of the trainee.

Figure 151

In a way, the general objectives describe the **behaviour,** or the **performance,** expected of the properly trained person at the end of the course, a sort of "ideal trainee" who is a more efficient and effective employee. This trainee is one who has learned more about the job and achieved the objectives of training.

A DEFINITION OF SPECIFIC OBJECTIVES

> SPECIFIC OBJECTIVES are precise statements of the learning outcomes of training and express the specific behaviour/performance which is to be observed overtly in the trainee.

Figure 152

Usually, of course, this specific behaviour/performance is related to a definite and specific task.

Each of the three definitions, which we have just made, has an orientation towards either the trainer, or the trainee. Which is which?

- *Aims are directed towards the trainer*
- *General and Specific Objectives are directed towards the trainees*

We can show this by a diagram.

AIMS AND OBJECTIVES: RELATIONSHIPS

Figure 153

We have added a couple of arrows in Figure 153 to show increasing detail and the fact that Aims and Objectives are not separated from each other. Indeed, Objectives are derived from Aims and we will discuss this in detail, later.

At this point it will be useful if we consider some examples to illustrate what we mean.

Write down two examples each of Aims, of General and Specific Objectives.

Compare what you have written against the examples which we have shown below. Work through the exercise and check the answers at the end.

Read the following, identifying whether they are Aims, General or Specific Objectives.

1. (The trainee) appreciates the part played by the supervisor in production.
2. It is the intention of training to describe the basic concept of selling.
3. (The trainee) can develop 35mm black/white film.
4. The course will consider the principles of planning theory.
5. (The trainee) knows the basic principles of planning theory.
6. (The trainee) defines accurately the theory of planning, in own words.

Answer :   **Aims – Numbers 2 and 4**
       General Objectives – Numbers 1 and 5
       Specific Objectives – Numbers 3 and 6

In the examples shown above, you can see that we have put the words "the trainee" in brackets. This is because you should always try to begin an objective with a suitable verb eg. "Appreciates", "Knows", "Defines". Adding other words is superfluous and objectives should be as concise as possible.

You should also note how examples 4, 5 and 6 become increasingly specific as you move from an Aim through a General to a Specific Objective.

Now revise what has been said so far in this Component and then answer the following question.

What is the relationship between a training course and the learning outcomes of training?

A training course is the **process** *of providing learning experiences for trainees and results in desired end* **products** *called* **learning outcomes***; these outcomes are what the trainees have learned and can do.*

AIMS

It is now time for us to examine each part of the Objectives Model of Training in detail, beginning with Aims. We shall use the headings:
Where do Aims come from?
Functions of Aims
Characteristics of Aims
Procedure for writing Aims
So let's begin with:

Where do Aims come from?

Aims come from a wide variety of sources some of which are shown in the following Figure.

AIMS: SOURCES OF INFORMATION

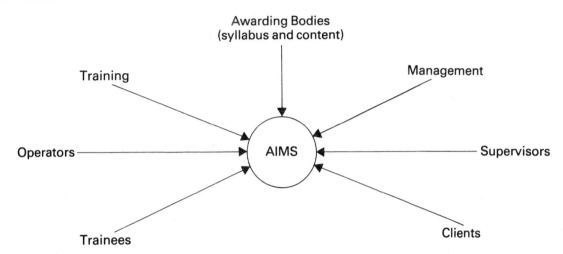

Figure 154

Checking back to Figure 147 will show you where information for your Aims (and Objectives) comes from in the systematic approach.

When you have looked at Figure 154, reflect on it carefully; of what does it remind you?

Well, you have already talked to most of these people about your training, when you did your Needs Analysis and your Entering Behaviour Analysis. This is an important link between the parts of our design system. The Aims of your training must be to fulfill the Needs which you identified in Needs Analysis. To a lesser extent, you will wish to shape your Aims so that they take cognizance of the information gained from your Entering Behaviour Analysis, especially in meeting the Pre-Course Expectations of the trainees. Figure 154 might be modified as follows:

AIMS: FURTHER SOURCES OF INFORMATION

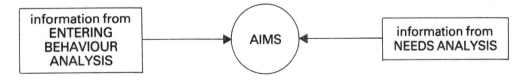

Figure 155

We will examine this in more detail, but first we shall have a look at the functions and characteristics of Aims so that we will have a good background when we come to actually writing them.

131

Function of Aims

Aims are required for a number of purposes:

1. They express how your training can fulfill the requirements of Needs Analysis.
2. They give a general summary of the purpose of training.
3. They are a starting point for the development of your training.
4. They provide information from which you derive your general objectives.
5. Therefore, they give guidance and direction over the **whole** of training or the **whole** of a Course.

Characteristics of Aims

They are written in terms of:

1. General intentions, purposes and extent of training.
2. Trainer intention.

How do these two characteristics differ from objectives?

Objectives are more specific.
They are written in terms of trainee behaviour.

Returning to the famous Sprigg's Cannonball Factory, we will examine how this works in practice.

Here are two statements; which is the better statement of Aims?

1. *The Aim of training is that cannonball operatives shall be able to produce smooth cannonballs.*
2. *The Aim of training is to improve the processes of cannonball production.*

Number 1 is not a good statement of an Aim, because it is expressed as trainee behaviour. Number 2 is more acceptable, expressing as it does the general intentions of the trainer and covering the whole of training.

Procedure for Writing Aims

When you are writing your training Aims, your procedure must ensure that you bear in mind several cardinal principles. These are shown in the Figure 156.

Before examining the next Figure, write down for yourself what you think these important principles to be. You will find that we have included several which we have not considered before, but which you can identify for yourselves if you bear in mind the whole of our Design System considered so far.

1. Write the statement for each Aim in general terms.
2. In each statement say what is the trainer's intention.
3. Ensure that your Aim statements cover all aspects of your content of training (eg. course syllabus)
    Use your Units of Analysis, from the Task Analysis which you made of the training job, topic or skill as a basis to indicate the extent of the content.
4. Make sure that your Aim statements cover, in general terms,
    a) the Need Statements of your Needs Analysis.
    b) a consideration of the relevant aspects of Entering Behaviour when formulating Aims, eg. entering behaviour expectations and pre-requisites.
    c) a regard for the availability of Resources as indicated by your Resource Analysis.
    d) a recognition of those Constraints upon your training which are exposed by your Constraints Analysis.

Figure 156

However, a word of warning; don't over-elaborate your Aims and **try not to include training problems in them.** *Remember statements of both Aims and Objectives are not just for your own personal guidance; others will read them too.*

Turn back to Figure 155. You can see that this Figure can now be expanded using information drawn from Figures 156 and 147. Try drawing your own diagram before examining ours.

AIMS: SOURCES OF INFORMATION FROM THE DESIGN SYSTEM

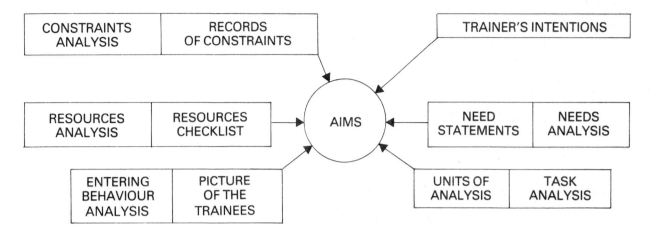

Figure 157

Figure 157 is an important one because it shows, once again, how our Design System fits together and how information is fed one part of the system into another, through the various System Functions. These relationships and interactions become even more important when considering Objectives.

WRITING AIMS: TRAINER'S GOOD INTENTIONS

Figure 158

Let's take an example of writing Aims, using some of the material which we produced previously. Turn back to Figure 52, Component 4 and look at the Need Statements written there.

Make up Training Aims from the Need Statements of Figure 52.

Here are our suggestions:

1. *Training is to be provided in the operation of certain audio-visual equipment.*
2. *Training is to be given to the writing of training materials.*

And concerning Sprigg's factory:

1. *Training is to improve the processes of cannonball production.*
2. *It is the intention to demonstrate techniques which will generally improve efficiency in the iron workshops.*

We have varied the phrasing of the Aims to show different styles of describing them. You can develop your own Aims statements which suit your training and your organisation best.

Using our examples and making reference to Figure 156, try developing some training Aims statements for your own courses.

The remainder of this Component continues with the System Activity of Analysis, System Function Aims and Objectives, by concentrating on how you write General Objectives.

GENERAL OBJECTIVES

Can you give a definition of General Objectives and where they appear in our design system?

Check with Figure 151 which shows our definition and with Figures 147 and 153, which show their location in our System Function of analysing Aims and Objectives.

The Systematic Design of Training Courses

In this part of the Component, we will follow the same procedure for examining General Objectives as we did for Aims ie.:

Where do General Objectives come from?
Functions of General Objectives.
Characteristics of General Objectives.
Procedure for writing General Objectives.
So, first of all we deal with:

Where do General Objectives come from?
There are two main sources:
1.   Training Aims
2.   The Content of your training

1.   **Deriving General Objectives from Training Aims.**
General Objectives translate your training Aims into learner, or trainee, behaviour. They are also part of the process of analysing the Aims so that they are both classified and amplified as shown in the next Figure.

FROM AIMS TO GENERAL OBJECTIVES

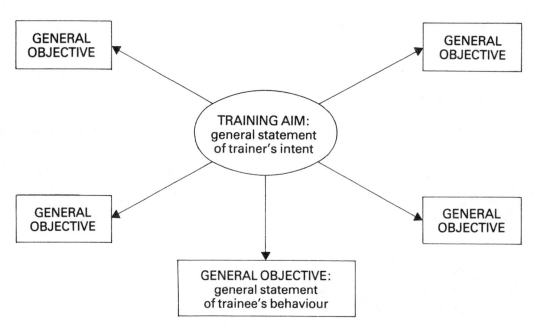

Figure 159

Let's take an actual example now with which we are all familiar: failure of your car engine. We show how you derive General Objectives from Aims, as follows:

Training Aim: To provide trainees with the basic knowledge and skills required to deal with engine faults.

General Objectives: After training, trainees will be able to trace a fault and restart the engine when the
a)   Engine cuts out suddenly
b)   Engine splutters and dies
c)   Engine will not start
d)   Engine overheats
e)   Engine runs rough and noisy.

GENERAL OBJECTIVE: TRACING A FAULT

Figure 160

Now let's take an Aim which we have met before. Have another look at the last Checkpoint but one, "Make up Training Aims from the Need Statements of Figure 52".

Training Aim: "Training is to be provided in the operation of certain audio-visual equipment."

General Objectives: After training, trainers will be able to operate the following a-v equipment in the classroom, efficiently and effectively:
a)   Video equipment
b)   16mm projector
c)   35mm projector
As you can see, we have derived three General Objectives from one Aim. Clearly, we have based our General Objectives on the Need Statements of Figure 52.

▨▨

Before we go on, can you derive General Objectives from the other Aims shown in the last Checkpoint but one?

We shall concentrate on our favourite Spriggs, as follows:
First Training Aim: *"The Aim of training is to improve the processes of cannonball production".*
General Objectives: *After training, operators will*
a)   *Achieve correct tolerances on cannonballs.*
b)   *Perform moulding process efficiently.*
c)   *Pour pig iron to correct weight accurately.*
d)   *Achieve correct cannonball hardness.*
Second Training Aim: *"It is the intention to demonstrate techniques which will generally improve efficiency in the iron workshop."*
General Objectives: *After training, operators will be*
a)   *Proficient in the techniques which reduce wastage rates of pig iron.*

b)   *Proficient in methods of reducing cannonball reject rates.*

Once more, we need the information which we have available from the Need Statements of Needs Analysis, see Figure 52. Often you can write your General Objectives by slightly modifying the actual Need Statements and this demonstrates again how the different parts of the Design System interlock and supply material to each other.

2.   **Deriving General Objectives from the Content of your training.**
An alternative way of producing General Objectives is to take them from the content of your course. This is a useful method when you are working to a set syllabus for an external examination or where you haven't had time to carry out a full Needs Analysis.

However, if you have the results of a Task Analysis of your training topic to hand, they will be very useful.

▨▨

Study Figure 59 again and see if you can write both Training Aims and General Objectives from that information.

We derived the following from Figure 59:
Training Aim: *"To improve the training skills of trainers".*
General Objectives: *After the training programme, trainers will, efficiently and effectively:*
a)   *Apply the precepts of learning theory and learner psychology to their training.*
b)   *Operate a range of video equipment.*
c)   *Use and select computer software.*
d)   *Carry out simple programming on computers.*
e)   *Operate reprographic equipment.*
f)   *Produce graphic learning materials.*
g)   *Apply appropriate methods of training and learning.*
h)   *Design courses.*

i)   *Appreciate the context of training in their own organisation.*
j)   *Assess their trainees.*
k)   *Evaluate their courses.*
l)   *Value programmes in training skills.*

So we have here a perfectly valid set of General Objectives taken from our Task Analysis of a training topic ("training skills") i.e. the course content.

One important word of warning: although derived from the content of training, you will notice that each Objective is still written as an action, or behaviour, rather than in terms of content.

Functions of General Objectives

General Objectives
1.   Summarise the learning outcomes of training.
2.   Describe the expected terminal trainee behaviour in broad terms, e.g. to apply, analyse, perform, use.
3.   Describe terminal learner attitudes e.g. to appreciate, to value, to volunteer.
4.   Link Aims with Specific Objectives, by interpreting Aims more closely.
5.   Form a starting point for the writing of Specific Objectives.
6.   Offer a method of ensuring that all of the course content is covered.
7.   Give guidance and direction over the **whole** of training or the **whole** of a course.
8.   Help to identify training time allocation.

BRIDGING THE GAP

Figure 161

Characteristics of General Objectives
1.   They are derived from the Training Aims, or
2.   The Training Content.
3.   They are learner orientated.
4.   They are more precise than Aims, but not as closely defined as Specific Objectives.
5.   They are more numerous than Aims, as each training Aim produces something in the range of from two to ten General Objectives; this is a very rough guide.
6.   Break down readily into Specific Objectives.

Procedure for Writing General Objectives
In a way, provided that you keep your terms and descriptions general in flavour when writing your training Aims, it doesn't matter too much which words, especially verbs, you choose. It matters a lot, however, when you are writing Specific Objectives.

When writing General Objectives, you may use verbs which have **several meanings;** when writing Specific Objectives your verbs must have a **single,** or at most, a few meanings. Therefore, verbs used for General Objectives may be imprecise in their meaning. Specific Objective verbs, as their name implies, have to be much more precise or specific and convey meaning much more accurately. Confusion must be avoided by trainees and other trainers not knowing what you mean when you write objectives.

WHAT DO YOU MEAN, DEAR?

Figure 162

Think of some verbs which you could use to express training outcomes, which have several meanings and which you could use for stating General Objectives. Think of another list of words with few meanings, useful for Specific Objectives.

Now read through our next list and decide whether each verb has few or many meanings. Our answers are at the end of the list.

1.	Understand	9.	Simplify
2.	Apply	10.	Appreciate
3.	List	11.	Use
4.	Comprehend	12.	Compare
5.	State	13.	Organise
6.	Name	14.	Indicate
7.	Interpret	15.	Create
8.	Perform	16.	Assemble

Useful for General Objectives: 1, 2, 4, 7, 8, 10, 11, 15.
Useful for Specific Objectives: 3, 5, 6, 9, 12, 13, 14, 16.

Let's conclude this Component by further examining the procedure for writing General Objectives, as we did for training Aims.

WRITING THE GENERAL OBJECTIVES: PROCEDURE

---

1. Try to begin each General Objective with a **verb** (appreciates, knows, understands etc). You can preface your list of General Objectives with a statement such as, "After training, trainees will . . . . .".
2. State each Objective as **Trainee Behaviour or Trainee Performance** (not trainer intention or performance.)
3. State each Objective as **Learning Outcome, or a Learning Product,** rather than in terms of the training process.
4. State each Objective so that it broadly identifies expected or desired **Terminal Behaviour,** even if it is derived from the content or syllabus of training. (Terminal Behaviour is the behaviour or performance shown by the trainee at the end of training).
5. State each Objective so that it indicates one **General Learning Outcome.** Objectives which contain a combination of outcomes, or products, should be broken down further into simple outcomes.
6. State each Objective at a level of **General Learning Outcomes** later to be further broken down into specific sorts of trainee behaviour.
7. State as many Objectives as are **necessary** to cover all of the expected trainee terminal behaviours, but **do not overdo it.** Too many General Objectives lead to a multiplicity of Specific Objectives and the whole process then becomes unwieldy.

Figure 163

In the next two Components we will give you a lot of examples of verbs which are suitable for expressing General Objectives and Specific Objectives. Write a list of your own before you tackle the next Component.

Identify a couple of final checks which you can make when you have written your General Objectives. What might such checks be?

Our suggestions are:
1. *If the trainees achieve all of my stated General Objectives will they have attained the Aim(s) of the training?*
2. *Do my General Objectives accurately reflect the broad scope of the knowledge, mental skills, motor skills and attitudes which the trainees are to acquire through training?*

Summary

*   Continuing with System Activity, Analysis, Step 6 involves the System Function of Aims and Objectives Analysis. This is a very important Step in our Design System. In it we are undertaking the process of identifying the Learning Outcomes, or End Products of training, embracing the knowledge, mental skills, motor skills and attitudes which we want the trainees to learn. Usually, these Learning Outcomes are expressed as overt behaviour on the part of the trainer.
*   We begin this process by identifying our training Aims, stating these in accordance with certain principles shown in Figure 156. Aims state trainer intention in broad terms covering the whole of training.
*   General Objectives are expressed in less general terms and concentrate on what the trainee, as distinct from the trainer, is to do. General Objectives are derived either from the training Aims, or sometimes training content and are written in accordance with the principles expressed in Figure 163.
*   When writing General Objectives, care must be taken to use suitable verbs and not to overdo the number of Objectives produced.
*   In their turn, Specific Objectives are derived from General Objectives.
*   When writing both Aims and General Objectives, a great deal of invaluable information can be obtained from previous Analyses made in our systematic approach, especially Needs Analysis and the Task Analysis of training content.

STUDY UNIT TWO

Step 6   Aims and Objectives Analysis (1)
Aims and General Objectives
Component One

Step 6
AIMS AND OBJECTIVES ANALYSIS (2) Specific Objectives
Component Two

 **YOU ARE HERE**

Step 6   Aims and Objectives Analysis (3)
Specific Objectives
Component Three

Component 2:

Analysing the Specific Objectives of your Training

Key Words

Specific objectives; deriving objectives; functions; characteristics and procedures for writing specific objectives; performance; behaviour; conditions and criteria; condition and criteria categories and statements; verbs for objectives; sequencing objectives; enabling and terminal objectives; key words and objectives.

Introduction

> **Considered in this Component**
> **System Activity: Analysis**
> **System Function:**
> **Aims and Objectives Analysis**

We said at the beginning of the last Component that this System Function of Aims and Objectives Analysis is one of the most significant sections of our Design System. The stating of Specific Objectives is, in turn, one of the most important sections of Step Six of our systematic approach.

In this and the next Component we will consider first how to write Specific Objectives, then move on to the sequencing of Objectives, have a look at examples of the sort of verbs which are useful when writing Objectives and then finish off by considering some of the advantages and disadvantages of the Objectives Model of course design.

We shall now follow the same procedure for examining Specific Objectives as we did for Aims and General Objectives, ie

Where do Specific Objectives come from?
Functions of Specific Objectives.
Characteristics of Specific Objectives.
Procedure for Writing Specific Objectives.
So, first of all we deal with

Where do specific objectives come from?

They are derived from General Objectives, See Figure 147. Specific Objectives translate General Objectives into detailed statements. Don't forget that your previous Design System Analyses can help in deriving and writing Specific Objectives. Reflect on how this happens; we will consider these sources of information at the end of this Component.

DERIVING OBJECTIVES CAN BE HARD WORK!

Figure 164

▨▨▨ **Checkpoint**

What do the letters "S.O." and "D.S." stand for in Figure 164? Who is the pickman?

S.O. = *"Specific Objectives"*.
D.S. = *"Design System"*.
The Pickman = *You, the trainer.*

Here is a General Objective:

"The (trainee) understands the dangers which are present in the workshop".

Make a list of Specific Objectives from it. Don't worry about writing them in the correct way, just have a go.

Specific Objectives:
1. *Labels the workshop dangers as a plan of the workshop is provided.*
2. *Lists the safety rules.*
3. *Identifies the reasons for observing each safety rule.*
4. *Explains the reasons for the presence of machine guards.*

5. *States the dangers associated with the moving parts of machinery.*
6. *Describes suitable clothing for the workshop.*
7. *Suggests types of unsuitable clothing, hairstyles.*
8. *Gives reasons why jewellery is not worn in the workshop.*
9. *Checks out list of workshop electrical hazards.*
10. *Demonstrates a positive attitude towards avoiding dangers.*
11. *Values the importance of the safety measures which are used in the workshop.*

At this stage you probably haven't written your Specific Objectives in quite the correct form and those shown above aren't perfect anyway. Keep the list which you wrote and have another look at it when you have completed the Component to see how you could have bettered it, just as safety could be improved in the Workshop shown in the next figure.

FULFILLING SPECIFIC OBJECTIVES IN PRACTICE?

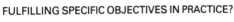

Figure 165

Before we consider the Functions of Specific Objectives, read through the Checkpoint which follows.

We list the Functions of Specific Objectives next. As you read them through, check each of the Specific Objectives 1 to 10 listed under General Objective, "understand the dangers which are present in the Workshop" above and see if they fulfil the Functions which we list.

Functions of Specific Objectives

Specific Objectives carry out the following important functions:

1. Breakdown General Objectives into groups of shorter statements which describe recognisable trainee behaviour (an action or a performance) either at the conclusion of training or at the end of discrete parts of training.
2. Identify the intended learning outcomes, or end-products, of training, ie, knowledge, skills and attitudes.
3. Provide a blueprint for the trainer upon which he can base the details of his training and which let him know where the training is going.
4. Deal with overt learner behaviour, or performance, which is measurable, so allowing the trainer to assess the trainees, gauge their progress accurately and evaluate the success of training.

5. Allow the trainer to be accountable to his firm for the measured success of training.
6. Provide information for the trainees as to where they are going in the training and what is involved so that they know where they are at any time.
7. Give the trainees an idea of what is to be accomplished and the level of accomplishment required to complete training successfully.
8. State, to management, in detailed yet summary form, what the training is about.
9. Therefore, give guidance and directions for **parts** of the training or **parts** of a course, eg. discrete units or individual lessons.
10. Guide the trainer in the selection of learning activities which provide opportunities for the specified behaviour to be learned.

To help you remember these functions of Specific Objectives, we are illustrating them in the next Figure.

ILLUSTRATING THE FUNCTIONS OF SPECIFIC OBJECTIVE

1. Recognizing Trainee Behaviour

2. Identifying the Learning Outcomes
a) Knowledge

b) Skills   c) Attitudes

3. Providing a Training Blueprint

6. Helping Trainees know where they are and where they are going.

4. Measuring Trainee Progress

7. Explaining Accomplishment

5. Ensuring Accountability

8. Informing Management

9. Giving Guidance

Figure 166

10 Selecting Learning Activities

1. *Are they precise?*
    YES
2. *Are they detailed enough, but short?*
    YES
3. *Do they specify the Performance/Action which the trainee is to take?*
    YES?
4. *Do they contain only one Action verb?*
    YES
5. *Do they describe the Conditions of accomplishment?*
    NO
6. *Do they describe the Criterion, or standards, of success to be met?*
    NO
7. *Are they related to the course content?*
    YES

As you can see, the list of functions for Specific Objectives is formidable and this underlines their importance in the Design System. Let's move on now to look at their characteristics.

Characteristics of Specific Objectives

These are as follows:-

1. They are precise.
2. Although detailed, they are short, usually not being longer than one sentence.
3. They specify the ACTION, BEHAVIOUR OR PERFORMANCE, which the trainee is to take.
4. Usually they contain only one action verb.
5. They describe the CONDITIONS under which a trainee is to accomplish the desired learning performance by achieving the appropriate learning outcome.
6. They describe the CRITERIA which must be met by the trainee in successfully completing the objective.
7. They are always written in relation to some definite piece of course content, ie knowledge, skills or attitude.

▨▨▨

Have another look at the list of eleven Specific Objectives written for the General Objective, "understanding the dangers which are present in the Workshop". Bearing in mind what we have said about the characteristics of Specific Objectives, what do you notice about those objectives?

Well, we said the Specific Objectives which we wrote weren't perfect and they seem to be deficient in two ways: they do not describe the Conditions of accomplishment and the Criteria to be met.

Each fully complete **SpecificObjective should contain a description of the**:-

Performance (action) which the trainee has to take at the end of training, or as a part of training. This action is explained as the **behaviour** which the trainee shows or a **performance or action** which the trainee must undertake.

Conditions in which the trainee will be accomplishing the performance. The trainer can include any restrictions which have to be placed upon the performance action, any stimulus to be made to the trainee and any information, equipment or materials which the trainee has to have.

Criteria of success. These state a successful standard of accomplishment for the behaviour described in the objective. The criteria, or one criterion, are the level against which the actions of the trainees are judged as acceptable or not.

▨▨▨

Let's look at a humorous example of putting A, B and C into practice. Can you write out a specific objective for a course in burglary?

Here is ours: "At the end of this training in burglary, trainees should be able to enter, undetected, any type of domestic dwelling, disconnect any form of protective device and, using only the standard burglar's kit, steal within 30 minutes, re-saleable goods with a fence value of not less than two hundred and fifty pounds."

Objectives which contain these three elements are called Mager-type objectives, after the American who described them first. We will examine them in greater detail later in this Component.

MAGER-TYPE OBJECTIVES

> SPECIFIC OBJECTIVES WHICH CONTAIN:
> PERFORMANCE ie. Action/Behaviour of trainee.
> CONDITIONS of accomplishment.
> CRITERIA of success.

Figure 167

■■■■

There is one problem for the trainer concerning Mager-type objectives. Consider what we have told you and say what you think it may be.

Writing down details about Performance, Conditions and Criteria certainly gives the sort of information required for you to know exactly what your trainees will be doing, but a major disadvantage is that it does take a long time to do. Imagine a course with five

General Objectives and imagine that you derive six Specific Objectives from each; as every single Objective has three parts (Action, Conditions, Criteria) you are writing out 5 x 6 x 3 = 90 separate items of information. Well, writing down 90 carefully considered pieces of information might be thought to be reasonable, but we'd suggest that anything over, say, 100 items would be starting to get rather heavy in terms of time and effort expended by the trainer. Having said that, the information put together by Specific Objectives is extremely important and you'll have to generate this information in some shape or form when planning.

We will look at some examples of complete Specific Objectives and you can then decide just what sort of detail you wish to use, personally, and what detail your training requires.

A MAGER CAUSE OF FATIGUE

Figure 168

Using the General Objective, "understands the dangers which are present in the Workshop" we derived eleven Specific Objectives, but we did not identify them fully by stating Conditions and Criteria as well as Actions. Complete these objectives now under the headings Performance/Action, Conditions, Criteria. *Our full objectives are shown below.*

	PERFORMANCE/ACTION	CONDITIONS	CRITERIA
1.	Labels the Workshop dangers	on a plan of the Workshop provided, within ten minutes	to 100% accuracy.
2.	Lists the Workshop safety rules	in 25 minutes	identifying all twelve rules.
3.	Identifies the reasons for observing safety rules	in a gapped handout	with 90% correct responses.
4.	Explains the reasons for the presence of machine guards	to the instructor in the Workshop on the machinery	clearly and comprehensively and naming five out of six reasons.
5.	States the dangers associated with moving parts of machinery	by pointing out the dangers to the instructor on five machines	and stating correctly six out of the eight major points.
6.	Describes suitable clothing for the Workshop	to the instructor and the group	with a clear idea of appropriate clothing.
7.	Suggests types of unsuitable clothing, hairstyles	in a group discussion	giving four apt examples.
8.	Gives reasons why jewellery is not worn in the Workshop	to the instructor and the group	with a clear knowledge of dangers.
9.	Checks out a list of workshop electrical hazards.	to the instructor in the Workshop	with no more than two errors.
10.	Demonstrates a positive attitude towards avoiding dangers	at all times when in the Workshop	
11.	Values the importance of the safety measures which are used in the Workshop	at all times	

By comparing our original list with that shown above, we think you will agree that Specific Objectives written this way are more useful and usually worth the extra effort, provided the extra detail is necessary and helpful.

In Specific Objectives 10 and 11 above, we did not fill in the Criteria column. Why is this?

Because it is very difficult to describe Criteria for measuring attitudes. We could have stated, under Criteria, 'by maintaining a good safety record'', but we felt that it was worth making this point on writing objectives about attitudes now, in this way.

Let's revise some of the material which we've covered by your answering the following Checkpoint.

Below are a series of statements about Specific Objectives. Decide whether you agree with these statements or not; if you disagree with a statement, then explain your reasons, in writing.

"Specific Objectives":
1. provide an outline for trainers about how an individual lesson may be taught.
2. indicate what students must achieve by the end of training.
3. are statements of general intentions about the training.
4. explain the scope of training to management, administrators, parents, clients and trainees.
5. give a basis for student assessment.
6. give a basis for course assessment.
7. indicate to trainees what they have to do and learn in each part of training.
8. describe to each trainee how he or she will learn a particular piece of training.

We make the following comments:-
1. **Disagree** *Specific Objectives describe trainee not trainer performance. The trainer has to select learning experiences and activities which will help the trainee to fulfil an objective.*
2. **Agree**
3. **Disagree** *Specific Objectives are written in detail and do not deal with general intent. They are action-orientated and describe what a student will be doing in each training period.*
4. **Agree**
5. **Agree**
3. **Agree**
7. **Agree**
8. **Disagree** *Specific Objectives identify learning outcomes but not how the learning will happen. How the trainees will learn depends on the sort of experience of learning which the training provides and the trainees' individual styles of learning, all of which differ. See Figure 169.*

DIFFERENT LEARNING EXPERIENCES AND LEARNING STYLES

Figure 169

We will now move on to examining how you write objectives.

Procedure for Writing Specific Objectives

There are three major parts to a Specific Objective, as we have seen: Performance; Condition; Criteria. We shall now examine these in greater detail, but before we do so, revise what we wrote previously about Performance in this Component.

Performance

As we know, this is the part of an objective which describes what the trainee will be doing. This means that it describes a behaviour which is to be seen or a performance which can be observed. Each Specific Objective describes the performance and behaviour which is to be achieved and uses an action-orientated verb to do so.

For example, after working through this and the next Component the trainer will be able to:-

a. **Justify** the reasons for developing Specific Objectives for trainees.
b. **List** the characteristics of Specific Objectives.
c. **Explain** the function of Specific Objectives.

d. **Identify** whether objectives on a given list are primarily concerned with knowledge, skills or attitudes.
e. **Write** effective Specific Objectives.
f. **Sequence** a list of Specific Objectives.
g. **Value** the use of Specific Objectives.
h. **Value** the use of the Objectives Model of course design, upon which the use of specific objectives is based.

You'll recollect what we said about writing "complete" Specific Objectives which contain information about which Performance you expect of the trainee, which Conditions the trainee works under and which Criteria he or she is to fulfil. The objectives written above are not complete, but they would be good enough to work from, if you didn't have the time to do a more detailed analysis of each Objective.

You have to decide on the sort of detail you want in your objectives and only you know how much time you háve for writing. You can vary the amount of detail which you use when writing objectives; maybe "short" objectives of the type shown above would do for some parts of your training, whilst you would use complete Specific Objectives where you felt them to be necessary.

THE THREE 'WHICHES'

Figure 170

So it is a matter of the **Three 'Whiches'**
Which Performance
Which Conditions?
Which Criteria?

To help you decide on which of the Three "Whiches" you are going to use or whether all three, we will continue our detailed examination of the procedure for writing Specific Objectives by examining Conditions and then Criteria.

Conditions

This part of the Objective describes the circumstances under which the trainee has to perform the activity required. It is possible to categorize these Conditions broadly and we will give examples of suitable phrases which you may use to describe the Conditions in Figure 171.

STATEMENTS ABOUT CONDITIONS

Category	Examples of Conditions
Conditions in which the performance is to be made	• In the Workshop/Machine Shop etc. • In the laboratory. • In the classroom. • On the factory floor. • Behind a counter. • In a work situation.
Equipment or materials given to trainee	• Using workshop/laboratory equipment. • Using a lathe. • With a cash register. • With an Apollo computer. • Making reference to the brief provided. • Given a blueprint. • Using the company manual.
Information with which the trainee is provided and which guides the performance.	• Using a gapped handout. • Provided with lists of terms and of definitions. • Using a case study provided by the trainer. • Involving two set problems.
Time allowed for completion of performance	• After completing the training. • When finishing the planning course. • By the time you have accomplished Objective Five.
Materials which the trainee cannot use	• Without using any training computer readouts. • Using only the materials provided. • Without references. • Using the tool kit given. • Without making reference to the fault-finding chart.

Figure 171

These are only examples, of course, intended to give you the general idea of how to define conditions.

Criteria

Before you move on to looking at our list of Criteria Statements, revise what we have said about conditions before and then have a try at writing some out for yourself on the lines of Figure 171, using "category" and "examples".

STATEMENTS ABOUT CRITERIA

Category	Examples of Criteria
Speed	• Complete within 10 minutes. • Finish within the time alloted for each job in the Service Manual. • Ready for the customer within 8 hours of delivery to Workshop. • At 100 cannonballs per shift.
Errors: maximal number/ proportion allowed.	• With a reject rate of no more than 1 in 200. • With a wastage rate of less than 5%. • With a typing error of not more than two words in a hundred.
Accuracy	• Within a tolerance of not more than 1/10mm. • With a tolerance of +/− .002 inch as measured on a micrometer. • To the nearest penny. • With 90% correct responses. • 49 out of 50 items to reach British Standard.
Reference to other material which states specific criteria.	• In accordance with procedures for filing. • Using manufacturer's specifications. • According to the standards set out in the written brief. • Based on standard practice. • In accordance with instructions.
Standard	• To withstand a pressure of 100 lb per unit. • With a pulling strain of 100 lb/foot. • Stress machine indicates that weld can stand 104 pounds of pressure. • To the standards laid down in the company's customer relations manual. • To British Standard specifications. • With a personal appearance considered acceptable by the Head Supervisor.

Figure 172

Is there any linking statement which you consider that we could add to either Figure 171 or 172?

Perhaps a general comment that the statement of conditions, or criteria, can be extended if necessary, to identify the level of performance and the training environment even more accurately, eg.
Conditions: *"Without using references and with the aid of only the equipment provided".*
Criteria: *"At the rate of 30 per hour with 85% correct responses".*

REMEMBER THE PARTS

Figure 173

The message of Figure 173 is for you to remember that whilst a well-stated, complete, Specific Objective has all those parts which we have mentioned, if statements about Criteria and Conditions are **absolutely** necessary, you must write only to the level of detail required, ie. be as specific as needed, but don't overdo it!

Comment on the examples following, saying how far they are complete and well written.

Number 1. "The trainee will stitch Paradise Jeans so that they will pass company inspection standards".

Number 2. "Using form CT61 provided, you are to criticise each of three sales presentations within 25 minutes".

Number 3. "After scanning sample instructions you will know how to write similar ones".

Number 4. The trainee Operator is to read out aloud to the Supervisor four Maxi boiler room temperature guages in the boiler room to an accuracy of +/− 1° C.

Our Comments:

Number 1

Performance	*"The trainee will stitch Paradise Jeans".*
Criterion	*"so that they will pass company inspection standards".*
Comments	*Performance vague; absence of conditions.*
Suggested rewrite	*The trainee will stitch Paradise Jeans, on a workshop machine, given cut pieces and patterns, so that they will pass company inspection standards.*

Number 2

Performance	*"You are to criticise each of three sales presentations."*
Conditions	*"Using form CT61."*
Criterion	*"Within 25 minutes."*
Comments	*The Conditions are vague: are these live presentations? are they videotaped? is it a training simulation? The Criterion is OK, but is it not more important to be accurate rather than speedy?*
Suggested rewrite:	*"After watching three live sales presentations you will criticise each presentation on Form CT61 provided, comparing your observations with those of the supervising salesman immediately afterwards.*

MAKE SURE YOUR OBJECTIVES ARE REALISTIC

Number 3

Performance	*"You will know how to write similar ones".*
Conditions	*"After scanning sample instructions."*
Comment	*"Know" is too vague an action verb for performance: what you mean by "know" might not be what we mean by "know". There is no criterion. With this in mind, try rewriting this Specific Objective yourself.*

Number 4

Performance	*"The trainee Operator is to read out aloud to the Supervisor four Maxi boiler room temperature guages."*
Conditions	*"in the boiler room."*
Criterion	*"to an accuracy of +/– 1° C."*

A Perfect Specific Objective! There is not a problem here. If you found one you had better reread this Component

---

Writing Specific Objectives in such detail is a fundamentally useful guide to preparing your training and in establishing realistic instructions. You know what you want to teach before you start and can discard the irrelevant at the beginning, so concentrating on the necessary.

Figure 174

We will now tabulate the important steps which you should follow when defining Specific Objectives. Remember that you are identifying the parts (Specific Objectives) which make up the whole (the General Objective).

WRITING THE SPECIFIC OBJECTIVES: PROCEDURE

1. State the General Objective from which you are to derive the Specific Objectives which follow. Usually this statement will be in terms of expected Learning Outcomes.
2. List underneath the Specific Objectives which break down the general statement of the General Objective into detailed learning outcomes. Each Specific Objective describes the terminal performance – the final behaviour – which trainees are to demonstrate when they have achieved the objective.
3. Begin each Specific Objective with a verb which specifies trainee performance, or behaviour; this is an action which is usually measurable and certainly observable.
4. Include in each Specific Objective a statement of the Conditions in which the Specific Objective is to be achieved.
5. Include in each Specific Objective a statement of the Criteria whereby the successful achievement of the desired trainee behaviour may be judged.
6. Describe enough Specific Objectives in the form of learning outcomes to ensure that the actual training content in each Specific Objective is covered by trainee behaviour.
7. Check to ensure that the actual training content in each Specific Objective is kept to a minimum; you are concentrating on actions rather than content.
8. Make sure that each Specific Objective is relevant to the General Objective from which it is derived.
9. Refine the original General Objective(s) if necessary, having defined the Specific Objectives.
10. Check your Specific Objectives to ensure that duplication has been avoided.
11. Sequence your Specific Objectives.
12. Ensure throughout all stages of this procedure that you use information already obtained through your previous Design System Analyses.

Figure 175

We have included in the procedure shown in Figure 175 three steps which we require to examine more carefully. Which are they?

Items 3, 11 and 12. We need to have a closer look at the selection of appropriate action verbs; at how we sequence Specific Objectives and how we incorporate information from previous Analysis into our procedure for defining Objectives. The consideration of these points will be made in the next Component, although you can begin to work on them now, especially the last one, using material available already.

Before we do this, we will illustrate the procedure for writing Specific Objectives in a diagram.

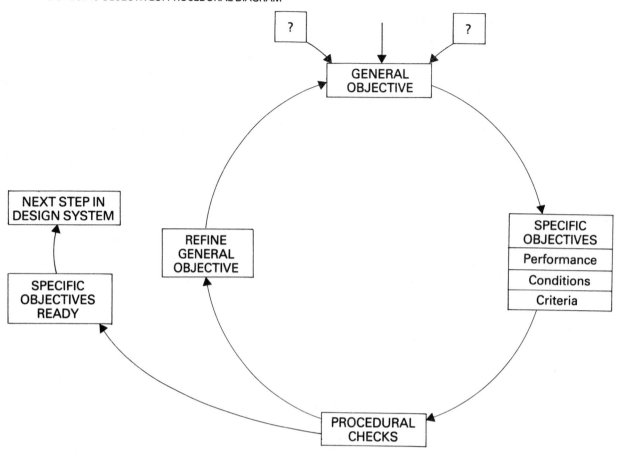

Figure 176

What do the two unlabelled boxes with ? in them indicate.

The box labels are "Needs Analysis" and "Task Analysis". They show information which is fed into your General Objectives, via your Aims.

What are the procedural checks shown in Figure 176?

They are the checks shown in Numbers 6, 7, 8 and 9 of the procedure for writing Specific Objectives, Figure 175.

Incidentally, you will meet quite a large number of synonyms for the name "Specific Objectives". They really are all variations on the same theme, but we show them below so that confusion will be avoided. Most of the names are reflections of how different authors highlight different aspects of Aims and Objectives Analysis. The alternative names for Specific Objectives are:

Training Objectives; Performance (Objectives); Behavioural; Learning; Measurable; Instructional; Criterion Referenced; Enabling; Terminal.

The last pair of names are not really synonyms; they express a different point of view about how objectives may be used.

Some users of the Objectives Model of Course Design begin by deriving Terminal Objectives from a General Objective. Terminal Objectives describe the behaviour/performance which the trainee is to achieve at the end of training and they are much the same as Specific Objectives.

Enabling Objectives are different in that they outline the intermediate behaviours which a trainee shows, or the different levels of performance to be realised, on the way to fulfilling the Terminal Objective. The idea is that a trainee must achieve each Enabling Objective, usually in a recognised sequence, before passing on to the next and finally to the last or Terminal Objective.

Sometimes trainers and course designers prefer this idea of using sequential Enabling Objectives, especially where a skill is to be learned.

We show this idea in the next Figure.

154

ENABLING AND TERMINAL OBJECTIVES

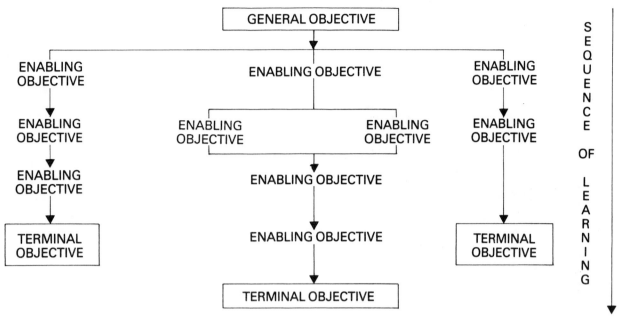

Figure 177

TERMINAL STEPS

Figure 178

▰▰▰

As an example of enabling objectives, when calculating a sales discount, there are certain mathematical procedures which you have to follow. Achieving competence in each procedure, each marked by an enabling objective, enables you to pass on to the next procedure and finally to being able to make a sales discount which is the Terminal Objective.

Would you agree that Terminal Objectives, being last in achievement, are prepared last by the training designer?

Not necessarily; when preparing objectives, trainers frequently begin with the Terminal Objectives and then develop Enabling Objectives to provide a series of intermediate steps to reach the Terminal Objectives.

▰▰▰

Casting your mind back over what you have read in this Component, can you suggest any difference between achieving a **behaviour** (as in Behavioural Objective) and achieving a **performance** (as in Performance Objective)?

There is a slight difference in that achieving a Behaviour means that all trainees must exhibit pretty much the same behaviour after training; there isn't much room for differences here. However, achieving a similar Performance _ and here the trainer is checking and measuring the performance of some act and not measuring and observing a behavioural change in the trainee _ may be attained by a variety of different behaviours.

A single example: if the Terminal Objective is "winning tennis matches", then the performance is similar, ie, it is a winning performance. But think of the different behaviours which actual tennis players exhibit when making a winning performance! The result is the same; the behaviour can vary. See what we mean? Whilst the conditions of performance are the same, eg. the Centre Court at Wimbledon, some players fail to achieve the criteria expected of good behaviour, eg. good manners. So performance and behaviour are not the same.

Consequently, as it is really "performance" which we are after improving and achieving, especially in the skills and knowledge areas, the term "performance objective" is more commonly used now instead of "behavioural objective".

We have elected to use "specific objective" as we are concentrating on stating the detail and the increasingly specific detail of our objectives' performance, or behaviour. In the area of trainee attitudes, behaviour is paramount, however.

The next Component deals with the selection of suitable verbs used in describing Specific Objectives, the sequencing of objectives and some views on the advantages and disadvantages of their use.

Summary

- Specific Objectives are derived from General Objectives and are used to break down the General Objective into clusters of specific behaviours or performances which the trainee has to attain by the end of training, see Figure 147.
- Put another way, Specific Objectives identify closely the learning outcomes, or end products, of the training.
- Each Specific Objective contains a detailed, but succinct, statement of Performance/ Behaviour, of Conditions in which the objective is to be achieved and of Criteria standards for judging the success of performance.
- Important steps in writing Specific Objectives are checking that all of the behaviours embodied in the General Objectives are covered by the Specific Objectives; that duplication is avoided between objectives; that you sequence the objectives properly and that information is used from other analyses which have been made when undertaking each System Function in the System Activity of Analysis.
- Enabling and Terminal Objectives offer a slightly different method of structuring your objectives, offering a ready-made sequencing.
- Finally, before the next Component, try this Checkpoint.

▨▨▨

Obviously, we are advocating the use of objectives in our systematic approach to training. However, in the place where you would normally expect to find Objectives, we use "Key Words". Why do you think this is?

Think about it and check with your Programme Study Guide to find out where our objectives are, should you have forgotten.

As for the answer to why we have used this "Keywords – Objectives" system, please wait until the end of the next Component. This will give you plenty of time to discover or reason through your answer.

So, "See this space" at the end of Component 3, Study Unit 2.

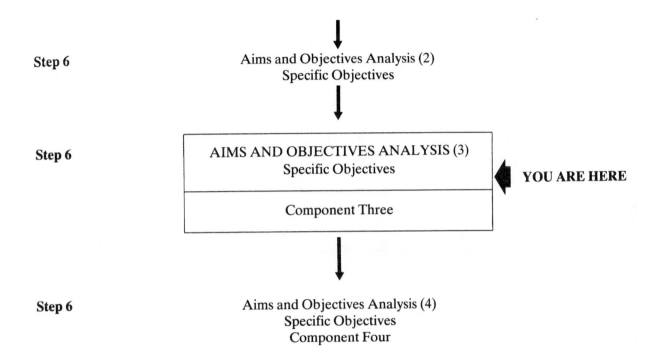

Step 6   Aims and Objectives Analysis (2)
Specific Objectives

Step 6

AIMS AND OBJECTIVES ANALYSIS (3)
Specific Objectives

Component Three

YOU ARE HERE

Step 6   Aims and Objectives Analysis (4)
Specific Objectives
Component Four

Component 3:

Further Analysis of the Specific Objectives of your Training

Key Words

 Sequencing specific objectives; chronological sequencing; logical sequencing; skills sequencing; domain sequencing; rules sequencing; domains; cognitive; psychomotor; affective; categories in the domains; sequencing process.

Introduction

> **Considered in this Component**
> **System Activity: Analysis**
> **System Function:**
> **Aims and Objectives Analysis**

In this Component we are going to continue our examination of SpecificObjectives by considering the one topic only:

How to sequence Specific Objectives

Checkpoint

Let's practise what we preach. For the topic mentioned above, write down four Mager-type Specific Objectives, beginning "On completion of the next two components the trainer will be able to ____" then state your Specific Objectives.

Here are ours:-
- *"Sequence a series of Specific Objectives (1) from a list which he or she has prepared (2) with complete accuracy (3)."*

- *"Select action verbs (1) from lists given in the Component (2) which are entirely suitable for the Specific Objectives being developed (3)."*
- *"Compare the advantages and disadvantages of using Specific Objectives (1) from information given in this and the next Components (2) with a balanced perspective (3)."*
- *"Demonstrate a positive attitude towards the use of the Objectives Model (1) when planning and when writing training materials (2) by preparing Objectives to a high standard of accuracy and efficiency (3).*

We have placed bracketed numbers in each Objective to show:-
(1) The Performance (observable action or behaviour) which the trainer is to achieve; thus, in the first Objective, the performance is, "Sequence a series of Specific Objectives."
(2) The Conditions, eg "from a list which he or she has prepared."
(3) The Criteria (or Standard) eg "with complete accuracy."

PRACTISING WHAT YOU PREACH

Figure 179

So let's begin.

How to Sequence Specific Objectives

Having learned various techniques so far in this Programme, we should always try to apply them in our thinking. At the beginning of this Component we used the technique of structuring Objectives, although we have not completed our work on this process yet, as you know. A suitable technique which we can use here is that of Task Analysis; try it out for yourself in the following Checkpoint.

Make a Task (Topic) Analysis of the Topic "Sequencing' Objectives" using only a first Level of Analysis, see Figure 56, Component 5, Study Unit 1.

Our analysis is shown in the next Figure.

TASK ANALYSIS: TOPIC, "SEQUENCING SPECIFIC OBJECTIVES"

SEQUENCING SPECIFIC OBJECTIVES

| Chronological Sequencing | Concept Sequencing | Skills Sequencing | Domain Sequencing | Rules Sequencing |

Figure 180

We can deal with each of these in turn.

Chronological Sequencing

This is the Sequencing of Specific Objectives according to the chronology of the **events** with which the objectives are concerned; the Objectives are placed in the same order as that of the occurrence of the events.

So if you are arranging a presentation on the development of your organisation, you arrange your Objectives to cover each historical event as it happened in time order; your Objectives are sequenced in date order.

Chronological sequencing is restricted to Objectives dealing with material which has a basis in historical time.

CHRONOLOGICAL SEQUENCING

Events	Specific Objectives
Founding "Spriggs Cannonballs" 1801	Objective 1
By appointment to Duke of Wellington, 1808	Objective 2
Second Factory opened 1812	Objective 3
Founder, Geo. Spriggs dies 1820 Albert Spriggs, Chairman, 1821	Objective 4
Crimean War main official supplier 1853 to 1856	Objective 5 Objective 6
Conversion of Numbers 1 and 2 factories to shellmaking 1870	Objective 7
Albert Spriggs Retires, 1871. Clarence Spriggs, Chairman	Objective 8 Objective 9
Boer War, official suppliers 1899 to 1902	Objective 10 Objective 11
Great World War official suppliers 1914 to 1918	Objective 12 Objective 13 Objective 14 Objective 15 Objective 16
Number 2 Factory closes 1919	Objective 17

and so on

Figure 181

As an example of translating an Event into an objective, you could state: "Apprentice cannonball makers should be able to give the exact date of the founding of Spriggs Cannonballs at all times when asked, with complete accuracy."

Concept Sequencing

A concept is a "key idea" and concepts form the fundamental parts of knowledge. It is necessary for the trainee to understand Concept 1 before moving on to Concept 2 and so on.

CONCEPT SEQUENCING

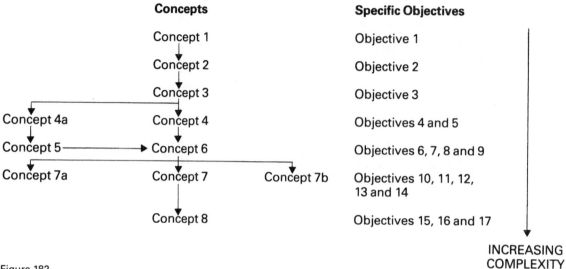

Figure 182

As the Concepts become more complex, they may require several Specific Objectives to cover the learning in them.

An example of a concept is "gunpowder compositions" and a specific objective derived from it could be, "Apprentice Cannonball makers should be able to state the compositions of five different types of gunpowder, at any time when asked to do so by the supervisor, naming the correct ratios of saltpetre, carbon and sulphur required for each composition".

Skills Sequencing

The idea of skills sequencing of Specific Objectives is much like that of Concept Sequencing. You begin with identifying either the simpler skills, or the simpler elements of a skill, which the trainee has to master before proceeding to more complex skills or building up a single complex skill.

SKILLS SEQUENCING

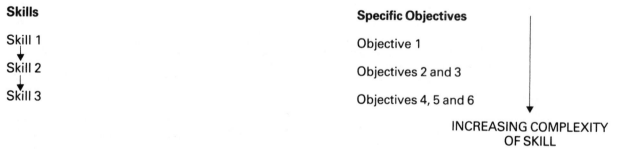

Figure 183

Objective 1 will test mastery or competence of the trainees for Skill 1; when achieved, the trainee moves onto Skill 2 and Objectives 2 and 3.

An example of a skill is "mixing gunpowder" and one objective derived from it could be: "Apprentice Cannonball makers must mix Number Three Gunpowder in the Factory Mixing Shop, to exactly the correct composition as laid down in British Standard G.4251, allowing five minutes mixing time per kilo of gunpowder and without making an explosion".

Plenty of criteria to be fulfilled in this objective and the Sprigg's trainers will certainly know explosively if their training isn't adequate to achieve the objective!

Both Concept and Skills Sequencing represent a fairly simple and straightforward approach to the problem of sequencing your Specific Objectives. What other way of sequencing can you suggest, based on these techniques?

A well-known method is to categorise the trainee performances into three major areas of activity, whether concerned with

> *Knowledge, or*
> *Skills, or*
> *Attitudes.*
Each of these areas of activity is called a **domain**.

The fundamental link between Concept and Skills Sequencing and Domain Sequencing is that all three deal basically with increasing complexity and consequently difficulty. However, Domain Sequencing is more sophisticated than either Concept or Skills Sequencing and we shall see why next.

Domain Sequencing

We have seen that there are three major Domains. Usually, they are distinguished by different names from those which we have used above; although the names are different, the sense is virtually the same:-

> Knowledge = **Cognitive Domain**
> Skills = **Psychomotor Domain**
> Attitudes = **Affective Domain**

Each of these Domains can be subdivided into categories and these categories themselves are scaled according to the difficulty and complexity of the actions and thinking which they contain. Here the greater sophistication of Domain Sequencing can be distinguished from any other sequencing technique.

The idea of Domains comes from an American educationist, Benjamin S. Bloom in 1960. He classified educational objectives in the cognitive area. Subsequently, Kratwohl produced a taxomony (classification) for the affective domain. Both men headed committees of teachers, psychologists and test experts. It is interesting to note that a complete classification system was not developed for the psychomotor domain, at that time.

Recently, taxonomies have been prepared by others for the psychomotor domain and we shall show a couple of these.

The taxonomies are very important in classifying learning outcomes and in helping the trainer sort out his sequences. After examining each, we shall go into more detail of the benefits which taxonomies confer on the trainer; they are the areas in which we all work as trainers.

KING TRAINER'S DOMAINS

Figure 183a

Express, in your own words, how Bloom graded Specific Objectives.

Bloom, as we suggested, graded objectives according to the level of thinking required to accomplish them. See if you can sort these levels out in the next Checkpoint.

Bloom named six levels of thinking or cognition for cognitive objectives. These are: comprehension, synthesis, application, evaluation, knowledge, analysis. Arrange these "famous six" into an order based on the level of thinking each requires.

The six were arranged by Bloom thus:

THE COGNITIVE DOMAIN

EVALUATION	HIGHER LEVEL OF THINKING/COGNITION
SYNTHESIS	
ANALYSIS	
APPLICATION	
COMPREHENSION	
KNOWLEDGE	LOWER LEVEL OF THINKING/COGNITION

Figure 184

This Figure shows a hierarchy (a ranking in grades one above another) which suggests that achievement of the higher grades depends on prior attainment of those lower. It can be argued that you have to first **know** the facts, then **comprehend** them before you can **apply** them. Finally, having achieved these lower order objectives you can **analyse, synthesise** and **evaluate** the highest level objectives.

How does this hierarchy relate to our design system?

Well, first of all we describe the facts, give examples and Checkpoints which help you comprehend them before you apply them in your work situation. Finally, we spend a great deal of time describing techniques of analysis before moving on in our systematic approach to synthesis and evaluation.

SO YOU THINK YOU KNOW IT ALL?

go to the bottom of the hierachy

EVALUATION

KNOWLEDGE

Figure 185

The Psychomotor Domain

Performance. This Domain measures the skill – sometimes called the motor skill – performance of trainees and involves the physical manipulation of equipment, tools, supplies and any other object in your firm. Here are some examples of motor skills performance.

use a computer,
type a letter,
operate a machine tool,
build a wall,
develop a film,
thresh corn.

Conditions in this domain are mainly concerned with the working environment and the materials necessary for the jobs, above, eg

given a Paragon computer,
in an office,
in the workshop,
given a building plan and construction materials,
following exposure,
in the granary.

The **Criteria** or standards to be achieved in this domain relate to the finished product, the actual performance and the standard of performance to be realised.

Once again you are advised to review Figures 171 and 172 before looking at our examples, these include:-

— to the standards described in the course handout.
— at 60 words per minutes with no more than one error per 60 words.
— to the manufacturer's user manual specifications.
— so that the finished wall meets the standards outlined in the building plan and will pass the company site manager's inspection.
— according to the company darkroom standards stated in "Instruction for Developing", Brief VFV689Y.
— within acceptable wastage rates.

A complete objective, using the information given in the last three sections would be, "Thresh corn, in the granary, within acceptable wastage rates." Work out the remainder from the examples given of Performance, Conditions and Criteria.

The Affective Domain

As **performances** in the affective, or attitudinal, domain involve the observation and demonstration of feelings, sensitivities, interpersonal relationships, attitudes, ideas etc., they are often difficult to measure because they sometimes cannot be seen easily. Unfortunately, the research on attitudes shows that a significant change in attitudes during and after training tends apparently to weaken over a comparatively short period of time. After two or three months, trainees have largely, if not completely, gone back to believing what they thought in the first place, anyway.

So with all of these difficulties in mind, the trainee might be required to:-
— show sympathy towards patients.
— comprehend dangers in the darkroom.
— demonstrate increased awareness.
— accept more responsibility.

The **Conditions** in which attitudes are shown is one of the least important considerations, because we hope that the feelings will be shown in all conditions, at least to some degree. However, conditions which could show the necessary feeling related to the performances shown in the last section, are:-
— when unobserved ie. during the admission procedure.
— in the laboratory.
— at work in the office.
— when unsupervised.

As we suggested, attitudes are not only hard to observe, but they are certainly not directly measurable. Sometimes trainers become ridiculous when trying to measure attitudes and we show an actual example, which we read about, in the next Figure.

ATTITUDES: GOING OVER THE TOP

Figure 185a

In trying to measure an improved attitude to reading on a statistical basis, a training department counted their trainees' use of the library before and after training. The specific objective related to "double the book usage as demonstrated by library withdrawals". Nobody found out if the trainees actually read the books they took out! So don't overdo it.

However, don't forget that you can always **ask** the trainees about their attitudes and the Paired Scales and Adjective and Semantic Differential Scales of Needs Analysis (Components 2, 3 and 4) are useful here.

The **Criterion** for achievement of an affective Specific Objective calls for **behaviour** which shows if an attitude or feeling is present. So both the performance and the criterion statements will each contain an action verb or word. For example:
— comforts a worried patient during pre-operation preparation.
— regularly reports on darkroom conditions.
— and takes account of colleagues' sensitivities.
— by volunteering for extra duties and by relating well to customers.

You will have to consider carefully the behaviour patterns which you might expect to see and be prepared to accept any one, or a combination of behaviours which show that you have achieved your objective(s).

Many skills in this area are social or life skills, much concerned with what the trainees are like as people, not only in the workshop or organisation, but also in the wider area of living with others, successfully.

▰▰▰

Do you consider that recognising objectives as purely cognitive, psychomotor or affective is an easy task?

Generally, Specific Objectives can be recognised readily for what they are **primarily.** *Many, however, are not "purely" of one type. Identify these by the sort of primary performance which is required.*

▰▰▰

In writing Specific Objectives, you allocate each to one of the three domains. What sort of objectives do you think that you would be writing primarily for the following trainees?
1. A sales assistant.
2. A bricklayer.
3. A packer.
4. A social worker.
5. An accountant.
6. A receptionist.
7. A fork-lift operator.
8. A laboratory technician.

Answers
1. *Primarily cognitive; an affective element (dealing with customers), some psychomotor (cash register).*
2. *Psychomotor.*
3. *Psychomotor.*
4. *Cognitive; some affective.*
5. *Cognitive; some psychomotor (computer: calculators etc).*
6. *Affective; cognitive.*
7. *Psychomotor.*
8. *Cognitive (processes) and psychomotor (apparatus).*

In the last few pages, we have been making sure that you have a firm understanding of the organisation of the three domains as a basis for Domain Sequencing.

Figure 184 shows Bloom's Cognitive Domain and the different **levels** of which it consists. We shall now look at the various levels for all three domains.

OK. So you look at the levels. But how do they help the sequencing process?

*This is the **key** question. As the levels are graded according to difficulty and complexity, you should* **sequence your objectives so that you begin,** *as far as possible,* **with the lower, less difficult levels,** *subsequently writing objectives which are concerned with more complex behaviour.*

Our next four Figures show the major categories in each of the three domains. We have shown two breakdowns for the Psychomotor domain so that you can pick the one which is most useful to you and for training in your firm. Both of the Cognitive and Affective Domain diagrams are very well known, but there is variation for the Psychomotor.

CATEGORIES OF THE COGNITIVE DOMAIN

HIGH LEVEL

EVALUATION
Ability to judge value of material involving decision-making, selecting or judging based on reasons and definite criteria.

SYNTHESIS
Ability to put parts together to form a new whole, or entity from the original, eg producing a unique communication, building up a classification. Learning outcomes stress creative behaviours, emphasising the formation of **new** structures and patterns.

ANALYSIS
Ability to break down material into parts until relationships between the parts are clear, eg identification of parts and their organisation.

APPLICATION
Ability to use learned material by applying it to the job and in new situations different from original learning context, eg application of techniques, rules, principles, concepts, laws, theories.

COMPREHENSION
Ability to grasp the meaning of material, ie interpreting translating, estimating, summarising, or paraphrasing given information.

KNOWLEDGE
Remembering of previously recalled material, recognition and recall of facts, theories.

Figure 186

LOW LEVEL

166

CATEGORIES IN THE PSYCHOMOTOR DOMAIN 1

HIGH LEVEL

NATURALISATION
**Skill or skills
become automatic**
with limited mental
or physical exertion:
easy skill user.

ARTICULATION
**Harmony and consistency used
to combine two or several
skills** in one major skill
sequence.

PRECISION
**Reproduces a skill with accuracy and
proportion.** Generally, an exact
performance independent of original
source.

MANIPULATION
**Performs skill in accordance
with an instruction**
rather than by
observation.

IMITATION
**Sees a skill and
tries to repeat it.**

Figure 187

LOW LEVEL

The Systematic Design of Training Courses

HIGH LEVEL

ORIGINATION
Highly developed skills
allowing operator
creativity in originating
new patterns of movement
to fit a new situation or
problem.

ADAPTATION
**Skill so well developed that
operator can modify movement
patterns** to fit new
requirements or meet
problems.

COMPLEX OVERT RESPONSE
**Skilful performance of a complex
skill**: quick, smooth, accurate
performance; minimal energy used.

MECHANISMS
**Various skills where the performance
is habitual** and is made with some
confidence and proficiency.

GUIDED RESPONSE
Early stage of learning a complex skill,
eg imitation (copying act by demonstrator)
and trial-by-error (identifying a
suitable response).

SET
Readiness to take an action
ie mental set (mental
readiness to act) physical
and emotional set (willingness
to act).

PERCEPTION
**Sense organs pick up cues
which guide motor activity.**
Selecting cues and using
cues in performance.

LOW LEVEL

Figure 188

CATEGORIES IN THE AFFECTIVE DOMAIN

HIGH LEVEL

CHARACTERISING
Trainees behaviour becomes consistent with internalised values: develops a characteristic "life style". Behaviour consistent and predictable. Learning Outcomes: reliable behaviour which is typical and characteristic of the trainee.

ORGANISING
Trainee brings together different values and resolves conflicts between them; becomes committed to a set of values and displays this in behaviour. Learning Outcomes: trainee becomes a responsible person and develops a reliable philosophy.

VALUING
The worth or value a trainee places on a particular object, happening, or behaviour. **Trainee displays behaviour consistent with a single belief** or attitude in situations where he or she is not forced to comply or obey. Learning Outcomes: consistent and stable behaviour.

RESPONDING
Active participation on the part of the trainee. Attends and usually reacts to stimuli or happening in classroom/workshop. Learning Outcomes: willingness to respond (and reads voluntarily) and satisfaction in responding (reads for pleasure, does extra work). Develops personal interests.

RECEIVING
Trainee willing to attend to stimuli and to particular happening (workshop activities, reading a manual, music, simply listening). Learning Outcomes: simple awareness to selective attention.

LOW LEVEL

Figure 189

What is a taxonomy? Give examples.

A taxonomy is a categorisation or classification borrowed from biologists who classify plants and animals from the simple to the complex.
Examples are the categories of the three domains.

Figures 186 to 189, in a way, show levels for trainee competency, as a sequence for the performance of a task. As the levels increase in complexity of performance, they provide a guide to sequencing and progress, from the simpler to the complex.

Describe the process whereby taxonomies help the sequencing of Specific Objectives. How does this sequencing assist training?

The process of sequencing and relating this sequencing to help our training is:-

Step 1:   *Identify the domain to which the Specific Objectives belong.*

Step 2:   *Determine the category to which an objective belongs, ie decide on the taxonomic level shown in the appropriate Figure 186 to 189.*

Step 3:   *Sequence your Specific Objectives beginning with the lower levels and then proceed to the higher levels.*

Step 4:   *Develop your training so that you begin by instructing in the lower levels, where this is necessary. With trainees of high calibre you may be able to omit the earlier and therefore lower-level stages. Your Entering Behaviour Analysis will tell you where to start.*

Step 5:   *As trainees master the objectives for each level then proceed to the next higher level for which you have written Specific Objectives.*

We show this process in the next Figure.

SEQUENCING OBJECTIVES AND TRAINING
Cognitive Objectives only used in this example.

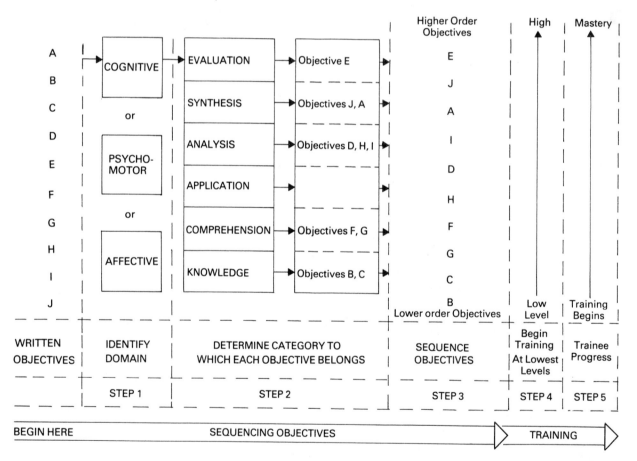

Figure 190

What strikes you as unusual about Step 2 of Figure 190?

No objectives are shown for the Application category. In practice it happens frequently that a level, or levels, in a taxonomy do not have related Specific Objectives. Very often the higher levels are not reached by training, because the course is a short one and there is insufficient time for development, or simply because the knowledge or skills which are the focus of the training are of a lower order.

In Figures 187 and 188, we offered you two charts showing categories of objectives in the psychomotor domain. Why is this?

The classification in the psychomotor area is not as well defined as in the cognitive and affective areas, where the categories of Bloom and Kratwohl's taxonomies are famous and accepted. We are offering you a choice in the psychomotor area.

To revert to Figure 180, you will recollect that we have one type of sequencing left; what is it?

As the Figure shows, it is

Rules Sequencing
If you glance back at Figure 65, you will see what we mean immediately by Rules Sequencing.

Figure 65 shows the "Rules" for sequencing Rules and numbers 1, 2, 3, 4, 5 and 6 offer some very commonsensical, simple rules for sequencing. If you apply these Rules to your Specific Objectives in the fashion of the Figure which follows, your objectives sequencing will never go far wrong.

Rules Sequencing is a quick and commonsensical way of sequencing Specific Objectives. Always make sure an objective is essential before you write it.

Don't forget that when you have sequenced your objectives you might find that some of the higher order objectives include the material covered by lower order ones which you have written first. Delete the latter.

Our next Component concludes System Function, Aims and Objectives Analysis.

Before you begin work on it, reread the last two Components, so that you are thoroughly familiar with them. We shall include quite a lot of exercises in Component Four so that you can practice what we preach.

Summary

Much of the material in this Component, especially the information concerning the three Domains, is very widely applicable in training. You will find the terms cognitive, psychomotor and affective used throughout this Training Technology Programme and the details which we have included will give you a sound basis for comprehending, applying, analysing, synthesising and evaluating all training materials.

RULES SEQUENCING

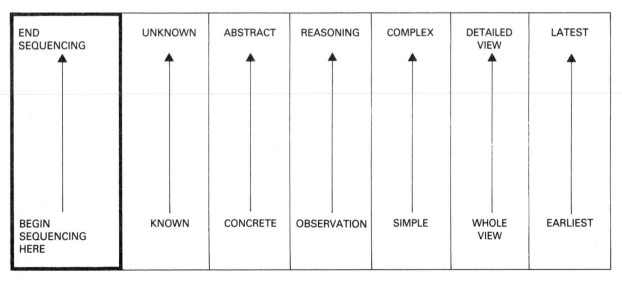

Figure 191

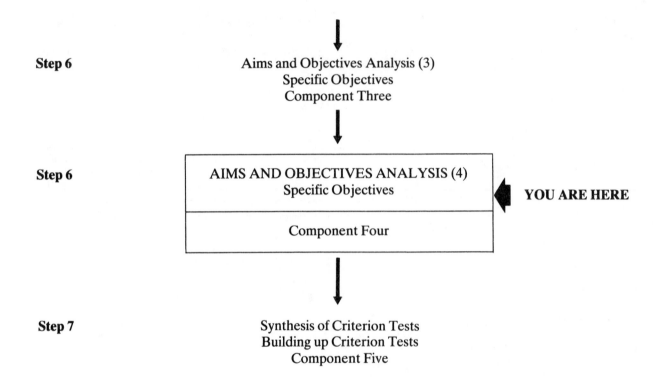

Step 6   Aims and Objectives Analysis (3)
Specific Objectives
Component Three

Step 6   AIMS AND OBJECTIVES ANALYSIS (4)
Specific Objectives   **YOU ARE HERE**

Component Four

Step 7   Synthesis of Criterion Tests
Building up Criterion Tests
Component Five

Component 4:

Final Analysis of the Specific Objectives of your Training

Key Words

Suitable action verbs and phrases; samples for general objectives in the cognitive, psychomotor and affective domains; linking the system functions with aims and objective analysis; advantages and disadvantages of using objectives; key words and objectives.

Introduction

"AN OBJECTIVE DETACHMENT"

> **Considered in this Component**
> **System Activity: Analysis**
> **System Function:**
> **Aims and Objectives Analysis**

We have spent a lot of time on Objectives and particularly Specific Objectives, because they are so significant a part of our design system.

Having clear objectives is an important part of any trainer's armoury. If you know exactly where you are going, you can apply an objective "yardstick" to what you ought, or ought not to be doing and have a "compass" which guides you through your training (and life!) activities.

So remember your objectives.

Figure 192

In the last Component on the System Function of Aims and Objectives Analysis, we are going to consider

Using suitable action verbs, and phrases when writing Objectives.

Linking up Aims and Objectives Analysis with the other Functions of our Systematic Approach to Training.

The Objectives Model : Advantages and Disadvantages.

We shall start with

Using Suitable Action Verbs and Phrases when writing Objectives

The next Figures 193, 195 and 197 are charts which show suitable action verbs and phrases for both General and Specific Objectives.

These charts are extremely useful when you are composing Objectives.

COGNITIVE DOMAIN:
SAMPLES OF GENERAL OBJECTIVES AND OF VERBS FOR STATING SPECIFIC OBJECTIVES

General Objectives	Verbs for Stating Specific Objectives
KNOWLEDGE	
— Knows definite facts — Knows methods & techniques — Knows principles — Knows simpler concepts — Knows operation function — Knows purpose and function	Cognises, enlightens, learns, identifies, labels, matches, gives, sketches, lists, describes, defines, names, underlines, outlines, selects, states, reproduces.
COMPREHENSION	
— Comprehends methods/data — Understands facts — Makes estimates — Interprets diagrams — Interprets written material — Understands procedures	Discerns, comprehends, rewrites, solves, infers, explains, defends, converts, distinguishes, estimates, generalises, compares, discusses, determines, predicts, gives examples, extends, interprets.
APPLICATION	
— Applies new concepts — Solves new problems — Solves problems not met before — Constructs diagrams/graphs — Shows correct usage of new methods — Applies new procedures	Attends, practises, studies, perseveres, changes, manipulates, prepares, computes, demonstrates, operates, produces, discovers, modifies, shows, uses, verifies, solves, relates, applies.
ANALYSIS	
— Recognises assumptions — Analyses a structure — Analyses the organisation of a plan, design, experiment — Recognises fallacies in reasoning — Sees the differences between facts and inferences — Breaks down material into sub units — Breaks down information in parts — Breaks down knowledge into procedures	Diagnoses, breaks down, identifies, outlines, analyses, recognises, distinguishes, categorises, differentiates, diagrams, graphs, discriminates, points out, chooses, separates, subdivides, infers, outlines, sketches out, illustrates, clarifies, elucidates.

SYNTHESIS

— Develops new ideas
— Gives an organised lesson/talk
— Writes a creative piece of work
— Builds up a new plan
— Makes up a design
— Integrates training in different areas into a problem-solving plan
— Makes up new schemes
— Puts together ideas from training into new procedures
— Suggests a plan for an experiment

Combines, explains, builds up, organises, appraises, composes, designs, engenders, plans, tells, explains, creates, re-arranges, modifies, revises, re-orders, re-writes, devises, reconstructs, re-states, compiles, summarises, writes, synthesises, puts together, suggests, makes, integrates, enlarges, extends.

EVALUATION

— Judges the consistency of a plan or design
— Judges the adequacy of a course
— Judges the value of supporting data on which conclusions are based
— Judges the value of conclusions
— Judges the work of a plan by using internal criteria
— Judges the efficiency of a design by using external standards

Appraises, criticizes, judges, explains, compares, discriminates, contrasts, describes, summarises, justifies, concludes, relates, points out, questions, attacks, defends, supports.

Figure 193

Figure 193, like 195 and 197 are **samples** of verbs and phrases which you might like to use, depending on the subject of training which you are doing. There is some overlap, naturally, because of the suitability of some of the verbs for both general and specific objectives and for different domain categories.

Try using some of the suggested examples in writing general and specific objectives for your own courses. Make sure that you use all of the different **categories**, or **levels** of the taxonomy.

COGNITIVE VERBS IN ACTION

Figure 194

For details of each category in the domains shown in Figures 193, 195 and 197 and for explanations of what they mean, refer to appropriate Figures in Component 3, Study Unit 2, Package 1.

PSYCHOMOTOR DOMAIN:
SAMPLES OF GENERAL OBJECTIVES AND VERBS FOR STATING SPECIFIC OBJECTIVES

General Objectives	**Verbs for Stating Specific Objectives**

PERCEPTION

— Recognises when equipment is functioning properly by visual cues	Discerns, senses, recognises, identifies, selects, describes, distinguishes, relates, isolates, separates.
— Recognises when equipment is functioning properly by auditory cues	
— Recognises when equipment is functioning properly by tactile cues	
— Recognises when equipment is functioning properly by olfactory cues	
— Recognises that a product is satisfactory by sense of taste	
— Identifies machinery malfunction by sensory cues	
— Can distinguish between different cues	
— Can select relevant cues	
— Can relate cue perception to performance	

SET

— Demonstrates wish to type efficiently	Starts, shows, displays, responds, proceeds, demonstrates, knows steps, offers.
— Shows proper walk when modelling	
— Knows sequence of steps in making a dovetail joint	

GUIDED RESPONSE

— Performs proper sequence of hand movements as demonstrated	Writes, applies, determines, sequences, draws, compiles, puts together, performs, copies, assembles, organises, works, places, manipulates, builds, dismantles, measures, manoeuvres, mends, mixes, calibrates, takes to pieces, constructs, displays, cuts, fastens, grinds, moves, produces, heats, repairs, sketches, dissects, fixes, unfastens, operates.
— Copies the trainer's demonstration of bandaging a sprain	
— Uses trial and error to determine the best sequence for preparing a pudding	
— Makes a tennis stroke as demonstrated	
— Follows emergency procedures for switching off machinery, watched by trainer	

MECHANISM

— Operates on overhead projector
— Writes with a legible hand
— Demonstrates simple operations with
  a power saw
— Goes through the basic procedures to plane
  a piece of wood
— Reads an ammeter

Same as for Guided Response

COMPLEX OVERT RESPONSE

— Repairs a-v equipment efficiently
— Shows skill in driving a heavy goods vehicle
— Demonstrates correct use of a precision tool
— Works telephone switchboard quickly
  and accurately
— Demonstrates the correct way to shoot at goal
— Performs skilfully with welding equipment
— Makes out a guest's hotel account efficiently

Same as for Guided Response.

ADAPTATION

— Uses lady's tights when fan belt is broken
— Makes a substitute when proper machine tool
  is broken
— Modifies driving techniques in bad weather
  conditions
— Adjusts waitressing procedures when demand
  becomes unexpectedly heavy
— Carries out makeshift repairs when proper
  materials not available
— Changes room allocation procedures when
  extra guests arrive
— Modifies operation of pumping machinery to
  meet overseas conditions

Adjusts, changes, varies, rearranges, revises, alters, modifies, adapts.

ORIGINATION

— Designs new equipment techniques
— Creates a new fashion style
— Creates more efficient assembly procedures
— Derives new cooking methods for feeding
  foreign guests
— Originates a more cost-effective method
  of machining garments

Creates, designs, devises, originates, makes, generates, constructs, arranges, engenders, organises, initiates, develops, progresses, emanates.

Figure 195

 **Checkpoint**

You will have noticed that some of the verbs used for Specific Objectives are also used for General Objectives. Does this matter?

Not really, provided that you keep the **statements** *of the General Objectives what they are supposed to be:* **general**. *Your Specific Objectives might use the same verbs, but they would be much more* **precise and detailed statements**.

In Component Three, we gave two charts for the Psychomotor Domain in Figures 187 and 188. Here we have given examples of one only, Figure 188. You will be able to translate the material shown in Figure 195 for use with both of our psychomotor charts. We picked the more complicated one for our example.

PSYCHOMOTOR VERBS IN ACTION

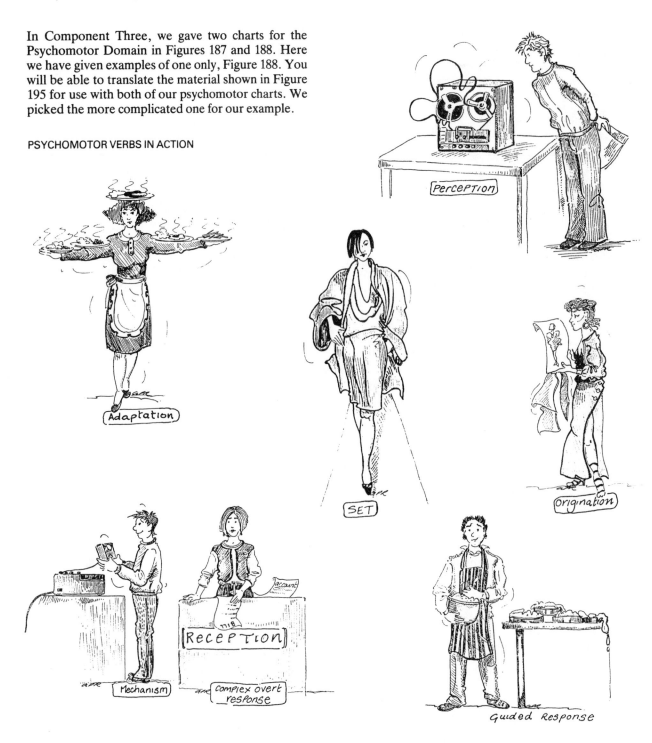

Figure 196

The next Figure shows samples which you may wish to use in the Affective domain. Here we are trying to show how you may write objectives for a **change of attitude** and the Figure gives examples of how this may be brought about. Examples of such changes of attitude might be: to work unsupervised; to demonstrate commitment to safety procedures; to value the efficiency, accuracy and speed of a particular machine tool; to realise and appreciate the importance of good relationships with customers.

AFFECTIVE DOMAIN:
SAMPLES OF GENERAL OBJECTIVES AND VERBS FOR STATING SPECIFIC OBJECTIVES

General Objectives	Verbs for Stating Specific Objectives
RECEIVING	
— Listens with attention — Shows awareness of the importance of training — Watches machinery demonstrations with care — Shows sensitivity to colleagues' problems	Chooses, shows, asks, gives, identifies, describes, names, distinguishes, points out, selects, locates, follows, holds, replies, attends, picks.
RESPONDING	
— Obeys workshop rules — Takes an active part in training — Completes assignment tasks — Shows an interest in following correct procedures — Asks questions during training — Finishes experiments in the laboratory — Follows blueprint with special care and interest — Follows safety regulations methodically — Volunteers for extra duties — Seems to be enjoying the course — Helps other trainees	Helps, responds, complies, answers, replies, recites, gives, assists, presents, obeys, selects, reports, tells, practises, conforms, greets, reads, writes, forms, labels, follows, completes, finishes, offers, discusses, performs, operates, corresponds, communicates, ends.
VALUING	
— Appreciates the course — Tries to improve group skills — Appreciates the role of the operator — Shows interest in the progress of others — Prepared to accept some responsibility for effective work of group — Will have a go at solving problems — Demonstrates committment to improving the firm's image — Values hard work	Describes, values, tries, completes, initiates, reads, joins, defends, explains, follows, proposes, invites, differentiates, works, selects, shares, appreciates, chooses, justifies, demonstrates, reports, studies, weighs.
ORGANISATION	
— Recognises the responsibility of each trainee for improving working conditions/production quotas/the product/service — Accepts personal responsibility — Recognises the need for individual freedom within the structure of the firm's rules — Recognises the importance of the systematic approach to training — Knows own strengths and weaknesses — Formulates sensible plans for his/her future	Accepts, recognises, formulates, organises, adheres, combines, identifies, defends, alters, integrates, modifies, completes, explains, changes, prepares, arranges, orders, alters, finishes, takes, shapes, compares, relates, ends, modifies, gets ready, puts together, generalises, synthesises.
CHARACTERISATION	
— Uses the Objectives Model of training design — Shows reliable awareness of safety in the workshop — Demonstrates reliability, consistency, industriousness, punctuality — Exercises self-discipline — Shows independence and self-reliance — Co-operates with others — Practises a characteristic, reasonable "life-style"	Acts, listens, practises, revises, reforms, shows, discriminates, demonstrates, verifies, maintains, qualifies, modifies, questions, performs, does, exercises, displays, proposes, influences, serves, listens, solves, validates, preaches, co-operates.

Figure 197

The highest level of the Affective Domain is hard for trainees and trainers themselves (you and us) to achieve, or course. You won't be setting many objectives in that area except for your most mature and senior trainees, but the preceding level, Organisation, is achieved commonly.

And so to our last illustration of the three domains.

AFFECTIVE VERBS IN ACTION

Figure 198

Much of the material given so far in this Component is useful for reference purposes. When constructing your own objectives you will find it extremely useful in both structuring, sequencing and picking the correct verb.

At this point it would be beneficial to revise Components 1, 2 and 3. The process of identifying and writing objectives is based on information from other aspects (Functions and Activities) of our design system. Suggest which aspects are particularly helpful and explain why.

We examine these links in the next section of this Component.

Linking up Aims and Objectives Analysis with the other Functions of our Systematic Approach to Training

We will deal with the System Functions which we have examined already, one at a time, beginning with Needs Analysis.

Links with the System Function of Needs Analysis

The **goals** of Needs Analysis give you a lead to writing your Aims and sometimes the General Objectives. This may be a direct lead, in the sense that a Goal which you have written will suffice for an Aim without much modification. At other times the Goals will require re-formulating; this is because Goals are more loosely structured, thus making them a basis only for writing Aims. This looseness comes from the fact that many of your Goals are written by non-trainers and although acceptable for Needs Analysis, need tidying up for Aims and Objectives Analysis. You will remember that we discussed this before in Component 2, 3 and 4 of Study Unit 1, Package 1.

In Figures 28 and 29 of Component 3, the Goals stated there would be quite adequate Aims or General Objectives in themselves, especially in Figure 29, which are excellent General Objectives.

Similarly, the Output of Phase One of Needs Analysis, Figure 33, Component 3 offers a good basis for writing Aims or General Objectives, as do the surveys carried out in that Phase.

You have a further list of useful Goals in the Ouput from Phase Two, shown in Figure 37, Component 3, "Rank Order and Weight of Goals."

In Phase Three of Needs Analysis, the Performance Statements of Figure 43, "Perception Survey, Establishing Needs", can be used when formulating General Objectives, as do the Needs in the "Need Statements" shown in Figure 49 and the "Need Statements in Order of Priority for Action", Figure 52.

Let's take an actual example of how this might work in practice, using the famous Sprigg's Cannonball Factory.

Need statements: in Study Unit 1, Component 4, Figure 52, we saw that under the heading Need Statements, a need was established for Jack Bloggs, a cannonball pourer, to have training in pouring pig iron to the correct weights. When making a Task Analysis of exactly what Jack has to do when pouring, we would make sure that we knew the sort of details required by Figure 71 and 74 of Component 5, Study Unit 1.

From this information we would then proceed to write the general, and specific objectives which would ensure that we got the training right for Jack himself.

Naturally, when thinking about Jack and his training and that of the other cannonball pourers, we would bear in mind the information found from **Entering Behaviour Analysis,** ensuring we have a clear picture of Jack as a person and as a trainee. We would know that resources we had from **Resources Analysis** to guarantee that proper training would take place and we would have dealt with the obstacles which we identified in **Constraints Analysis.**

From the information given already in Aims and Objectives Analysis, you should have no problems in translating this information into appropriate Aims and Objectives.

Links with Task Analysis

Task Analysis offers much information on structuring your objectives, as well. The first level Units of Analysis can be easily translated into Aims. Take Figure 59, Component 5, Study Unit 1, Package 1, "Task Analysis: Training Skills", for example. You can translate the Units of Analysis shown into Aims like this:

"The Course will consider the use in training of learning theory;
learner psychology;
A-V equipment;
computers;
graphics and reprographics;
course design;
methods of training and learning;
assessment and evaluation;
the training context."

Figure 68, Component 5, Study Unit 1, Package 1, "Writing Rules: Sequence & Style" is a good example of how the earlier units of Task Analysis, "Duties" and "Tasks", help formulate Aims and General Objectives, whilst those Units analysed last, "Task Elements" or "Rules", can help produce Specific Objectives. Sometimes the Units of Analysis are so detailed that they require little modification and serve as an excellent basis for the stating of the objective when you have added suitable verbs saying what the trainee has to do.

Using Figure 68 as a basis, translate the information provided by Task Analysis into Aims, General and Specific Objectives.

Aim (Topic). *The course is to offer training in "Black and White Film Processing"*

General Objectives (Duties and Tasks) *Examples are: "The trainee accounts for personal safety in the darkroom". "The trainee recognises the importance of maintaining safety in the darkroom".*

Specific Objectives (Task Elements or Rules). *Taking the first of the two General Objectives above, the Specific Objectives which can be derived from it, using*

the Task Analysis of Figure 68 as a basis, are:
"After the completion of training, the trainee will be able to:
1. Describe risk exaggerated because of darkness.
2. Explain the importance of orientation in the darkroom.
3. Name the chemicals in use in the darkroom.
4. Describe the individual dangers of each chemical.
5. State the dangers arising from spillages.
6. Point out the need for consideration of the safety of others.
7. Demonstrate the importance of awareness in the dark.
8. Explain clearly the emergency procedures for the darkroom.

As you can see, Task Analysis has given us a useful start. Why is it only a start?

As we suggested previously, in this Study Unit, you have a decision to make: how far to develop your Specific Objectives? You may consider those specified above to be adequate, but they do lack both conditions and criteria. Your decision depends upon their adequacy when measured against the use to which you are going to put them and the time which you have available to write fuller objectives. Time is, of course, always a vital consideration.

TIME, THE VITAL INGREDIENT

Figure 199

Select two or three of the objectives shown above and develop them with statements of conditions (2) and criteria (3) added to the performance (1) shown.

Here are our completed Specific Objectives:
Number 1   *"Describe risk exaggerated because of darkness (1) in the darkroom to the training officer (2) with complete accuracy and identify every danger (3)".*
             "Name the chemicals in use (1) to the instructor (2) without error (3)".
             "Explain clearly the emergency procedures for the darkroom (1) orally to the training officer (2) naming and describing each procedure with 100% accuracy (3).

You should have noted that Figure 68 even gives a **sequencing** for your Specific Objective, although you may wish to check this against a sequencing procedure which we described in the last Component.

When carrying out a Skills Analysis, the type of material shown in Figure 73, Component 5, Study Unit 1, Package 1, clearly helps, for starters, when writing objectives; the Acts described all form the basis for writing the performance element of your Specific Objectives.

If you examine Figure 74, the questions which you ask yourself there, about Units of Analysis, could also serve as checks to be made against your objectives.

Links with Entering Behaviour Analysis
Turning now to links with Entering Behaviour Analysis, Figures 114, 115 and 116 Component 7, give a helpful background for writing objectives in that they provide clear indications about where your incoming trainees' knowledge, skills and attitudes require careful attention in training because of short-comings. Consequently, your Specific Objectives would require particular care in these areas and you would have to be certain of covering them with pertinent objectives.

Your "Summary of Entering Behaviour Analysis", Figure 119, Component 7, gives a wealth of background information ensuring the writing of appropriate objectives.

Links with Resources and Constraints Analyses

Finally, how do the results of Resources and Constraints Analyses help writing objectives?

They are helpful in assisting you write your Criteria and Conditions Statements of Specific Objectives. If you examine the lower level Units of Analysis in Resources Analysis, Component 8, Study Unit One, you will see how they provide a framework within which to specify your **Conditions.** *Take Figure 133, as an example; at Level 7 of Analysis your Conditions Statements could include the terms "by using gapped handouts", or "answering multiple choice questions", or "by means of a problem-solving paper", or "using the diagrams provided". These are only examples capable of being developed for all of the Level 7 Units of Analysis.*

Criteria *statements follow on naturally, eg "answering multiple-choice questions* **achieving not less than 90% correct answers",** *or "by means of a problem-solving paper,* **solving correctly not less than four of the six problems set."**

Similarly, your Resource Checklists, Figures 136 and 137, show how the Conditions of your Objectives are affected by availability of Resources. Just as pertinently, your Conditions Statements must be written within the context of your Constraints, summarised in your Record of Constraints, Figure 146, Component 8.

Remember that the results of your Analyses will all be to hand, usually in a single file and sorting through them to find this supportive and indicative information is not a time-consuming task. Indeed, you will find that just scanning the analyses can be inspirational, when writing Aims and Objectives.

USING INFORMATION FROM YOUR ANALYSIS

Figure 200

(Incidentally, congratulations, you have now scored a double-century in viewing our Figures!)

Draw a diagram to show how the information which we have given in linking with the system functions, assists the writing of Aims and Objectives.

Our linking diagram is illustration in the next figure, Figure 201.

LINKING ANALYSES WHEN WRITING AIMS AND OBJECTIVES

SYSTEM FUNCTIONS	ASSIST IN WRITING	FIGURES FOR SPECIAL REFERENCE
NEEDS ANALYSIS		
Goals	Aims	28, 29
	General Objectives	28, 29
Phase 1 Output	Aims	33
Phase 2 Output	Aims	37
Phase 3, Performance Statements	General Objectives	43
Phase 4, Need Statements	General Objectives	49, 52
TASK ANALYSIS		
Units of Analysis	Aims	59
Duties and Tasks	Aims	68
	General Objectives	68
Task Elements/Rules	Specific Objectives	68
Acts	Specific Objectives (performances)	73, 74
ENTERING BEHAVIOUR ANALYSIS		
Background	General Objectives	114, 115, 116
	Specific Objectives	116
Summary	General Objectives	119
	Specific Objectives	119
RESOURCES ANALYSIS		
Lower levels of Analysis	Specific Objectives (conditions)	133
Resource Checklists	Specific Objectives (conditions)	136, 137
	Specific Objectives (criteria)	133
CONSTRAINTS ANALYSIS Record of Constraints	Specific Objectives (conditions)	146

Figure 201

The relationships shown in Figure 201 are indicators of the links between the System Functions involved in the System Activity of Analysis. When you are writing your Aims and Objectives, you'll find that many other links and pieces of information spring to mind spontaneously and naturally.

Finally, in this Component we have to discuss the advantages and disadvantages of using the Objectives Model of course design.

The Objectives Model: Advantages and Disadvantages

As the advantages and disadvantages of basing your training on the **Objectives Model, that is a systematic approach which uses Aims and Objectives as a basis,** largely speak for themselves, we shall list the pros and cons, without a great deal of comment until we get to our Summary.

ADVANTAGES OF USING OBJECTIVES

OBJECTIVES ARE:-
- The only rational method of planning training which has been worked out systematically and tried in practice.
- Encouraging to trainers to plan and think in a specific, detailed manner.
- Measurable and so give a rational basis for assessment and evaluation.
- Prescriptive of the choice of training methods.
- A self-improving system.
- A reliable, consistent system.
- A means of translating theories into practice.
- An excellent means of communication between trainers, between trainers and trainees, between trainers and management.
- Delimiters of the training task which are unambiguous.
- Easy to interpret and understand by trainers and trainees.
- Providers of feedback, helping the evaluation of training and accurate assessment of the student.
- A good basis for selecting training content and materials.
- A technique for helping trainers distinguish the sort of performance and behaviour likely to yield best results from the training.
- Of assistance in identifying optimal learning strategies.
- Providers of a summary of the training.
- **Essential signposts for telling the trainees where they are going and when they have got there.**
- Advantageous, in a large training project, in giving a basis for:-
  - assigning work to team members.
  - reviewing developed materials.
  - organising and managing the work.
  - ensuring clarity of direction.
  - assisting sequencing of material production.
  - informing trainees of the purpose of training.
  - telling trainees what they should be able to do.
  - helping trainees to work selectively.
  - protecting the trainer from unjustified criticism that exams are unfair, unexpected or irrelevant.
  - the reviewing and improving of the training.
  - providing information to management on what the training is about.
  - giving a basis for pre-testing, including the testing of pre-requisites.
  - offering identification of difficult material, needing research to improve.

Figure 202

It's a formidale list. To offer a balanced view, let's examine the disadvantages.

DISADVANTAGES OF USING OBJECTIVES

- Training and learning outcomes are not as predictable as claimed.
- Some areas of training are difficult to write objectives for accurately.
- Some objectives are not of more use than more easily constructed, broad syllabus aims.
- Objectives can be constricting and if written before training prevent "voyages of exploration" in training.
- Objectives do not show trainers how to deal with unexpected events in training.
- There are many paths through learning and training; objectives offer only one, partly restricted way and may be blinkering.
- Many objectives are difficult to write without ambiguity.
- Deciding on the level of specificity can be very difficult; they can become over-detailed.
- Trivial objectives are easiest to write; consequently complex training materials may be avoided or "short changed".
- Objectives raise the question of whether training is all about lists of behaviours and performances.
- Objectives rigidly prescribe trainee-trainer interaction.
- Objectives can take a long time to write and maybe the trainer could be better employed elsewhere.

Figure 203

We have tried to be fair by describing both sides of the objectives "coin".

Overall, we very firmly believe that using objectives is greatly advantageous, that it is an essential part of a systematic approach to training and that it is the only model of training which offers a rational, organised and methodical approach. The advantages are large, often unique and organise training in a far more effective and efficient way than any other method even begins to do.

Nevertheless, it is wise to bear the disadvantages in mind and to avoid them by using commonsense; a **balanced view** on the part of the trainer nullifies most of the disadvantages. In any case, many of the disadvantages which we have mentioned are matters of opinion. Some are not supported by strong evidence of any kind.

DECIDING ON USING OBJECTIVES

Figure 204

So, in Figure 204 we are firmly convinced that the trainer is sensibly using a double-headed coin!

Now you remember that at the end of Component Two, Study Unit Two we asked you to think about the way we have used objectives and key words in this Programme. Normally, Aims, General and especially Specific Objectives are written at the beginning of a course, a Package, a lesson, a unit, as appropriate. Yet we have placed key words at the start of our Components, and the Aims and Objectives at the end of the Package!

We have done this because there is one more disadvantage of using objectives which we have not mentioned and practice shows it to be a real one: a list of tough-looking and demanding objectives at the beginning of a piece of work can be "off-putting" to the readers.

There is no problem if the instructor is there to work through them with trainees, because he or she can explain the objectives in simple terms and reassure anyone who feels he or she is being faced with a formidable list of expectations. In distance learning material, like the Training Technology Programme, there is no trainer to help the student accommodate immediately to the objectives themselves, so we have substituted a list of Key Words for the list of objectives.

Key Words and phrases are really cues which alert you to important items as they come up in the text. You know you have to watch out for them and understand them when reading through the material. They act as "mini-objectives".

Placing the objective at the end of a piece of work allows you to check that you have met the performance which they require of you, act as a method of revision and give you the chance of checking back through the Package to revise any points about which you are not certain.

Summary

When writing General and Specific Objectives every effort should be made to use the correct type of verb and these differ according to the Domain to which the Objective belongs primarily, whether cognitive, psychomotor or affective.

Similarly, it is important when constructing Aims and Objectives to ensure that information is used which is already available from previous analyses made in the System Activity of Analysis. Material is to be found in Needs Analysis, Task Analysis and the analyses of Entering Behaviour, Resources and Constraints which can be used directly in the process of writing objectives, provided that it is modified suitably.

Using the Objectives Model in the design of training has many advantages, which outweigh the few disadvantages; using objectives is the only systematic method of approaching course design and the only way of providing clear-cut statements of the performance and the behaviour which trainees are expected to achieve as measurable learning outcomes.

The Objectives Model is used in this Training Technology Programme, but is modified to include the additional strength of using Key Words.

The System Function "Analysis of Aims and Objectives" is the last of the analyses which we make when designing our training. Steps 1 to 6 are concerned primarily with analysis; the next Step in our systematic approach is concerned with the **System Activity of Synthesis**, see Figures 10 and 12, Component 1, Package 1.

However, you must remember that each System Activity is only **primarily** concerned with the Activity which bears its name, eg. analysis, synthesis, assessment etc. In the Analysis of Aims and Objectives, for example, whilst we have been concerned mainly with analytic methods, elements of other Activities appear; the actual writing of the objectives is in some ways a building-up process, involving synthesis.

You will see, throughout the rest of this Package, that this mixing is commonplace; all you have to do to avoid any confusion is to bear in mind the **primary nature** of the Activity with which you are concerned in each Step of the Design System.

You may wish to use a Checklist to decide if your Objectives are comprehensive enough; an example is given in the next Component. Work out your own before you look at ours.

Finally, when making an Aims and Objectives Analyses let's have a look at an illustration which we hope says it all in a humorous way.

FAILING TO ACHIEVE YOUR OBJECTIVES

Figure 205

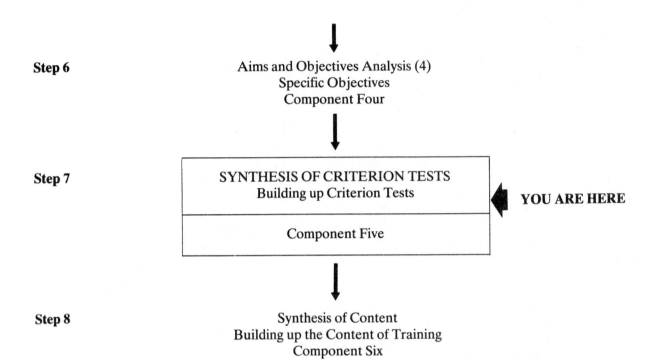

Step 6 Aims and Objectives Analysis (4)
Specific Objectives
Component Four

Step 7 SYNTHESIS OF CRITERION TESTS
Building up Criterion Tests **YOU ARE HERE**

Component Five

Step 8 Synthesis of Content
Building up the Content of Training
Component Six

Component 5:

Building up Criterion Tests

Key Words

Objective checklist; synthesis of criterion tests; types of test; characteristics of the tests; linking content to objectives and to tests; writing test specifications; when to test; reliability and validity of tests; test items.

Introduction

Considered in this Component
System Activity: Synthesis
System Function:
Synthesis of Criterion Tests

In this Component we are considering one system Function, Synthesis of Criterion Tests. These are Steps 7 and 8 of our design system, see Figure 147.

Before we begin with the study of Criterion Tests, we shall revise our last three Components by examining the process of building up a Checklist which tells us whether or not the objectives we have written are adequate for the job.

Bear in mind that when evaluating your final list of objectives you will want to know how adequate it is, as well as how clearly the statements say what you and the trainees are about. So we have incorporated criteria in the Checklist not only for assessing the objectives themselves, but also for checking if the specific learning outcomes are covered adequately.

▰▰▰▰ Checkpoint

Try your hand at writing out your own Checklist first, making reference to Figures 163 and 175.

Mainly, you should use the Checklist as a diagnostic tool for identifying and then correcting errors in your objectives. However, the Checklist is a useful 'shorthand' guide for helping you write your objectives in the first place.

Remember, any tick in the 'No' column identifies an area which you have to improve.

OBJECTIVES CHECKLIST: QUESTIONS TO ASK YOURSELF

	YES	NO

ADEQUACY OF GENERAL OBJECTIVES (G.O.'s)

1. If the trainees acquire all of my stated G.O.'s, will they have **attained** the Aim(s) of the training?

2. Does each G.O. indicate a **suitable learning outcome** for the training?

3. Does the list of G.O.'s cover all **knowledge, mental skills, (psycho)motor skills** and **attitudes** which I wish to include in the training?

4. Are the G.O.'s **achievable** by the trainees? i.e. have they enough time, resources, facilities, ability etc?

5. Have the G.O.'s been **approved by management**?

6. Do the G.O.'s establish a **clear relationship** between the objectives and the information provided by the previous steps of my design system, especially Needs and Task Analysis?

7. Have the G.O.'s been **seen and agreed** by other **trainers** who may be involved in the training?

STATEMENT OF GENERAL OBJECTIVES

8. Does each G.O. begin with a **verb**?

9. Does each G.O. state **trainee behaviour** or a **trainee performance**? (Not trainer performance).

10. Does each G.O. state a **general learning outcome,** or a **learning product**? (rather than a training process).

11. Does each G.O. identify trainee **terminal** behaviour? (rather than content to be covered).

12. Does each G.O. indicate **one general learning outcome** only? (rather than a combination of outcomes).

13. Is each G.O. stated at a **general** level of learning outcomes? (not in specific detail).

14. Is each G.O. free from **overlap** with other G.O.'s?

15. Have I written **too many** G.O.'s?

16. Do my G.O.'s **incorporate** all of the **relevant information** obtained through **previous system analyses**?

STATEMENTS OF SPECIFIC OBJECTIVES (S.O.'s)

17. Is it clear from which of the General Objectives each of the S.O.'s come?

18. Does each S.O. describe the **terminal performance** or behaviour which trainees are to demonstrate when they have achieved the objective?

19. Does each S.O. begin with a **verb** which specifies a trainee performance which is **desirable**?

20. Does each S.O. incorporate a performance which is **measurable**?

21. Does each S.O. include a statement of **conditions**?

22. Does each S.O. include a statement of **criteria,** or **standards,** to be achieved?

23. Does each S.O. describe **enough learning outcomes** to cover the whole of the G.O. by trainee behaviour?

24. Is **training content** in each S.O. kept to a **minimum**?

25. Is each S.O. **relevant** to the G.O. from which it is derived?

26. Do my S.O.'s **incorporate** all of the **relevant information** obtained through **previous System Analyses**?

27. Are any of my S.O.'s **trivial**?

28. If any are, have I planned to **remove** them or incorporate them into other S.O.'s?

29. Have I **too many** S.O.'s?

30. If I have, have I planned to **remove** them?

31. Have **other trainers** involved in the training **seen and agreed** the S.O.'s?

Figure 206

Quite a formidable Checklist, but worth using, as writing your objectives correctly is fundamentally important to your design system.

After you have practised the use of the Checklist a few times, you will be able to scan it quickly, concentrating on the important words indicated in heavy case. Pruning your Objectives can save you time. Also, this Checklist can help you write your Objectives in the first place.

PRUNE OR PRUNER?

Figure 207

What is the main difference between the System Activity of Analysis and that of Synthesis?

Analysis is a breaking down process whilst the next System Activity of Synthesis is mainly concerned with building up. We have just engaged in analytic activity geared to checking the quality and validity of our objectives.

SYSTEM FUNCTION: SYNTHESIS OF CRITERION TESTS

We now begin the System Activity of Synthesis, **beginning with the building up of Criterion (or Criterial) Tests.** The idea behind these tests is that they check the trainees' progress through training by testing their achievement of the objectives.

Basically, each Specific Objective has a test, or test items attached to it, the degree of success of each trainee in each test item indicating their degree of progress. Therefore, Criterion Tests are progress tests.

In this part of Component 5, we shall examine:
Types of criterion test.
The characteristics of criterion tests.
Linking Content to objectives and criterion tests.
Writing Test Specifications.
When to test.

Types of Criterion Test

We are only giving a general outline here of the sorts of criterion test which you might wish to apply. Further details of tests are included later in this Study Unit and in the Package on Assessment and Evaluation in Training.

Broadly speaking, there are eleven basic ways of testing for us to consider and they are:

Multiple Choice questions
"Gapped" Handouts
Short Answer questions
Problem Solving papers
Skills performance
Practical Written
Assignment/Project
Oral/Aural
Question papers
Laboratory practical
Essay/Dissertation or Thesis

A few words of explanation about each:
Multiple Choice questions offer a choice of statements, one of which is correct and which the trainee has to identify. Usually, the trainee has to select one from four or five statements. Those statements which are not correct are known as "distractors."
"Gapped" (or incomplete) handouts make a statement, or statements, in which key words are missing; these key word gaps must be filled in by the trainee.
Short answer questions are mini-exam papers in which a series of short statements are each succeeded by four or five blank lines for the trainee to fill in with an answer.
Problem solving papers include a series of problems which the trainee has to solve.
Skills performance tests are where the trainee is required to demonstrate competence, or mastery of a skill by practising the skill itself. Marks are awarded by the tester observing the process, which the trainee follows, or by marking the finished product of the skill process, or both.
Practical written are tests in which the trainee writes answers to questions about a practical or skilled procedure; this tests the cognitive element of a motor skill.
An Assignment is a set piece of work which the trainee completes individually; this may be either of a practical nature (e.g. make a video tape) or theoretical (e.g. write a case-history). A Project is a long assignment.
Oral tests are conducted face-to-face between trainer and trainee, the trainee answering questions put to him by the trainer. **Aural tests** involve the trainee listening to an audio tape and answering questions either in writing or on to another tape; the process is basically the same as for an oral test.
Question papers are the normal type of "answer-any-five-from-eight" question papers set in examinations.
Laboratory practicals are conducted in laboratories and involve setting up equipment and making experiments.
Essays, we all know about. For our purposes, we shall consider an essay to range up to about 10,000 words

and call the work a thesis or a dissertation over that length. Normally, of course, essays range from 1,000 to 5,000 words in length. In setting essays you can allow trainees to pick their own titles, or set a subject. If they pick their own, the trainees can often make them more appropriate to their own interests, but this type of essay can be more difficult to mark. These are called "open-ended" essays.

"Structured" essays are those in which the trainer sets the subject and lays down specific criteria which the trainee has to achieve. Such criteria can also be incorporated in "open-ended" essays and give guidance in both types of essay about the requirements which the trainees are expected to fulfil.

NOW, WHAT HAVE WE FOR TODAY?

Figure 208

Don't forget that to cover all categories of objectives (and domains) it may be necessary to combine different types of test until you are satisfied that all aspects of the training and learning are covered.

The Characteristics of Criterion Tests

Figure 208 shows that the trainer has to make a choice of the most suitable criterion test, and we have included a table of questions which you should ask yourself when selecting a suitable method of testing. The questions underline the characteristics of the different types of test, but do remember that they are only guides, are a little 'crude' and can be modified if you wish.

Before looking at this table, shown in Figure 210, we must discuss the meaning of two terms:
Validity
Reliability
The Validity of a test is whether or not it **actually tests what it is supposed to be testing**, i.e. the extent to which the test fulfils the purpose for which it was designed. For example, for a test linked directly with a Specific Objective, does the test really measure the behaviour, or the performance, which the Objective specifies? If it does, it is described as being valid.

Reliability is the measure of a consistency of a test. Does it produce the same results in similar but not exactly the same conditions? For example, if you gave the same test to a different group of trainees of the same course, would the results of the two testings be comparable? Or if you gave it next year to trainees who have followed the same course, would you have similar results? If you do have a reasonable comparison in these cases, then the test is reliable.

SPRIGG'S CANNONBALLS:
RELIABILITY OF A SKILLS PERFORMANCE TEST

Good training produces

Poor training produces

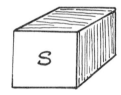

Figure 209

From the lower half of this Figure, you can see that we identified that something is wrong with the training. We carry out this identification by **measuring the products** (the cannonballs) **with a criterion test**. In this case, it would be a **template** which would fit over perfect cannonballs, but not bad ones. We can illustrate this by the second half of Figure 209, shown overleaf.

A reliable Test Instrument: perfect template.

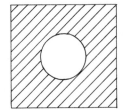

Here we show how a test instrument which measures cannonballs (the outcomes of training) perfectly, is reliable. The template must also be a valid test instrument, because it certainly tests what it is supposed to be testing. Only perfect cannonballs will fit the template.

An unreliable Test Instrument: imperfect template.

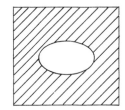

Even a perfect cannonball would not pass through this template.

There is an important lesson here. What is it?

Your training might be entirely suitable in achieving its objectives, but you must be sure that your test instrument is both valid and reliable. If it is not, then it may be reporting that the end products of your training are unsatisfactory, when it is actually the test instrument itself which is at fault and not the training.

There are other factors to be considered; have a look at the next Checkpoint to see what they are.

Of course, in checking the reliability of skills tests, 'all other things have got to be equal'. What do we mean by this?

You have to make sure that the trainee's length of training is the same; the workshop environment has not changed between testings; the equipment functions exactly as before; the materials are the same; the length of time given for the test and the instructions are precisely as they were before. If they are, then the products of the skilled performance should also be the same if the test is reliable. Obviously, Sprigg's reliability (Figure 209) isn't too good.

We can now move on to look at test characteristics, expressed in tabular form in Figure 210.

The key to this Figure is as follows:

Column Number	Quality
1	Are they **easy** or difficult to mark? Easy to mark = 5 points Difficult to mark = 1 point
2	Can they be **self-marked** by the trainees? Yes, they can be self-marked = 5 points No, trainees cannot mark them = 1 point
3	Are they easy to **prepare** by the trainer? Easy to prepare = 5 points Difficult to prepare = 1 point
4	Do they require any **special equipment?** No, they do not need special equipment = 5 points Yes, they do need special equipment = 1 point
5	Are they easy to **handle, physically?** Yes, they are easy to handle = 5 points No, they are not = 1 point
6	Are they **costly** to organise? They are cheap = 5 points They are very costly = 1 point
7	Are they likely to **cover** all aspects and categories of your Objectives? They are likely to cover all aspects = 5 points They are unlikely to cover all aspects = 1 point
8	Are they likely to **involve** more than one trainer in marking? (e.g. to check the accuracy of the first marker) Only one marker involved = 5 points More than two markers involved = 1 point
9	Are they likely to be **valid?** They are usually valid = 5 points They are not usually valid = 1 point
10	Are they likely to be **reliable?** They are usually valid = 5 points They are not usually valid = 1 point
11	Are they **objective?** They are objective = 5 points They are subjective = 1 point

In the key shown above, is it better for the type of test characteristic to score 5 points or 1?

We have arranged the key so that the higher the score (4 or 5), then the more desirable are the qualities shown by the test. A low score (1 or 2) shows that type of test to be poor in that characteristic. Scoring 3 points is an in-between mark, which is neither good nor bad.

CRITERION TEST CHARACTERISTICS: QUESTIONS TO ASK ABOUT EACH TYPE OF TEST

Characteristics / Type of Test	1. Easy To Mark?	2. Self Marking?	3. Easy To Prepare?	4. Special Equipment?	5. Physical Handling	6. Cost?	7. Cover?	8. Trainer Involvement?	9. Validity	10. Reliability?	11. Objectivity?
Multiple Choice	5	5	1	5	5	3	5	5	5	5	5
Gapped Handout	5	5	3	5	5	4	5	5	4	4	4
Short Answer	4	1	3	5	5	4	4	5	3	4	4
Problem Solving	4	1	2	5	5	3	3	5	3	4	4
Skills	2	1	1	1	1	1	5	1	5	5	4
Practical Written	4	1	3	5	5	3	4	5	4	4	4
Assignments	3	1	3	5	4	4	3	1	3	3	3
Oral/Aural	2	1	4	5/2	4	3	5	1	5	2	2
Questions	2	1	3	5	4	4	2	1	2	2	2
Laboratory	3	1	1	1	1	1	4	1	5	5	5
Essay	1	1	5	5	3	5	1	1	2	1	1

Figure 210

Let's try expressing in words what Figure 210 tells you.

State what the chart shown in Figure 210 tells you about the following types of test:
- Multiple choice
- Skills
- Essay

Here are our interpretations:

Multiple Choice Tests. This type of test scores very highly in most areas: it is easy to mark because the answers are either right or wrong (1); may be self-marked by the trainees (2); requires no special equipment (4); handles easily as the answer sheets are well organised and they are not bulky (5); moderately costly in that the materials are cheap, but can be quite costly in trainer's preparation time (6); covers your objectives closely (7); requires only one trainer to mark (8); is valid in that the multiple choice questions can be very directly related to the objectives and so it is easy to ensure that it is testing each objective and the sense of each objective (9); reliable because exactly the same test may be given elsewhere (10); and objective in that the answer is either right or wrong, so eliminating the trainer's opinion and therefore his or her subjectivity (11).

However, this type of test has drawbacks: multiple choice questions can be demanding, as they must all be of roughly the same length and degree of difficulty; they must be concise and clearly understood; the correct answer must be unambiguous; the distractors must not be obviously wrong, or silly, or "makeweight" and it is sometimes difficult to even think up two or three distractors; no distractor must contain sufficient "truth" to be a reasonably correct alternative answer to the true answer; although multiple choice questions can be constructed fairly easily for lower-level objectives, they can be exceedingly difficult to mount for higher level objectives like Synthesis and Evaluation categories.

So, multiple choice questions have many advantages, but you can only select them as a suitable type of test if you have a lot of time in which to prepare them.

HAVE YOU GOT THE TIME, MATE?

Figure 211

YET ONE MORE TIME: SKILLS CAN BE DIFFICULT TO MARK

Figure 212

Skills Tests

Here you are watching and marking a trainee who is carrying out a skilled process. You estimate the trainee's success by the level of competence he or she displays in the skill which you are observing and/or by the quality of the end product produced by the skill. So, to take making a dovetail joint as an example, you guage the expertise with which the tools are handled, use of the materials, accuracy and fit of the completed joint, time taken for the job, or you may mark for the quality of the completed job.

Whilst the joint itself, i.e. the end product of the skill is quite easy to mark, the process of making it and the expertise shown in that process, isn't (1). The trainee cannot mark his or her own skill, although they may have an accurate idea of the quality of the end product (2). Skill tests are not usually easy to prepare, requiring equipment and materials to be available, set up and timetabled for use (3). Certainly special equipment is needed (4); the handling of the end products, which are usually bulky, isn't easy (5); cost of materials, equipment and time (taken to test) can be high (6); although you would expect to cover all aspects of the skill in the test so covering your objectives (7). Usually, more than one person is involved in marking, especially as some skills require a trainer or master operator to gauge (8); although validity is high because tests of skill have to test what the skilled process is about (9) and so is reliability, e.g. making a dovetail joint is the same this year as next or with one class or another (10).

Essay Tests

Finally, in looking at test characteristics, let's examine the use of the essay and its advantages and disadvantages as a form of test. Essays tend to be either good or bad, ie they score 5 or a low mark in our Figure 210. They are comparatively easy to prepare; require no special equipment; may be a little difficult to mark if they are especially long; cost little except the paper they're written on.

However, they have serious faults: they are difficult to mark being time-consuming, sometimes fatiguing and often cause a problem in sorting out what aid the trainee has had and what he or she really means. Certainly all objectives aren't covered, this being too time-consuming a method to test each one. Essays usually require another trainer to moderate and often don't test what we expect them to, especially so when trainees interpret the essay title widely. They are completely unreliable, producing different answers to the same essay subject from group to group.

A major drawback is that the marking of essays is highly subjective and it is very difficult to keep personal opinions about essay relevance, style and organisation out of the assessment.

SUBJECTIVE DIFFICULTIES IN MARKING ESSAYS

Figure 213

Linking Content to Objectives and Criterion Tests

In some training which is designed for awards which are approved or validated by external bodies, the syllabus is laid down for you already, sometimes to the extent of relating it to General and Specific Objectives which have already been decided for you. External validating bodies vary greatly as to the amount of information which they provide, of course: some give a syllabus only; some define objectives only; some do both. Obviously, you will read this Component and make the appropriate interpretation necessary.

However, much training is "home-made" by the organisations which are preparing trainees to meet those needs which have been identified as important by the firm itself. So you will often find yourself having to carry out most of the Steps of our design system yourself, frequently to the extent of designing your own syllabus or course content. We are considering training content more extensively in the next Component, so will view it in general terms only here.

We will work on the premise that you have finalised the outline of your course syllabus with enough detail to cover the requirements of your Specific Objectives. The matter of linking content to objectives and to an appropriate test then becomes fairly simple.

First you ask yourself

Question One: "Which area of my general course content or syllabus meets the requirement of each General Objective?"

Next, you ask

Question Two: "Which particular piece of my syllabus or course content meets the requirement of each Specific Objective?"

Next you ask

Question Three: "What Criterion Test Type/s best suit both Specific Objectives and content or syllabus?"

And finally,

Question Four: "What sort and number of Test Items should I include in each Criterion Test?"

Where you have your content provided for you by an external body, or available already from previous courses, you may follow the order of the Questions shown above ("Questions which you ask yourself", One to Four).

If you have to build up your content yourself, when designing a new course, for example, then you may wish to follow the sequence recommended in our Design System, ie. organising your Criterion Tests **before** you synthesise content.

Either way works well. You pick the order which suits your training best. This flexibility is inbuilt into our Design System. Further examples of it are given in the next Component.

///

Express the relationships which we have described between Question One to Four by means of a diagram.

Here's ours:

THE CRITERION CONNECTION

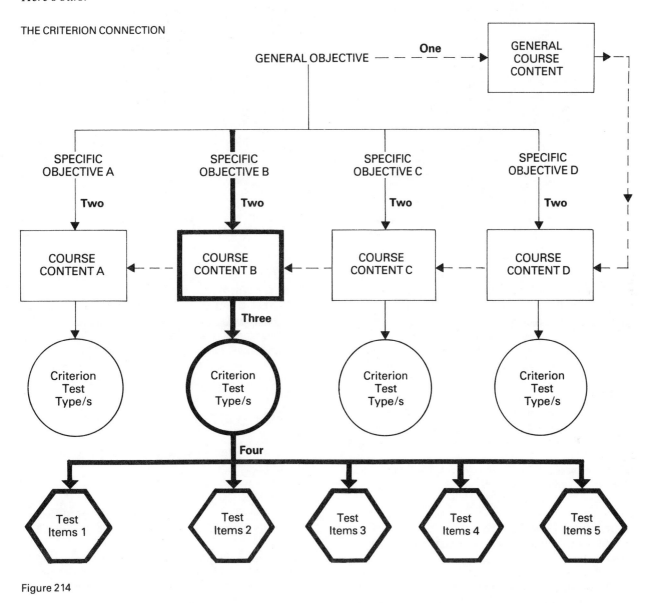

Figure 214

The numbers are those of the "Questions which you ask yourself" (One, Two, Three and Four shown) and **where** you ask them. The Criterion Test examined in detail in Figure 214 has five Test Items included in it.

///

You will have noticed how we keep asking you in Checkpoints to draw diagrams to illustrate what we have just been saying. We also introduce numerous graphics ourselves, sometimes humorous. Why do you think we do this?

We ask you to draw diagrams to help imprint the written material in a visual form in your memory. The act of translating the information into diagrams which encapsulate the meaning, the thinking that is part of this process, the fact that the diagrams summarise the text and show relationships more clearly, are all aids to memory and understanding.

Our graphics are an extension of this process. Many are humorous or unusual because a funny connotation or an incongruous way of presenting information helps retention. Have a look at the next Figure to see what we mean.

INCONGRUITY AIDS ATTENTION AND RETENTION

Figure 215

So, summarising the process of linking content, you select your general content area related to the General Objectives, then choose specific parts of the general content area for each Specific Objective, finally picking a type of criterion test and test items which examine the content most suitably for deciding if the requirement of the objective have been met by the trainees.

▰▰▰

Try this process out for some of your own training, working through from a General Objective to test items.

We give our example below,, taken from one of our previous General Objectives.

GENERAL OBJECTIVE:
"Understands the dangers which are present in the Workshop"

GENERAL COURSE CONTENT:
Workshop dangers; safety rules; machine guards; moving machinery; clothing; electrical hazards; attitudes to dangers.

SPECIFIC OBJECTIVES (Conditions and Criteria omitted for brevity).
1. Labels the workshop dangers.
2. Lists the workshop safety rules.
3. Identifies the reasons for observing safety rules.
4. Explains the reasons for the presence of machine guards.
5. States the dangers associated with moving parts of machinery.
6. **Describes suitable clothing for the workshop.**
7. Suggests types of unsuitable clothing, hair styles etc.

8. Gives reasons why jewellery is not worn in the workshop.
9. **Checks out a diagram of workshop electrical hazards.**
10. Demonstrates a positive attitude towards avoiding dangers.
11. Values the importance of the safety measures which are used in the workshop.

COURSE CONTENT for SPECIFIC OBJECTIVE 6, above
a. Clothing must not have loose or partly attached pieces.
b. Belts should not be used.
c. Bootlaces should be tied tightly.
d. Boots with protective toe caps must be worn.
e. Protective issue goggles must be worn when necessary.
f. Elastic bandlets should be worn around cuffs.
g. Clothing should be kept as clean as possible.
h. (For women) Hair nets should be worn with long hair.
j. Clothing must not obscure vision.

COURSE CONTENT for SPECIFIC OBJECTIVE 9, above
a. High voltage areas.
b. Frayed cables.
c. Broken or damaged plugs.
d. Broken or damaged machinery connections.
e. Makeshift repairs.
f. Fuses.
g. Loose cables.
h. Running water/leaks.
j. "Cutout" Failures.
k. Poor insulation.
l. Overloading.

CRITERION TEST **TYPE** FOR SPECIFIC OBJECTIVE 6: ORAL

The Conditions specified for this objective are "to the instructor and the group" and the Criteria "with a clear idea of the appropriate clothing".

Therefore, this is an oral type of test.

CRITERION TEST **ITEMS** FOR SPECIFIC OBJECTIVE 6

1. "Each of the two model figures provided shows men and women who are unsuitably clothed for employment in the workshop. Point out to the instructor and to the group which items make the clothing unsuitable. Say how each item could cause an accident".
2. "Check the clothing of members of your group and identify to your instructor the items which are dangerous to the wearer in the workshop. Say why each item is dangerous".

As you can see, "test items" are the parts of a test. These parts can be the actions which a trainee has to perform, or questions to answer.

CRITERION TEST **TYPE** for SPECIFIC OBJECTIVE 9: PRACTICAL WRITTEN TEST

The Conditions specified are "on the diagram provided" and the Criteria "with no more than two errors".

The trainee is answering a test in writing which requires practical knowledge of the skill of identifying electrical hazards. **So this is a practical written test.** If the trainee had had to identify and repair the electrical hazards, or faults, this would have been a skills test and the test items would have been written accordingly.

CRITERION TEST **ITEM** FOR SPECIFIC OBJECTIVE 9

"The diagram which you have been given shows 6 electrical hazards in the workshop. Mark each hazard which you can identify with a red circle, placed around the hazard. Name the hazard alongside the circle."

RED CIRCLE HAZARDS

Figure 216

Next we come to writing test specifications.

Writing Test Specifications for Criterion Tests

The procedure which we have described for writing our tests is incomplete; we wrote items which covered each Criterion Test and each Specific Objective, but we have not explained a system for obtaining an overall balance between the Criterion Tests. This specification will allow us to decide on whether or not the Criterion Tests **as a whole** reflect the content of the training and the learning.

When writing the Test Items, we also wish to know what sort of **balance** we have between the different levels of the taxonomy which we are using, whether it be cognitive, psychomotor or affective (attitudinal).

So how do we set about gaining a perspective on this balance? How do we write a Test Specification?

CRITERION TEST SPECIFICATIONS:
TO BE TAKEN BY TRAINEES DURING TRAINING

Figure 217

Perhaps Figure 217 wouldn't be quite the correct way to administer Criterion Tests to trainees, but the illustration does make an important point: we must get the training prescription right for the trainees. A Test Specification helps us to do just that.

You'll be pleased to know that you have already done much of the basic work for writing out a Test Specification. Test Specifications for the cognitive, the psychomotor and the affective areas are basically the same but vary in detail. We will begin with a cognitive Test Specification.

Procedure for writing a Test Specification: Cognitive Domain
Have a look at Figure 218, which shows the sort of chart which is used in Test Specification.

Fill in the specifications as follows:
1. COLUMN 1: Write down the General and Specific Objectives which you have specified already.
2. COLUMNS 3 to 8: Mark the taxonomic category of each Specific Objective with a number 1 in the appropriate column, 3 to 8. Each 1 represents a Test Item.

3. COLUMN 2: Write down the **General** Course Content which you have allocated to your General Objectives (shown as a, b, c, d, e, and f in the Specification, Figure 218).
4. COLUMN 2: Write down the Course Content for Specific Objectives (shown as A, B, C, D, to Q in Figure 218).
5. Look at the balance of your Test Items shown by the Numbers 1. Decide if the balance is satisfactory and if the combined Text Items make up a Criterion Test (or Tests) which reflect adequately the training and learning. Remember that "balance" is achieving a spread of Test Items at all levels (categories) which you have decided to be the most suitable. If the balance is OK, then you have completed this part of your Specification.
6. If the balance is not suitable, then increase the number of Test Items eg you might decide that
    a. One Specific Objective requires two or more Test Items.
    b. You wish to include more Test Items in a particular category.
7. Having decided to increase the number of Test Items you mark in the appropriate column with a number in brackets, eg (1), (2) showing the number of questions which you are adding.
8. COLUMN 9: Total your Test Items for both vertical and horizontal columns, ie add together the single number 1's which do not have a bracketed number alongside them and then add all the numbers in brackets.
9. COLUMN 10: Work out percentages for the column totals. The percentages show the proportion of test items allocated.
10. Allocate marks to be awarded to each Test Item.
You now have a Test Specification which shows the balance of your Criterion Test. You know how many Test Items you have for each Specific Objective and for the content related to each General and each Specific Objective.

The process is the same for the Psychomotor and Affective Domains.

More examples of Test Specificatons are included in the Assessment and Evaluation Package of this programme.

What does Column 11 tell you?

The number of the actual questions as they appear on the question paper, when you have written it. Thus, General Objective 1, has 3 test items, forming 12% of the total test items. They appear as questions 1, 3 and 6 on the actual question paper itself.

Have another glance at the Test Specification, then answer the following Checkpoint.

TEST SPECIFICATION FOR CRITERION TESTS: COGNITIVE DOMAIN

1	2 Content	3 Know-ledge	4 Compre-hension	5 Appli-cation	6 Analysis	7 Synthesis	8 Evaluation	9 Total Test Items	10 %	11 Question Numbers
GENERAL OBJECTIVE 1 (a) S.O. 1 S.O. 2	 (a) A B	 1 1(1)						3	12	1, 3, 6
GENERAL OBJECTIVE 2 (b) S.O. 3 S.O. 4 S.O. 5 S.O. 6	 (b) } C } D	 1	 1	 1 1(1)				5	20	2, 7, 9, 11 15
GENERAL OBJECTIVE 3 (c) S.O. 7 S.O. 8	 (c) E F	 1			 1			2	8	5, 10
GENERAL OBJECTIVE 4 (d) S.O. 9 S.O. 10 S.O. 11	 (d) G H J	 1(1)		 1		 1		4	16	4, 13, 17, 22.
GENERAL OBJECTIVE 5 (e) S.O. 12 S.O. 13 S.O. 14 S.O. 15	 (e) K L M N		 1(1)			 1(2) 1	 1	7	28	8, 14, 18, 19, 21, 23, 25.
GENERAL OBJECTIVE 6 (f) S.O. 16 S.O. 17 S.O. 18	 (f) O P Q	 1			 1		 1(1)	4	16	12, 16, 20, 24.
TOTAL TEST ITEMS		8	3	4	2	5	3	25		
%		32	12	16	8	20	12	100		

KEY: SO = Specific Objectives.   (a) to (f) = Content for General Objectives 1 to 6.   A to Q = Content for Specific Objectives 1 to 18.

Clearly, the specification shown in Figure 218 has an important role in balancing and organising your assessment of the trainees. This specification is made more specific by including a column (shown on the right in Figure 218) which gives the numbers of the individual questions. These may not be numbered consecutively, of course, as we have shown.

Figure 218

In Figure 218 explain the following:-

a. Why some Specific Objectives have separate content areas (eg S.O.1 and S.O.2) but some share content (eg S.O.3 and S.O.4)?

b. What the Specification says about General Objective 5; explain in your own words.

c. What the percentage columns tell you. How does this help you plan training?

Our answers are as follows:

a. *Usually you try to carve up your training content so that each Specific Objective has its own discrete piece of the syllabus. Occasionally, you'll find that you need to write two (or more) Specific Objectives to cover different aspects of the same content.*

b. *General Objective 5, covering general course content (e) has four Specific Objectives covering specific course content, K, L, M and N. There are seven Test Items covering these Specific Objectives, ie 1 + 1 + 1 + 1 + (1) + (2) = 7. These represent 28% of the total number of Test Items (25) and are deployed as follows:-*
   Comprehension Category: 2 Test Items (8% total)
   Synthesis Category: 4 Test Items (16% total)
   Evaluation Category: 1 Test Item (4% total)
   Accordingly, General Objective 5 is quite a high level, or high order objective, embracing the higher levels of the cognitive domain taxonomy.

   When you reviewed your first distribution of Test Items you added another three (Comprehension 1 and Synthesis 2).

   Finally, the Test Specification confirms the sequencing of the Specific Objectives and therefore the probable order in which they would be taught. You would begin with S.O.12 (Comprehension) then to S.O.13 and 14 (Synthesis) and finally teach S.O.15 (Evaluation). This is in accordance with the order of the levels in the cognitive taxonomy.

c. *The percentage columns tell you that the ranking order of General Objectives, as shown by the percentage of the total of Test Items which they contain. The order is as follows:-*

1.	*General Objective 5*	*28%*
2.	*General Objective 2*	*20%*
3.	*General Objective 4*	*16%*
	General Objective 6	*16%*
5.	*General Objective 1*	*12%*
6.	*General Objective 3*	*8%*

These percentages give you a clear indication of the proportionate amount of time you should allocate to the training for each objective.

Additionally, the percentage columns indicate exactly the type of training upon which you are embarking. Here you are concerned primarily with the acquisition of knowledge (32%) and least with analysis (8%).

As you can see, Test Prescriptions offer a formidable amount of information. There are other ways of making these specification out and we describe these in Package 6, Study Unit 3, Component 3.

Incidentally, you might decide that the Test Specification, shown in Figure 218 might be best split into smaller Criterion Tests, should each of your Test Items be large, eg each one a fairly difficult problem to solve. So you could derive not one, but three Criterion Tests with a smaller number of Test Items in each. These decisions depend on the size and scope of your Test Items and how, say, three Criterion Tests would fit into your training.

TEST SPECIFICATIONS GIVE YOU PLANNING CONFIDENCE

Figure 219

When to Test

This leaves us with the decision about when to give the Criterion Tests. Always your experience will help you decide when to apply the tests in training, but the Test Specifications are also indicative.

Let's imagine that we do decide to give three Criterion Tests, rather than one, from the Test Specification shown in Figure 218. We may decide to test as follows:

General Objectives 1 and 2	Test One
General Objectives 3 and 4	Test Two
General Objectives 5 and 6	Test Three

We could show this series of testings by a diagram.

WHEN TO TEST

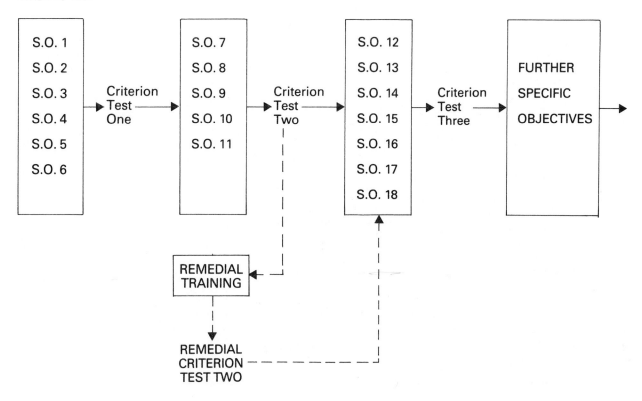

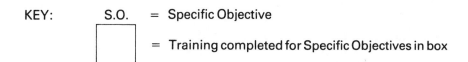

KEY: S.O. = Specific Objective

= Training completed for Specific Objectives in box

Figure 220

What do the pecked lines indicate in Figure 220?

Some trainees have failed Criterion Test Two, undertake remedial training on Specific Objectives 7 to 11, take another (remedial) Criterion Test and if successful, carry on with training.

Summary

An Objectives Checklist shows the adequacy of your General and Specific Objectives and areas in which they may need improvement.

Criterion Tests are progress tests used for the purpose of identifying where the trainees have got to in their training, which objectives they have achieved, how far they have progressed and where remedial action is necessary.

We have used eleven basic ways of testing and described the characteristic of Criterion Tests under eleven headings shown in Figure 210. Knowing these characteristics helps you choose the appropriate test for the job.

The content of your training can be linked to Specific and General Objectives and Test Items developed for both content and objectives, after an appropriate type of Criterion Test has been selected.

An important part of writing Criterion Tests is making out the Test Specification, which shows how balanced your tests are and how well they reflect the training and the learning.

Finally, experience and the Test Specification show you when to apply your Criterion Tests and give an indication of the place of remedial training when necessary.

Building up Criterion Tests is the first of our Functions concerned with synthesis and is succeeded by system step 8, Synthesis of Content.

Lastly, examine one of your current training courses and decide how you could introduce Criterion Tests or, if you have them, how they might be improved.

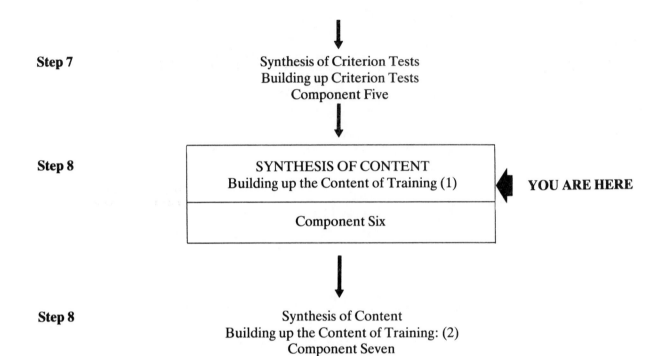

Step 7
Synthesis of Criterion Tests
Building up Criterion Tests
Component Five

Step 8
SYNTHESIS OF CONTENT
Building up the Content of Training (1)

YOU ARE HERE

Component Six

Step 8
Synthesis of Content
Building up the Content of Training: (2)
Component Seven

Component 6:

Building up the Content of Training (1)

Key Words

Sources of content; awarding and examining bodies; design system sources; trainer research sources; content mapping and spray diagrams; skills content maps; method content maps; sequencing content; circular sequencing; sequencing from the design system.

Introduction

> **Considered in this Component**
> **System Activity: Synthesis**
> **System Function:**
> **Synthesis of Content**

We are now considering the next step, number 8, in our design system, the synthesis of course content. Here, we are concerned mainly with the use and manipulation of content, although we do spend some time in finding out how to produce the information necessary for your training.

In many ways, this Component revises and builds upon the design system functions which we have considered previously. It will be useful to you to have these to hand so that referring back is made easy for you.

Incidentally, we must stress that we are presenting options in this Component. Don't imagine that you will use all of these techniques, in practice. When you have examined the alternatives then you ought to select those which suit your purposes best.

The structure of this Component is:

    Sources of Content

    Sequencing the Content

Remember that we are building up our content and therefore the System Function with which we are concerned is Synthesis. However, a word of warning: none of the System Functions is entirely discrete,

consisting purely of one type of activity such as analysis, syntheis or whatever. The Functions are broadly that of analysis, broadly that of assessment, etc, but containing elements of other functions as well. This mixing is particularly the case here, where much of our synthesis is built upon an analytical basis.

Sources of Content

Well, where does the content of our training courses come from? There is the traditional source for finding the riches of content and this is shown in our next Figure.

CONCEPTS GALORE?

Figure 221

205

Although we don't recommend the 'treasure chest' method of finding your content, nevertheless, the riches of content do dazzle us sometimes and we think that if we have the content of our courses organised that's all the hard work done. As you have seen from the systematic approach which we have advocated, there's much more to it than that.

▨▨▨ Checkpoint

Describe where you get the training course content from in your organisation.

Our sources are shown in the next diagram.

SOURCES OF CONTENT

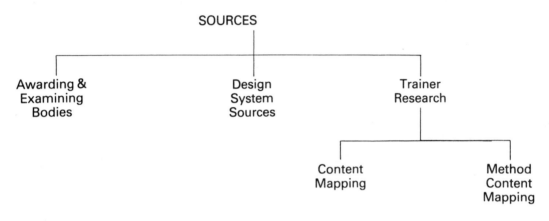

Figure 222

We shall deal with these individually.

Awarding and Examining Bodies

For course content, as for aims and objectives, you find frequently that your syllabus is laid down for you by the external examining body who approve the award for which your trainees are preparing. Usually, however, aims and objectives are stated in full and their definition is categoric: that is what you have to do. Content does not usually appear in such detail, although there are courses where you are not left much discretion in that area either. Generally, external examining bodies indicate an outline of content, as a fuller description would require altogether too much detail and therefore space.

Clearly, if the awarding body does give a lot of information on content then you only require to fill out the detail. However, in those cases where you have to generate the content completely or partially by yourself, the remainder of this Component will help you develop suitable methods.

Incidentally, don't forget the obvious, but Golden Rule: **check that your externally provided syllabus is up-to-date and kept amended.** It's easy to let the amending slide, as we all know.

KEEPING UP-TO-DATE WITH AMENDMENTS

Figure 223

Design System Sources
We know that we have said this before, but our design system will provide you with a lot of information about the content of your training.

Scan through the material which you have gathered so far in considering our systematic approach and consider how it might help in providing course content.

We shall deal with each of our System Functions independently, below.

- **Needs Analysis:**- Although information on content feeds through from all parts of this analysis, the most significant contribution is shown by your Need Statements in Order of Priority for Action (Figure 52). Here your Need Statements indicate the major areas of content **needed** by the trainees. A Need Statement indicates accurately the priority areas of content in outline; obviously you have to fill in the detail, which leads us to
- **Task (Topic) Analysis:**- remember, that Task Analysis is a universal tool which can be used for many different purposes.

THE UNIVERSAL TOOL: TASK ANALYSIS

Figure 224

Take Figure 68, Component 5, Study Unit 1, as an example; although this is only part of a full Task Analysis, of "Black and White Film Processing", nevertheless, you can see that detail of content is provided sufficient for you to use the material as a guide to lesson notes. Looking at the Task Elements, there is material there adequate as a useful guide for a couple of sessions, although you would have to expand each Task Element in your lesson notes, eg by listing the emergency procedures themselves, by naming each chemical and describing the individual dangers of each in detail and so on.

Figure 62 provides another good example of the part which Task Analysis plays in providing content. This provision can be very comprehensive.

How can Figure 62 be used to give you structure and content for the whole of a training course content?

Imagine that your course is divided into:
- Modules, sub-divided into
- Units, sub-divided into
- Sub-Units, sub-divided into
- Lessons
- and details of lessons

The relationship between the Task Analysis of Figure 62 and this course structure is shown in Figure 225. The system works like this:-

COLUMN 1. ELEMENT OF COURSE STRUCTURE. In this column the various elements, or parts, of our imaginary course structure (module, units etc.) are shown. From Figure 62, we have picked two examples to follow up: "A-V Equipment" and "Course Design" and we begin by naming the course Modules.

COLUMN 2. NUMBER OF LEVEL OF ANALYSIS. As you can see in Figure 62 we have taken our Modules from the first Level of Analysis. We picked A-V Equipment and Course Design as examples from the list of Units of Analysis shown in COLUMN 3 UNITS OF ANALYSIS. Each of the first level Units of Analysis from Figure 62 would be used as a module in our course.

We continue working down the chart shown in Figure 225 in the same fashion. Accordingly, you can see that when considering Lessons, against A-V equipment, in Column 3, we could take the Chalk Board as one lesson, the Charts as another and so on. These represent Level of Analysis 3 (Column 2).

Against Course Design we could take Level 5 Units of Analysis (Column 2) from Figure 62, each Unit representing say, one lesson on Determining the Goals, one on Ordering the Goals, etc.

RELATING TASK ANALYSIS TO COURSE CONTENT
(Refer to Figure 62)

1 ELEMENT OF COURSE STRUCTURE	2 NUMBER OF LEVEL OF ANALYSIS (from Figure 62)	3 UNITS OF ANALYSIS (taken from Figure 62)
MODULES eg A.V. Equipment eg Course Design	1 1 1	All Units, ie, Learning Theory and Learner Psychology; **A.V. Equipment;** Computers; Graphics & Reprographics; Methods of Training and Learning; **Course Design;** Training Context; Assessment & Evaluation.
UNITS for A.V. Equipment for Course Design	2 2, 3,	Still Media; Audio; Film media; Television; Projection media. Traditional & Systematic; Analysis; Synthesis; Implementation: Assessment & Evaluation; Improvement.
SUB-UNITS for A.V. Equipment for Course Design	Nil 4	Nil Need Analysis; Task Analysis; Entry Behaviour Analysis; Resource Analysis; Constraints Analysis; Aims/Objectives Analysis.
LESSONS for A.V. Equipment for Course Design	3 5	eg Chalk Board; Magnetic Board; Charts; Models; Slide Projector; Epidiascope; Microprojector; OHP eg Determining the Goals; Ordering the Goals; Measuring the Needs; Deciding on priorities
DETAIL OF LESSONS for A.V. Equipment for Course Design	4, 5, 6, 7,	eg Producing OHP Acetates; Types of OHP; Use of OHP; Advantages of Use; Disadvantages of Use; Materials; Pens, Instruments, Storing. Purpose; input; staff; methods; output. (Methods) Perception Survey; Data Survey

Figure 225

Figure 225 shows how you can use the Units of Analysis from Task Analysis to give a direct indication of the actual content which you may allocate to the various elements of a training course structure. Why do the work twice?

Under Modules, Units etc we have shown examples only.

All of this may seem like a lot of work, but it has to be done sometime when you are planning and producing a course.

RELATING TASK ANALYSIS TO COURSE CONTENT:
ANOTHER VIEW

Figure 226

Clearly, then, Task Analysis can provide you with a complete blueprint for your course content. As we said, you have to do it sometime; perhaps the only difference between the Task Analysis approach and "traditional" methods is that you do all the work at the beginning rather than as you go along. Another advantage of the Task Analysis method is obvious: you can see the outline structure of your course on the one or two sheets of paper which show your actual Task Analysis.

● **Entering Behaviour Analysis:-** In a general sense, you have a deal of information about the knowledge, mental skills, motor skills and attitudes of your trainees from this analysis, both in the individual pictures of each trainee's anticipated entering behaviour and from the composite picture of the entering behaviour of the whole group of trainees, see Figure 119, Component 7, Study Unit 1, Package 1. Obviously, you can relate your selection of content so that it is in harmony with this material.

However, it is in the consideration of the Entering Behaviour of Pre-Course Expectations, that you derive most benefit from this analysis. Figure 105 shows how you have actually asked questions on trainee expectations about the content and nature of training and how you develop this examination by looking at their general expectations of the nature of the training and their detailed expectations of the training content.

Glance through Component 7, Study Unit 1, Package 1, again. What parts of Entering Behaviour Analysis do you believe to be most useful when structuring your course content?

The techniques are those shown by the semantic differential questionnaires of Figures 107 and 108. The information which they produce could hardly be more on target, could it? You have a pre-view information about how the entering trainees actually feel about the "Topics" (Modules, Units, fields of Study etc), which you propose will make up the content of your training.

Obviously, as the trainees have not yet begun their training and can hardly know a great deal about the topics themselves you may have to take what they say with some caution, or a very small pinch of salt perhaps. Nevertheless, where you have trainees who have been working for your firm for a while, they will have talked to others who have completed your training previously and what they have to say could reflect accurately on how useful others have found the various parts of your training in practice. What they say could be well worth listening to.

TAKEN WITH A PINCH OF SALT

Figure 227

Certainly, reading the answers to your questionnaires on trainees pre-course expectations gives you another valuable perspective on what you are doing.

● **Resources Analysis:-** The work which you have done for Resources Analysis is more indirectly useful to establishing the content of your training. When you examine your Resources Checklists, eg Figure 137, Study Unit 1, you will find that you may be lacking certain items of equipment which you require to put across the material for part of the syllabus.

In Figure 137, is there any evidence of this?

You will note that item 24 on the Checklist shows that you have only one 16mm camera and there is no way of making another available. Should you have intended to convey part of your course content by an active exercise involving two 16mm cameras, then you will have to modify that content in some way. You are alerted to this by the "Action" column in Figure 137 which states "replan training" against item 24, "16mm camera".

- **Constraints Analysis:-** The procedures for dealing with a constraint on your training are shown in Figures 142 and 143, Component 8, Study Unit 1. In the latter you are advised to modify your training as a method of dealing with the constraint and "replan your training" for parts such as Content (and Aims & Objectives, Training Methods and Implementation).

▨▨

What does Figure 144 tell you about accommodating constraints, especially with regard to training content?

Stage one, your original plan, could represent, say, 10 items of content. Stage two of Figure 144 shows what would happen to that Content if the constraints which you have identified are not accommodated. Stage three shows what has happened to your training plan and your content when you have accommodated as many constraints as you can. The modified training plan, which we have selected to represent content for the purposes of this exercise, clearly has very strong implications for the material which you can teach, with the amalgamations of Content 1 and Content 2 and the omission of Content 7.

If you re-read Component 8, Study Unit 1, you will see that we said, "As each constraint which you can't remove means altered inputs, ie. altered content in this case, so you have to accommodate these changes in your planning".

- **Aims and Objectives Analysis:-** We have an important point to make here: having defined your Aims and Objectives, you have also identified the demands upon your syllabus, in the sense that you must produce content which covers the demands made by each Aim and General Objective (General content) and each Specific Objective (Specific content). To fulfil the requirements of each Specific Objective, you have to train the trainee in a skill, or knowledge, so that he or she can achieve what the objective says has to be done. In a way, you are attaching pieces of content to each General and Specific Objective.

MATCHING OBJECTIVES WITH CONTENT

Figure 228

Each Specific Objective indicates a content requirement and you ask yourself, "What do I have to teach to make this objective attainable by the trainee?"

So, continuing with our consideration of sources of content and design system sources in particular, it follows that the sources of your Aims must also be the sources of your content, to a large extent. These sources are shown in Figures 154, 155 and 157; some of these we have considered already. You can follow through the links to General and Specific Objectives by studying Figures 159 and 175, whilst Figure 201 provides a useful summary of one aspect of links throughout our design system.

▨▨

Summarise the information which we have given here under Aims and Objectives Analysis be means of a diagram.

Ours is shown on the next page, Figure 229.

SOURCES TO CONTENT

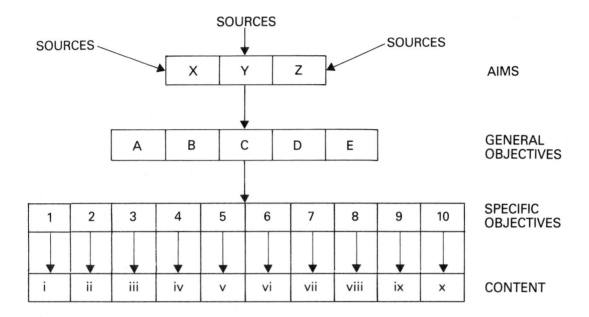

Key:
X Y Z   = Aims
A to E   = General Objectives for Aim Y
1 to 10   = Specific Objectives for General Objective C
i to x   = Content for Specific Objectives 1 to 10

Figure 229

● **Criterion Tests Analysis**:- If you glance back at Figure 214, you will see that it bears a logical resemblance to Figure 229. Much of Component 4, Study Unit 2 concentrates on establishing the link between General and Specific Objectives and course content and how the content is derived from the objectives. Examples of how this is done are shown after Figure 215 and there is no need to go over that ground again, except to emphasise the direct nature of these links.

If you glance back at Figure 222 you will see that our last area for examination when considering sources is "Trainer Research", and we shall do this now.

Trainer Research

These are two methods of research by trainers into content and these are:
1. Content Mapping
2. Method Mapping

These two are familiar: Method mapping is an extension of Content Mapping, so we shall begin with the latter.

1. **Content Mapping:** This is a technique which produces a diagram of your training. Beginning with your central topic, or concept, or skill, or job, you write down all of your related ideas, **spraying out from your**

central idea. You will see at a glance how this technique works when you look at the next diagram. We have used an example which we examined before, the "Human Body" external appearance Figure 57, Study Unit 1.

CONTENT MAPPING:
THE HUMAN BODY, A SPRAY DIAGRAM

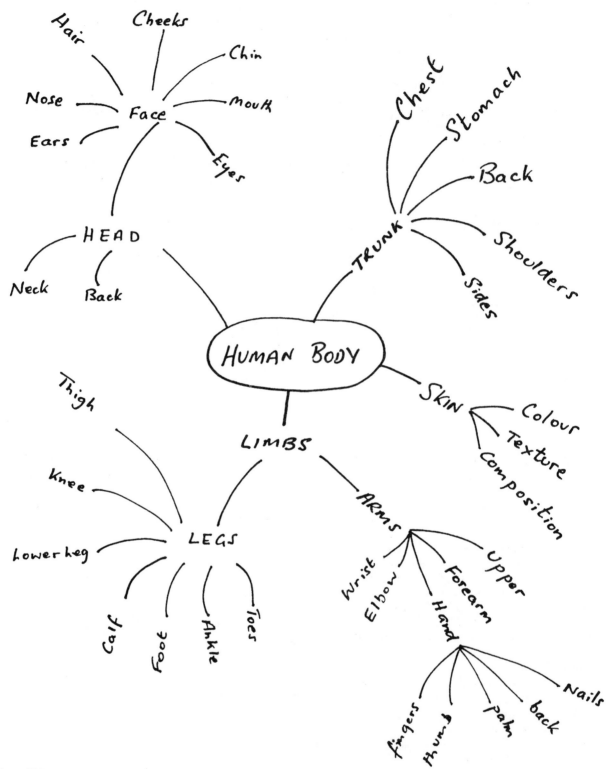

Figure 230

What are the major processes whereby you arrive at a spray diagram?

Well, there is a mixture of two processes: analysis and synthesis. Your preliminary thinking is analytic as you are considering of what parts the human body consists externally. However, your product, the spray diagram itself, is a picture which you have built up of the human body and this is synthesis. And it's the product which counts!

In a way, the product of drawing spray diagrams is not dissimilar from that of Task Analysis; the spray method can be quicker and often gives a more compact product, which you can often get onto one page of A4 (you can use a bigger sheet) but the two processes are equally efficient.

We will give you another couple of examples.

CONTENT MAP OF NEEDS ANALYSIS

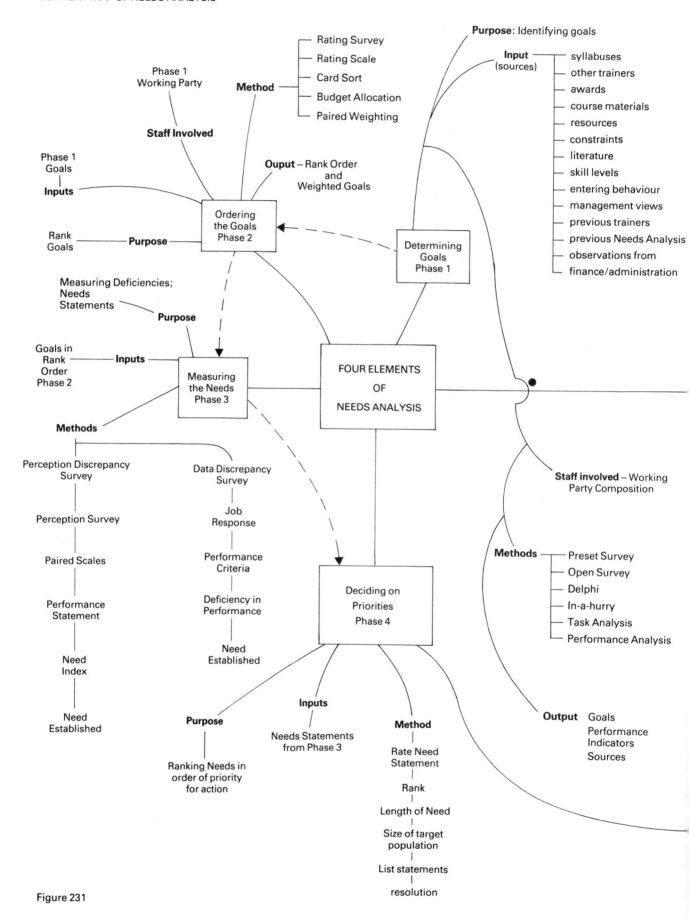

Figure 231

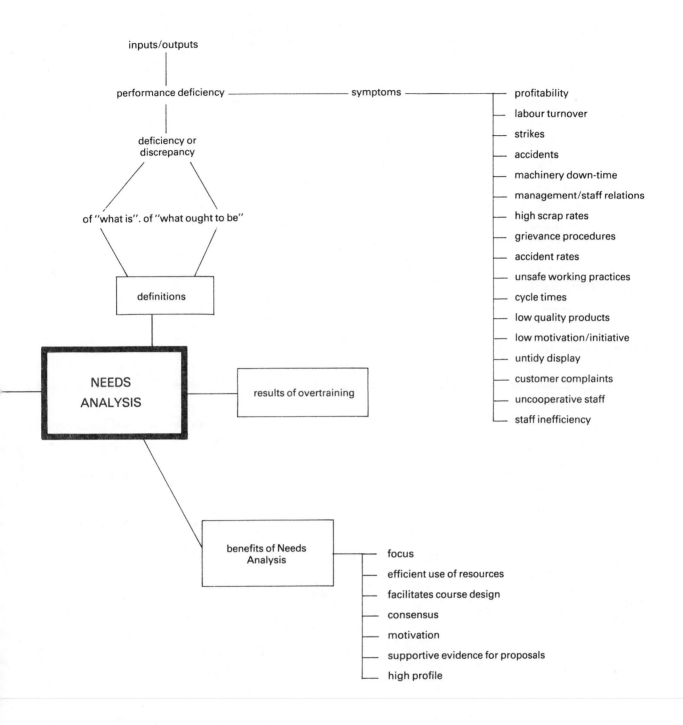

inputs/outputs

performance deficiency ———————— symptoms ——————— profitability

deficiency or discrepancy

of "what is". of "what ought to be"

definitions

NEEDS ANALYSIS

results of overtraining

- profitability
- labour turnover
- strikes
- accidents
- machinery down-time
- management/staff relations
- high scrap rates
- grievance procedures
- accident rates
- unsafe working practices
- cycle times
- low quality products
- low motivation/initiative
- untidy display
- customer complaints
- uncooperative staff
- staff inefficiency

benefits of Needs Analysis

- focus
- efficient use of resources
- facilitates course design
- consensus
- motivation
- supportive evidence for proposals
- high profile

Output
- Needs Statements in order of priority
- Target Population
- Training dates
- Type of training

How does Figure 231 differ from Figure 230 in its construction?

You can see that in Figure 231 we have aligned our writing horizontally and boxed the important points.

The direction of the process of Needs Analysis, ie. moving through the four elements, or Phases, from Determining the Goals, Phase 1, through Phases 2 and 3 to the final Phase, Deciding on Priorities, Phase 4, is shown by a pecked line. The topic of Needs Analysis itself, being central, is shown in a heavier box. In some

CONTENT MAP OF ENTERING BEHAVIOUR ANALYSIS

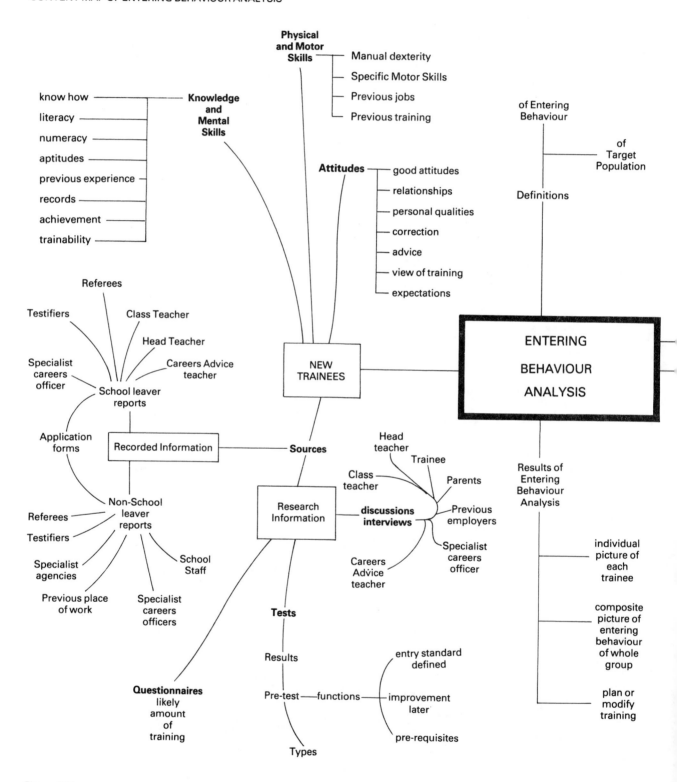

Figure 232

cases we have not given as much detail as possible, for example, we have not entered the results of overtraining. Such omissions are to save space, as we are restricted, but your own Content maps could include such detail. Notice how when one line crosses another you draw it as shown at ● in the diagram.

Now revise Components 6 and 7 in Study Unit 1 and draw your own Content map for the topic "Entering Behaviour Analysis". Figure 232, shows our diagram.

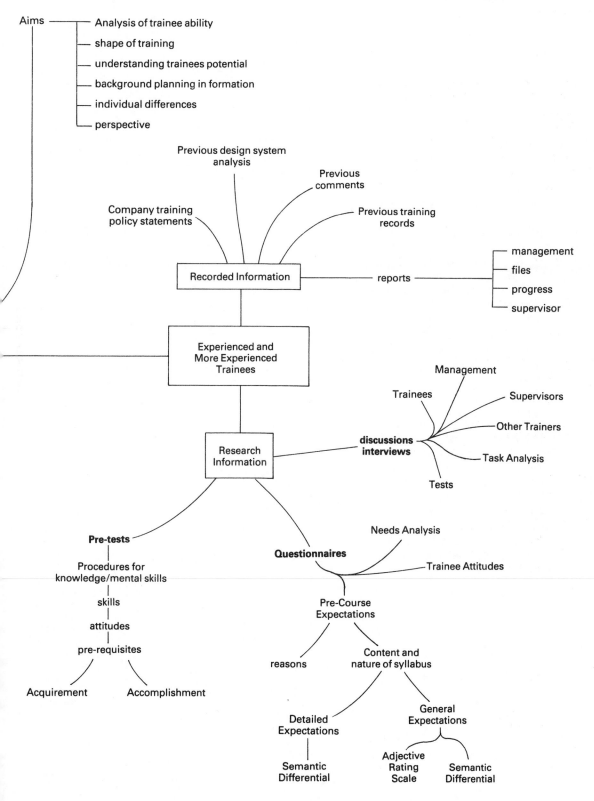

We think that content mapping is an excellent method of building up your training. If you are planning a modular course, a content map for each module shows exactly what content you are to cover and has many benefits. We use this technique very extensively ourselves.

What are the benefits of content mapping to a trainer who is planning the content of a course?

We believe the benefits to be as follows:-
a. *Content maps shows the content of training at a glance.*
b. *They are very compact in their format (compare the information in Figures 231 and 232 with the bulk of material you would have to write in traditional note form).*
c. *The process of content mapping helps you to develop your ideas about the content itself.*
d. *The maps can form the basis of revisionary exercises: by glancing at the map you can easily pick out any areas in which you are unsure of your facts.*
e. *They are a useful form of brief to issue to the trainees.*
f. *Content mapping is a useful exercise for the trainees to perform themselves, especially when they are breaking new ground and want to get their thoughts on paper quickly.*
g. *The maps themselves are a sound basis for the planning of training, giving a structure on which you can write in criterion tests, sequencing of content and indicating suitable subdivisions for planning individual lessons etc.*

So far we have concentrated on the content mapping of two areas which are a mixture of cognitive material, but also reflect skills. You have to know what Needs and Entering Behaviour are about and be able to comprehend and apply them. You must be capable of synthesising pictures of your training needs and trainees' entering behaviour, in addition to evaluating, during your planning, the material which these analyses produce. The process of carrying out these analyses is a mental skill. Now what about the content mapping of physical skills?

Consider a physical skill and draw a content map for it.

We have taken a skill which is useful to all of us: tracing a fault when your car engine overheats. Our content map is shown in the next Figure 233.

SKILLS CONTENT MAP: ENGINE OVERHEATING

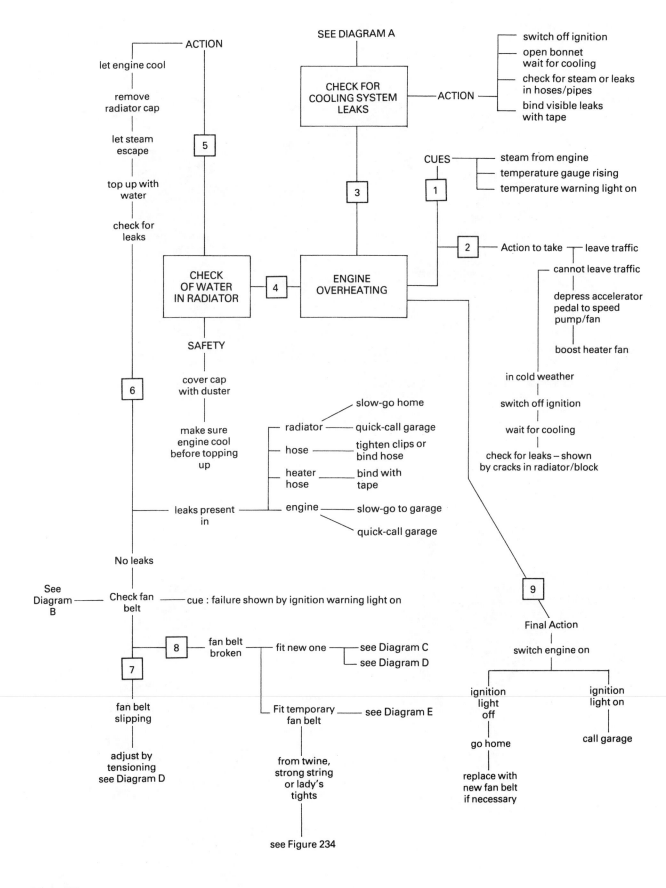

Figure 233

FIGURE 233 CONTINUED...

DIAGRAM A: CHECKING FOR LEAKS IN COOLING SYSTEM

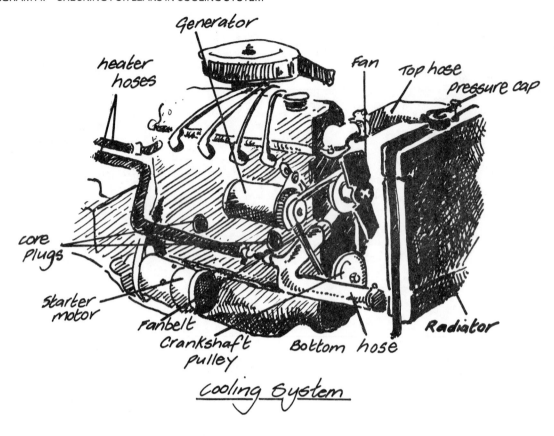

DIAGRAM B: CHECKING THE FAN BELT FITTING

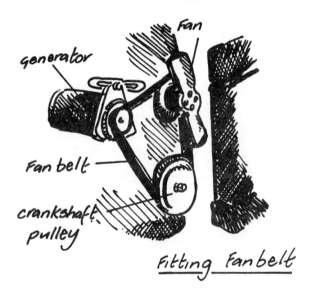

DIAGRAM C: FITTING AND ADJUSTING A NEW FAN BELT

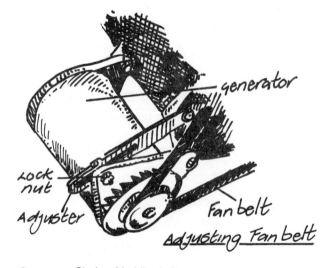

Sequence: Failure – ignition warning light comes on
Reasons for failure – broken or slipping

Sequence: Slacken 3 holding bolts
Push generator towards engine
Remove belt
Loop new belt over fan and onto water-pump pulley
Guide onto generator pulley by turning fan by hand

DIAGRAM D: ADJUSTING TENSION

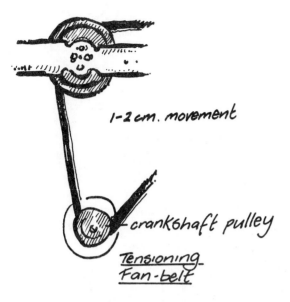

1-2 cm. movement

crankshaft pulley

Tensioning Fan-belt

Sequence: Adjust tension
Hold belt between thumb and finger
Move belt in and out
Movement should be between 1 cm and 2 cms
Adjust to correct tension by moving generator
Tighten bolts whilst holding generator

DIAGRAM E: FITTING A TEMPORARY FAN BELT

Pulley

pulley

Temporary fan belt

Fitting fan belt around two pulleys

Sequence: Make a slip knot loop at one end of a piece of
twine or strong string about 2 metres in length.
A pair of tights will also do the job.
Wind string around pulleys (not generator pulley)
Draw string tight
Wind string around pulleys tightly as many
times as possible
Tie the ends of the string
Cut off surplus string

▨▨▨

Note down the differences in the structure of the skills content map of Figure 223 and the content maps of Figures 231 and 232.

The differences which we note that are in the skills diagram:
a) *Numbers are included thus* $\boxed{3}$ *showing the* **sequence** *of actions in the skills procedure.*
b) *Diagrams are included with the content map to show the machinery with which you are concerned.*
c) *Details of the sequences of the skills process are included with each diagram. They could also be shown as the content map as numbered sequences (eg. "see Sequence 4") and shown alongside the skills content map.*

MAKING THE BEST OF A BAD JOB

This is the third pair of tights you've had off me this year

Figure 234

2.   **Method Mapping.** Finally, in Figure 222, you will notice that we have mentioned Method Mapping as a source of training content. This is a technique for making up your content notes (knowledge, skills or attitudes) by the usual means of referring to manuals and textbooks, but by showing your notes as a content map, together with references to your print-based resources.

You refer to your textbook, note the main points on a spray diagram and mark in the references on the diagram. Our next Figure shows what we mean.

METHOD MAPPING

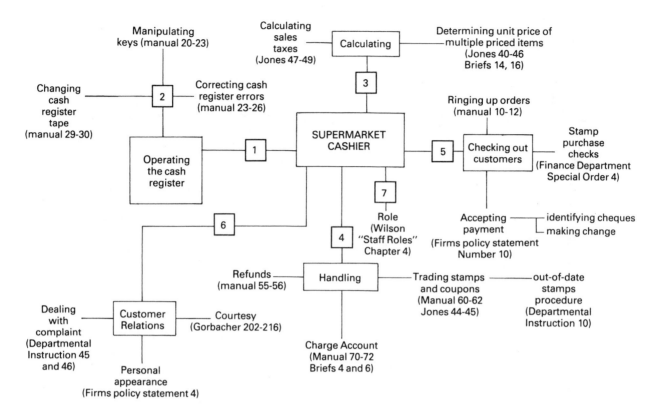

Figure 235

You can see how the references can be included in brackets after the content (Manual 10-12, Jones 40-46). The numbers indicate the appropriate pages, or the number of the briefs which are to be issued, etc, etc.

The sequence of dealing with the material follows the boxed numbers.

USING YOUR REFERENCES: ANOTHER VIEW

Figure 236

We have been concerned here, in examining sources of content to consider not only sources, but also techniques of finding and displaying content. We haven't really considered the traditional sources (textbooks, videos and films) with which you are all familiar, although further details of how to use sources and make lesson notes, are given in Package 2 of this Programme. Method mapping is not just a source of training content, it is also a technique for organising that content.

You will recollect that we also want to have a look at how to sequence your content and we will view this now.

Sequencing the Content

There are various ways of sequencing your content in the order in which you will present it to your trainees during training.

These methods are:
- The Circular Method
- The Design System Methods

The Circular Method

This is one of the simplest ways and is shown in the next Figure.

CIRCULAR METHOD OF SEQUENCING CONTENT

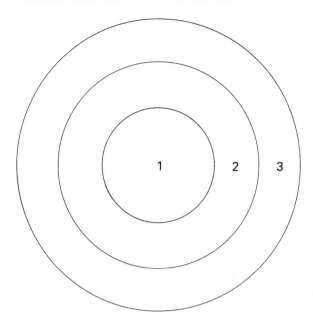

1 = What trainees MUST know
2 = What trainees SHOULD know
3 = What trainees COULD know

Figure 237

Under 1, what trainees must know, are the **core competancies** of any training curriculum and the essential skills which they require to do a job. Without this knowledge and these skills or steps in acquiring skills, the trainees cannot do the job at all.

Under 2, you would include all of the content in your training, whether knowledge or skills, that the trainees should know to become competent at their jobs.

Under 3, you include material in training which is not essential knowledge, nor are steps in a skills procedure which are really necessary for the job to be done competently. Sometimes, much attitudinal information is included here, perhaps unfortunately, the hope being that the trainees should pick up the right attitudes during training.

When sequencing course content, trainers often index the material 1, 2, or 3, so giving perspective to their planning. Deciding what falls into each category is a matter for trainers' experience, often based upon discussions with master and competent performers.

The Design System Methods
As we saw in the process of deriving content from sources within the design system, the systematic approach provides much useful information.

Scan the design system which we have established so far. Devise and draw a chart which shows which System Functions provide sequencing information which helps you sequence (and identify) content.

Our chart is shown in Figure 238.

SYSTEM FUNCTIONS WHICH PROVIDE SEQUENCING INFORMATION

Design System Function	Sequencing Information	Relevant Figures
NEEDS ANALYSIS	1 Rank Order & Weighting of Goals 2 Perception Surveys 3 Data Discrepancy Surveys 4 Need Statements 5 Need Statements in order of Priority for action	37 43 46 49 52
TASK ANALYSIS	1 Task Analysis: Breakdown into Units of Analysis 2 Task Analysis – Levels & Units of Analysis 3 Rules for Sequencing 4 Topic Analysis 5 Job Analysis: writing down the Task Element 6 Questions you should ask yourself when writing down the final units of analysis	56 62 65 68 71 74
AIMS & OBJECTIVES ANALYSIS	1 Enabling and Terminal Objectives 2 Sequencing Specific Objectives 3 Chronological Sequencing 4 Concept Sequencing 5 Skills Sequencing 6 Domain Sequencing: Cognitive Domain 7 Categories in the Cognitive Domain 8 Categories in the Psychomotor Domain 9 Categories in the Affective Domain 10 Process of sequencing 11 Sequencing objectives and training 12 Rules sequencing	177 180 181 182 183 184 186 187.188 189 189 et. seq. 190 191
SYNTHESIS OF CRITERION TESTS	1 The Criterion Connection 2 Test Specification for Criterion Tests	214 218

Figure 238

In each case, the elements of the System Functions (Needs, Units of Analysis, Objectives, Criterion Tests) have been sequenced and, consequently, so is the content which is attached to them. After viewing the relevant Figures again, you can select a method of sequencing useful for your purposes, or use the outline of sequencing provided by the design system.

Finally, let's summarise this Component.

Summary

We have been concerned here with the System Activity of Synthesis, System Step 8, Synthesis of Content.

In building up the content of training, there are three major sources of content and these are: awarding and examining bodies, design system sources and research by the trainer.

For some training, the external body which gives the awards and approves your courses also lays down the syllabus, but on other occasions you have to determine the content yourself. Especially useful in this area is the all-purpose tool of Task Analysis, whilst other Functions of the System Activity of Analysis provide useful sources of content.

When researching your content, the technique of content mapping provides summary diagrams of your material which are economical in time to produce and show the scope of your content at a glance.

Much of the sequencing of your content has already been provided by your various system analyses; you may select an appropriate method of sequencing from the various System Functions, or use the sequencing of the material which you have made already, especially in Aims and Objectives Analysis, as a basis for organising your content.

As a final exercise, select one area of content in your training and make a content map diagram of it.

ORGANISE YOUR CONTENT

Figure 239

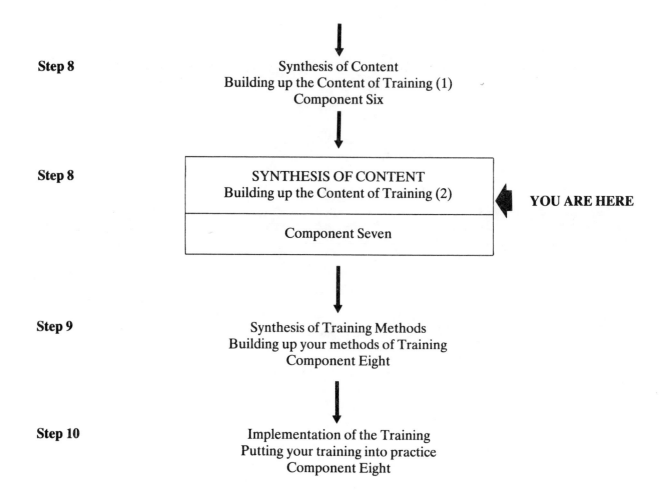

Step 8   Synthesis of Content
Building up the Content of Training (1)
Component Six

Step 8   SYNTHESIS OF CONTENT
Building up the Content of Training (2)

Component Seven

YOU ARE HERE

Step 9   Synthesis of Training Methods
Building up your methods of Training
Component Eight

Step 10   Implementation of the Training
Putting your training into practice
Component Eight

Component 7:

Building up the Content of Training (2)

 Key Words

Alternative approaches and starting points; beginning with aims and objectives; beginning with content; beginning with criterion tests; flexibility and accommodating changes; advance organisers; generality; interactions; structure of knowledge and cognitive structure; differing learning outcomes; content test specifications.

Introduction

> **Considered in this Component**
> **System Activity: Synthesis**
> **System Function:**
> **Synthesis of Content**

In this Component we will complete our considerations of the building up of the content of training by viewing a range of optional techniques from which you can make a suitable choice. We will consider three aspects of content:

Alternative approaches as starting points for the synthesis of content.
The Advance Organiser.
Content Test Specifications.

We will deal with each of these in turn

Alternative Approaches as Starting Points for the Synthesis of Content

Don't worry, we aren't going to reorganise the whole of our design system. You still begin with System Step One (Function, Needs Analysis) and carry on with Step 2 (Task Analysis) Step 3 (Entering Behaviour Analysis) Step 4 (Resources Analysis) Step 5 (Constraints Analysis) but at this point you can make a

change in the system if it suits you better to do so. The design system which we have described so far looks like the following Figure, in simplified form.

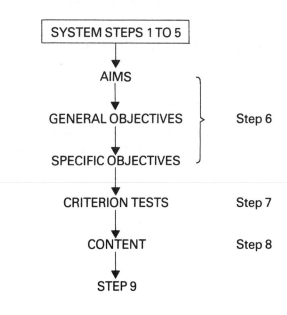

Figure 240

If you have a glance at Figure 229 and 214 again, you'll see this structure in different form.

▨▨▨ Checkpoint

What other ways can you think of to change the order above, **after** you have completed design system Steps 1 to 5?

Our alternatives are shown in Figures 241, 242 and 243.

ALTERNATIVE APPROACHES: BEGIN WITH CONTENT

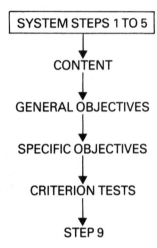

Figure 241

Now, why this format? Well, most trainers are expert in the content of their courses already and many of us have lots of notes from previous training and know many of the relevant reference books, manuals and skilled operations off by heart. So course content is often available from the start. In this approach we are suggesting that you begin with what you already know, the content. You then ask yourself, "What general objectives can I derive from this content?" We have discussed this in Component 1, Study Unit 2, Package 1. We then follow the procedures which we have described previously, working through specific objectives to criterion tests and then on to Step 9, Implementation of the Training.

ALTERNATIVE APPROACHES:
BEGIN WITH CRITERION TESTS

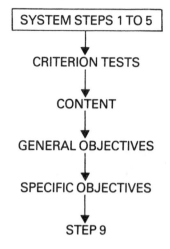

Figure 242

Often, when you have in mind the types of performance which the trainee has to attain, although you may not have written down your specific objectives yet, you can begin by devising your Criterion Tests. You then ask yourself what content you need to cover so that the trainees can complete the Criterion Tests successfully and from that proceed as described in Figure 242. This approach is especially useful when you are training in skilled procedures.

ALTERNATIVE APPROACHES:
BEGIN WITH CRITERION TESTS

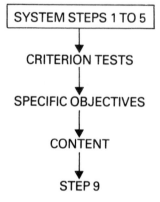

Figure 243

Here you begin with Criterion Tests again, but this time you ask yourself first what specific objectives must I formulate so that the trainees will be able to achieve the Criterion Tests? or, what performances or behaviours will the trainees have to do or show successfully to pass my Criterion Tests? Obviously, you will then need to cover each specific objective with the appropriate content.

You may feel the need to write general objectives after your specific objectives, or you may not and that will depend on whether or not you believe that you have enough guidance to plan your training without the extra information provided by general objectives.

Which method of planning the design of your training do you select? Figures 240, 241, 242 or 243?

Answer: whichever makes you feel the most comfortable. Initially, it is best to follow the "orthodox" routine which we have described in Study Units 1 and 2, so far, and in Figure 240. You can then try the other approaches to find out which one suits you best. You may find that one particular approach is superior for one course and yet another for different training.

After a while you will have a full repertoire of systematic approaches to designing your training. Be flexible and remember that the system is the servant not the master.

DESIGN FLEXIBILITY LEADS TO THE GOOD LIFE

Figure 244

Considering flexibility, remember that once having written your design system steps, **what you write for one step can influence the one before it.** If it does, then make a change in the preceding step to accommodate those which follow.

Show this process of change by a diagram.

Here is our diagram.

ACCOMMODATING CHANGES

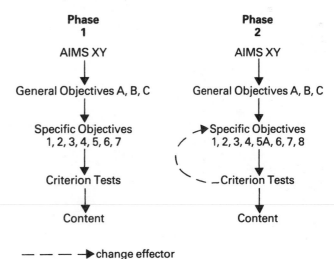

Figure 245

Figure 245 shows that when you wrote your Criterion Tests in Phase 2, they brought new information, or thinking, or a change of emphasis, or a different perspective, or identified something which you had omitted or hadn't covered adequately in your Specific

Objectives, Phase 1. You then changed one of your Specific Objectives (5 to 5A) and added a new objective (8) to accommodate the change. Thus your Criterion Tests caused a change in what went before, in this example in Specific Objectives and 5 and 8. Therefore, your Criterion Tests are "**change effectors**".

Changes can occur at any stage. Here is another example:

ACCOMMODATING MORE CHANGES

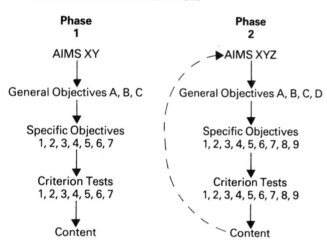

_ _ _ _ ➔ change effector

Figure 246

What does Figure 246 tell us?

You got as far as deciding your Content in Phase 2 and then considered a major change necessary. Maybe you read an article in a periodical which gave you a whole area of content which you had not been familiar with before, or which described a new way of improving a job performance and was so fundamental that you felt you had to incorporate it by changing your Aims.

Note that once you changed your Aims, you had to move down through each step of the system, making further accommodations for your changed Aim, viz another General Objective (D) and changes in Specific Objectives (8 and 9 added) and Criterion Tests (8 and 9). Usually design system changes are not as major as this, but minor changes occur all the time, especially when you are updating your training.

So remember the Golden Rule, "Be flexible: make changes".

ACCOMMODATE CHANGE: BE FLEXIBLE

Figure 247

Our design system is not only flexible but it is also **cyclic**. Perhaps we can summarise this Component so far with two diagrams which show how the parts interact.

DESIGN SYSTEM: BASIC INTERACTIONS

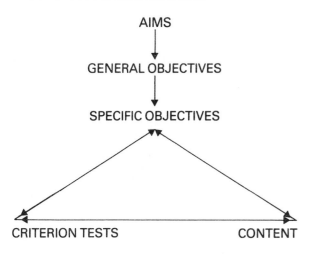

Figure 248

DESIGN SYSTEM: POSSIBLE INTERACTIONS

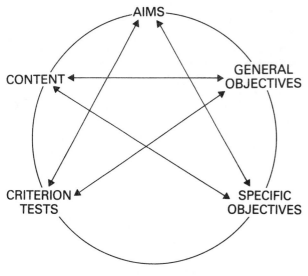

Figure 249

You'll recollect that we mentioned a preview, or advance organiser, at the beginning of this Component. Now, what is this?

The Advance Organiser

This is our last point on content and offers a further option to you when organising content. An Advance Organiser (a name originated by the psychologist David Ausubel) is a type of brief preview of the content which is to follow. If you like, it is a sort of "menu" (advance organiser) for the food (content) which is to follow during your meal (the training).

An advance organiser gives the trainees an indication of the content which is to be covered by the training and gives a **general** indication of the topics which are to be discussed subsequently. Our "keywords" are types of advance organisers for Components and so

are the introductory statements indicating which topics we are going to consider in each Component.

The important point is that an advance organiser gives a mental framework to which subsequent detailed learning can be related. This overview, or preview, must have meaning to the trainee and must take account of the trainee's existing knowledge which you have already acquired from your Entering Behaviour Analysis and pre-tests.

Advance organisers are not just an introduction, because they should **relate to what the trainee knows already,** usually called the trainee's **"cognitive structure". This cognitive structure is the organisation, stability and clarity of the trainee's existing knowledge.** By taking into account what the trainee knows already, the advance organiser is designed to become part of that structure of knowledge, skills or attitudes, ie part of the trainee's cognitive structure.

Advance organisers contain examples of the content which follows them and these examples may be practical, theoretical, metaphorical, give applications and use comparisons.

Our saying that advance organisers are a type of preview, or outline, is not strictly accurate. The advance organiser is much more concerned, than is the preview, with **conveying concepts** to the trainees. Using examples of concepts helps understanding. Even non-examples, ie. examples of what the concepts are **not,** are incorporated, eg. "Which of the following are colours? Brown, green, paint, red." Obviously, "paint" is a non-example of a colour.

Previews and outlines often merely list what is to be studied next. They do not aim for a general trainee understanding of the concept, at this early stage. Advance organisers do try to erect a broad structure in each trainee's mind, into which later detail can be fitted.

WE ALL HAVE A COGNITIVE STRUCTURE

Figure 250

So the advance organiser provides a well-organised, clear framework to which new skills of knowledge can be attached, with understanding. Consequently, advance organisers are written in more general and sometimes more abstract terms than the detailed information which follows.

We can diagram this information simply, as the next Figure shows.

Figure 251

Obviously, new information incorporated into a trainee's existing cognitive structure, will change the form of that structure slightly.

Advance organisers can be written for whole courses, parts of courses and for individual lessons.

How does this process of changing the cognitive structure affect objectives and learning outcomes?

You must have noticed when setting out to train a particular skill or piece of knowledge, perhaps even change an attitude, that the end products of your training or learning outcomes differ considerably from trainee to trainee. One reason is the difference in the cognitive structures of each trainee. When your input, the knowledge and skills of your training, become part of the trainees' cognitive structures, that knowledge and these skills become unique to each trainee. Therefore they become "different" and appear as slightly different outputs. Operators, when trained in the same skill, even if it is a simple one, always perform it differently from each other.

So, despite having the same objectives, your learning outcomes will differ between trainees. Whilst the specific nature of your objectives makes the prediction of learning outcomes a pretty accurate business there will always be final, "unaccountable" differences in performance, knowledge, skills and attitudes, see Figure 252.

SAME INPUTS, DIFFERENT OUTPUTS

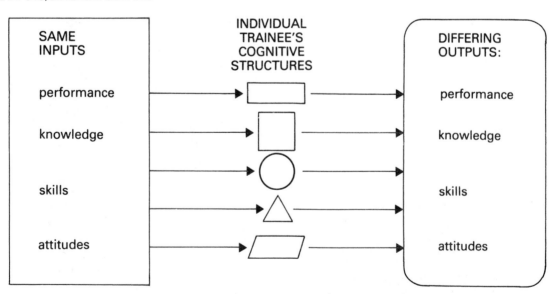

Figure 252

When organising content, it is useful to write down your advance organiser for your content in general terms and then for each part, or module in more detail. Finally you'll wish to consider advance organisers for each lesson or training session.

Diagrammatically, this procedure is shown in the next Figure.

ADVANCE ORGANISERS AND CONTENT

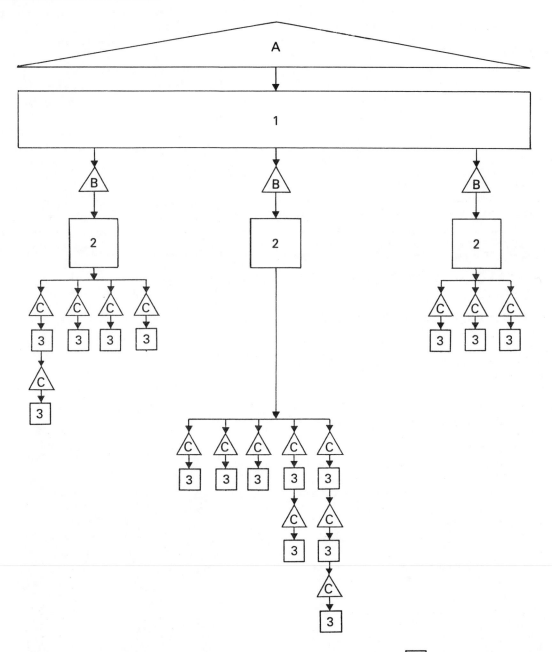

 ADVANCE ORGANISER

A Course Advance Organiser
B Module Advance Organiser
C Lesson Advance Organiser

☐ COURSE CONTENT

1 General Course Content
2 Module Content
3 Lesson Content

Figure 253

We'll look at a few examples of Advance Organisers now.

Course Advance Organiser (written at the beginning of the Course).

Example:

"This course will consider the development of a learning system tailored to meet the personal needs of trainees at Spriggs Cannonballs, plc. The main theme of the course is to consider all aspects of personalising, or individualising, training and will be entitled "Individualised Instruction at Spriggs"

There are seven modules in the training and they are:

1. introducing change;
2. designing the individualised training;
3. implementing individualised training;
4. resources for individualised training;
5. administration of the individualised training;
6. costing and funding the individualised training;
7. evaluation and improving the training;

Case histories are to be used to show how individualised, or personalised instruction can be effected; examples will be given to show how individualising instruction can succeed and where the process may fail; comparisons are to be made between courses where instruction has been personalised, for example the Cannonball Hardening Processes and where it has not, for example in the Pourer's Programme; the relative advantages and disadvantages of individualising instruction will be examined.

The course lasts for two weeks of full-time training."

(We can only take a couple of these modules for detailed examination, but they will show what we mean).

Module Advance Organisers (written at the beginning of each module)

Examples:

Module 4 "Resources for Individualised Training"

"This module will consider the space requirements and facilities for individualised instruction; how additional equipment will be provided; the place of resource centres in individualised instruction; special learning materials to be provided; resources and the priorities for individualised instruction; staff and other resources needed and available; the job of a resource person."

Module 6 "Costing and Funding the Individualised Training".

"This module will examine the costs of individualising instruction and where the funds are to be obtained from. Important topics are: extra equipment resources; the costing of tuition; assessment of fees from outsiders attending the training; "front-end" costing in the preparation of additional learning materials; gaining access to available funding; budgeting; comparisons of cost with courses which have not been personalised."

(We are describing here the use of Advance Organisers in an **outline form.** For more information on writing organisers and for greater detail on how they are structured, consult other Packages of this Programme. The examples which we have shown should build-up the concepts more and contain non-examples of the concepts. Try including this extra material for youself).

Lesson Advance Organisers (written at the beginning of each lesson).

Now a couple of Advance Organisers for single lessons. These examples are in outline form and non-examples of concepts are not given.

Lesson 25 (From Module 4) "The place of resource persons in individualised instruction".

"The lesson will cover: use of "resource persons"; training of resource persons; how a resource person sets about designing a resource centre; the place of a resource person in a training department."

Lesson 40 (From Module 6)

"This lesson will consider how you cost the preparation of additional print-based material resources, wall charts, handouts, briefs and overhead transparancies. After costing and the buying of materials, preparation costs will then be considered as part of an overall budget."

Module and Course Advance Organisers would be written; Lesson Advance Organisers could be either written, perhaps leading into the information in a handout, or spoken, depending on the nature of the lesson. Often in skills lessons parts of the skilled procedure may be demonstrated, or even the whole skill when a master or experienced performer is available. Often initial skill demonstrations are slowed down, so that trainees can distinguish each individual action, or so that they will not be put off by the speed and facility of the demonstrator.

ADVANCE ORGANISERS PREPARE THE WAY

Figure 254

From this discussion you can see how advance organisers give you a series of starting points from which you can build up succeeding content in increasing detail.

Content Test Specifications

You will recollect that we showed you how to develop a Test Specification in Component 5 of this Study Unit. Revise that Component now. There is another way, based primarily on a consideration of content.

Suppose you wish to test how well a student has learned about "Individualised Instruction at Spriggs", Module 5 of the course which we looked at before. Here are the steps for making out a **Test Specification** based on the content of that module, "Administration of the Individualised Training" (see under previous section on "Course Advance Organiser".)

1. **Divide the content into sections,** ours are:-
   a) Departmental reorganisation for individualised training.
   b) Policy changes supporting individualised training.
   c) Staff duties in individualised training.
   d) Staff training requirements.
   e) General organisation for individualised training.
   f) Keeping records of individualised training.
   g) Staff training loads.
   Each section represents a more-or-less discrete element of the content.
2. **Decide to which taxonomic Domain** (Cognitive, Psychomotor or Affective) **each section of the content belongs,** mainly. In this case let's accept that all seven sections are in the cognitive domain.
3. **Decide upon which categories in each domain you wish to test.** Our choice is:
   a) knowledge
   b) comprehension
   c) application
   d) analysis
   (We have decided to test the lower and middle order categories only).
4. **Give a weighting to each category** which indicates the relative importance of the abilities by these categories. Our selection is:
   a) knowledge   20%
   b) comprehension   20%
   c) application   30%
   d) analysis   30%
5. **Decide on how many questions you wish to set in the test** for each category to be tested, considering the time available for testing, etc.
6. **Allocate a proportion of your questions to each section of** your content.
7. Within each section, **allocate questions to each domain** category.
8. Bearing in mind the proportions shown in 4 above, **allocate %s of your total marks available to** the questions.

9. **Allocate actual marks** to each question.
10. **Fill in each of the steps** one to nine above on a Test Specification sheet as we have done in the next diagram, Figure 255.

░▓▓▓

What does this Content Test Specification tell you about a) "Reorganisation" and f) "Keeping Records"?

For a) Reorganisation, you are setting 3 questions, total value 7% of your marks. For f) Keeping Records you are setting 10 questions, total value 31% of your marks.

Obviously, you also know the total number of questions you are setting, as well as the % and number of questions which you award to each category.

Hopefully, you have a balanced test for both your sections of content and domain categories. If you don't like the look of what you've got, you can always change it around!

░▓▓▓

Making reference to Figure 255 say how you think the writing out of a Content Test Specification, in the manner which we have just described, helps you to synthesise your training course content.

From the Content Test Specification for Module 5, "Administration of the Individualised Training" you know three vital facts:
a) The number of test questions which you are setting for each section a) to g) of the content in Module 5 (see Figure 255).
b) The number of test questions in each category (Knowledge, Comprehension, Application and Analysis for each section of content a) to g).
c) The % of marks to be awarded to each category for each section.
Consequently, when selecting and developing your content, you have a complete description in your Test Specification of how to balance that content.
For example, in the section of the Module on a) Reorganisation, you know that you must develop content to cover the three questions which you are going to ask and that this content should form about 7% of the total content which you teach. These details are from Figure 255.

CONTENT TEST SPECIFICATION

COURSE: "INDIVIDUALISED INSTRUCTION AT SPRIGGS"
MODULE 5: "ADMINISTRATION OF THE INDIVIDUALISED TRAINING"

SECTION OF CONTENT	CATEGORY TO BE TESTED								NUMBER OF QUESTIONS IN TOTAL	%
	Knowledge		Compre-hension		Application		Analysis			
	%	Q.	%	Q.	%	Q.	%	Q.		
a) RE-ORGANI-SATION	3	1	2	1	2	1	0	0	3	7
b) POLICY CHANGES	3	1	2	1	2	1	0	0	3	7
c) STAFF DUTIES	3	1	2	1	2	1	4	1	4	11
d) STAFF TRAINING	3	1	2	1	6	1	4	1	4	15
e) GENERAL ORGANI-SATION	3	1	2	1	6	1	4	1	4	15
f) KEEPING RECORDS	3	1	8	2	10	5	10	2	10	31
g) STAFF LOADS	2	1	2	1	2	1	8	2	5	14
NUMBER OF QUESTIONS IN TOTAL		7		8		11		7	33	
%	20%		20%		30%		30%			100%

Figure 255

Q = Question

As another example, section f) Keeping Records of Individualised Training shows that you are asking a total of 10 questions, mostly on Application and that one half of your total content should be devoted to this section of the syllabus. Clearly, you are going to devote approximately one third (31%) of your total content to the actual practice of record keeping in this Module.

Actually writing out your questions, of which there are 33 for this Module shown in the Content Test Specification, will define your selection of Content even closer, at this stage.

However, what you have developed is a **test** specification primarily and it only serves as a guide which shows how you may select and balance your content.

So you have a framework in your Content Test

Specification which indicates how you may build up the content of the course in general, and any particular area within that content.

Do remember that the Content Test Specification offers indicators, not firm boundaries.

Summary

There are alternative approaches to the synthesis of content which do not follow the format shown in Figure 240 which begins with Aims and Objectives. Other starting points which may suit you better are Content (Figure 241) or Criterion Tests (Figures 242 and 243) and in each case the sequence you follow is different.

All starting points and sequences carry on to Step 9 of our design system. Retaining flexibility in your systematic approach is important for accommodating different styles of training and dealing with varying planning problems in a manner which suits your experience, style and material.

Advance organisers prepare a trainee for changes in the structure of his or her knowledge, skills or attitudes and are types of previews of the material which is to follow, couched in general terms. When written in full, they differ from ordinary previews by attempting to explain the concepts of your content, in broad terms.

As each trainee has a different structure of knowledge, or cognitive structure as it may be called, training affects each one differently. For this and other reasons you must always expect learning outcomes to differ from person to person, even though the training which they receive is the same.

Advance organisers are useful at course level, modular or sub-unit level and for each individual lesson.

Content test specifications help you to balance your content between the different sections, or topics, of your training. They also give a general indication of how you may select your course content and how far you may build up the detail of that content.

Consider a course which you have running currently or training which you have completed previously and consider how the use of content test specifications could have improved your training, or devise advance organisers for one of your training courses.

MAKE YOUR SYSTEM CHANGES IN GOOD TIME

Figure 256

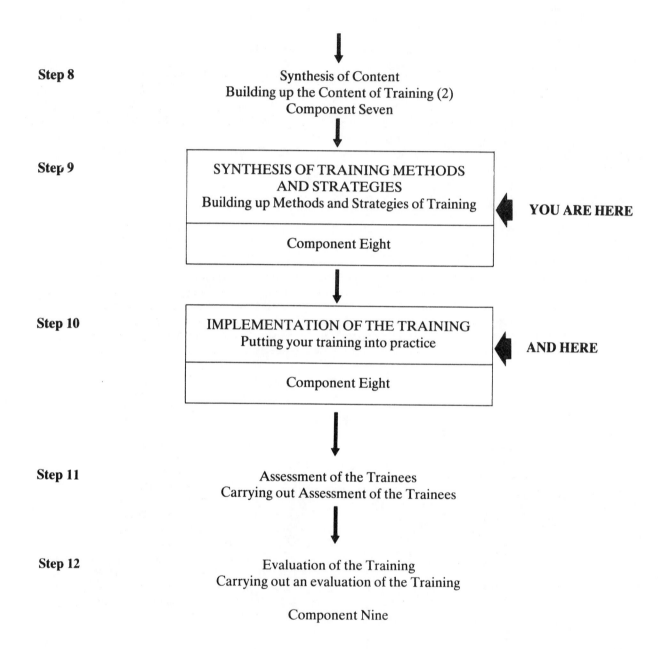

Step 8

Synthesis of Content
Building up the Content of Training (2)
Component Seven

Step 9

SYNTHESIS OF TRAINING METHODS
AND STRATEGIES
Building up Methods and Strategies of Training

Component Eight

YOU ARE HERE

Step 10

IMPLEMENTATION OF THE TRAINING
Putting your training into practice

Component Eight

AND HERE

Step 11

Assessment of the Trainees
Carrying out Assessment of the Trainees

Step 12

Evaluation of the Training
Carrying out an evaluation of the Training

Component Nine

Component 8:

Building up Methods and Strategies of Training, and Putting your Training into Practice

Key Words

Synthesis of training methods and strategies: trainer-centred and trainee-centred strategies; training strategies and instructional methods; advantages and disadvantages of both; interaction between trainers and trainees in both strategies; other sources of interaction; relating taxonomic domains to strategies; active trainees and effective training; expository and discovery training methods; learning procedures; implementation: events of instruction; expository; gaining attention; informing trainee of objective; stimulating recall; presenting the stimulus material; providing learning guidance; eliciting the performance; providing feedback; assessing the performance; enhancing retention and transfer; order reversal for discovery learning.

Introduction

In this Component we will consider both system Step 9, Methods of Training and System Step 10, Implementation of Training. However, we are really **making an overview in both of these system Steps of the much more detailed information which is available in Packages Two, Three and Four "Methods of Training" of the Training Technology Programme.** The information which we shall give here will be adequate for the purposes of our design system, but the close detail must wait until later Packages of the Programme.

Considered in this part of the Component
System Activity: Synthesis
System Function:
Synthesis of Training Methods and Strategies

Let's begin with:

SYNTHESIS OF TRAINING STRATEGIES AND METHODS

In this step of our design system, we will consider these main topics:

Trainer-Centred Training Strategy.
Trainee-Centred Training Strategy.
Selecting a Training Strategy.

There are two ways of viewing training: **the trainer-centred approach** and **the trainee-centred approach.** You must remember, however, that these methods are extremes and trainers use either one of them, or a combination of both. This situation is shown in the following diagram.

TRAINING STRATEGIES AND METHODS

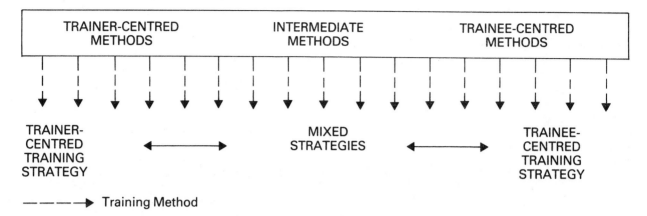

Figure 257

The two end positions in Figure 257 represent opposite ends of a continuum and in "traditional" terms most trainers and other educationists occupy the trainer-centred location. We are not being rude when we say "traditionalist"; both you and we have taught this way in the past. **Recent methods now concentrate on the trainee and this represents a development in which we are all participating.**

You will see from Figure 257 that each strategy subsumes a considerable number of training methods and that there are many intermediate, or mixed strategies.

Figure 258

▨▨ Checkpoint

What's a continuum?

The dictionary says "something continuous, uninterrupted." In this case we have a series of training strategies moving from one end (trainer-centred) to the other (trainee-centred) of a range of methods.

We will examine each of these strategies in turn.

Trainer-Centred Training Strategy

In this type of training, the trainer, the training institution and the firm are the **focus** of the action. This approach has other names which are used, eg. **didactic** and **expository** training, **reception learning.**

In this type of training, the trainer gives out information to the trainees either by:

● talking
● lecturing
● use of "chalk and talk"
● offering handouts
● setting exercises.

Many of us were taught at school this way.

Other characteristics are that the information which is given out usually comes from a set syllabus, often interpreted personally by the trainer; the instruction takes place at set times for set timetabled periods; the training is organised to fit neatly into the firm's requirements; not much trouble is taken to cope with individual learner requirements and differences between individuals.

As most of us have used or experienced this type of teaching, we will now ask you some questions about trainer-centred techniques to clarify your ideas.

Who makes decisions about what is to be taught?
Answer: the trainer, management of the firm, the outside body making the award for which the trainees are studying.

Who organises the timetable?
Answer: the training manager, in consultation with the firm's management. Training periods are closely timetabled and fit in with other courses.

Who makes the choice of teaching strategy?
*Answer: choosing a "strategy" means selecting a **major** style of teaching. Usually this selection is by the trainer, supported by management.*

Who makes the tactical decisions?
Answer: we are concerned here with "tactics". Using a war analogy, you should remember that the distinction between "strategy" and "tactics" is the difference between deciding on the theatre of operations in which battles are to be fought, which is the strategy, and the actual day-by-day and hour-by-hour conduct of the battles, which is tactics. So tactical considerations involve the selection and level of specific training material and subject matter, training methods and even the way in which each lesson is taught. In trainer-centred instruction it is the trainer who makes these decisions, by himself.

What part does the trainee play in making decisions about training?
Answer: very little, the trainees do what they are told to do and learn what is put before them.

Figure 259

If trainees have a particular way of learning things, then that personal style must go by the board to accommodate the decisions made by the trainer himself and the organisation's restraints.

Who decides on how fast the learning will go?
Answer: the trainer, who adopts a pace somewhere in between the speed of the quickest learners and that of the slowest. Obviously, there are disadvantages to both.

MEASURING THE PACE OF LEARNING

Figure 260

How is progress decided?
Usually, by a final examination, decided by the awarding body and/or the trainer. The trainees have no say in the form this test will take.

Now we may seem to have given a rather negative view of trainer-centred training and this has been deliberate. However, this method has many positive aspects and there is certainly a place for it in most training. It's all a matter of perspective; we are just saying that this method is best not overdone, or used exclusively, that's all.

Clearly, then, we consider trainee-centred training does have advantages. Here are some which we think are important.

Advantages of trainer-centred training
We believe that some of these are:
- Everybody knows how the traditional approach works. This is important: many teaching institutions and training departments are geared to this approach, they can operate this system smoothly, the administration and finance are organised to support it and trainers can get on with it with a minimum of guidance.
- Trying another approach often meets with opposition from the training staff and from the firm, anyway. Most people resist change, because it makes them feel insecure; they would rather rely on what their experience has taught them.

ACCEPTING CHANGE

Figure 261

242

Perhaps Figure 261 illustrates an extreme viewpoint, but you know what we mean!

- Mostly, training establishments have a well-organized training system which is fitted to meet the training requirements already existing. If it is proposed to change this, then that could mean a complete regearing and a lot of work for everybody concerned. It might be difficult to find the time and energy required to do this.
- Traditional, trainer-centred methods certainly "cover" the ground. If you have a set timetable you know exactly where you are. Accommodation, trainers' time and resources are used efficiently and you can make certain of meeting the requirements of tests which are set by external, awarding bodies.
- A big advantage is the control which the trainer has in designing training situations which are pitched at a suitable level and which contain an appropriate amount of material for the trainees to master.
- Similarly, the trainer can select training techniques already proved acceptable and can offer strong leadership.

So the trainer-centred methods are efficient in provision of trainer-controlled learning experiences. They do have disadvantages.

Disadvantages of trainer-centred training
- The trainer does most or much of the work. The trainees can be passive recipients of information only.
- A great deal depends on the experience and ability of the trainer. Consequently, he or she may rely heavily upon methods of training which are familiar; often these may not be suitable or the best available.
- The trainer has to make individual decisions about interpreting the syllabus, the amount of reinforcement given, the pace of presentation, motivating the trainees, reinforcement of the learning, obtaining feedback and structuring of the content. Often these decisions are correct; often they are not.

PACING YOUR TRAINING: DO YOU ALWAYS WIN?

Figure 262

- Traditionally timetabling is standard, usually 45 minutes or one hour per training session. The material has to be slotted into this timing, whether it is suitable or not for the nature of the material. Remedial classes may be difficult to incorporate into this timetable.
- Trainer-centred training is based upon the passive reception of information by trainees, although this situation may be alleviated in skills training which does require activity on the part of the learners. At worst, it becomes 'spoonfeeding' of trainees.

The efficiency of the trainer-centred strategy of training does depend upon the skill of the individual trainer. We all know that this dependence may be a strength or a weakness.

▨▨▨ Checkpoint

What training methods are used in the trainer-centred strategy?

*Methods where the trainer **gives out the information**, eg. lectures, skill demonstrations with little practice involved, "chalk and talk", dictating notes, reading through manuals or handouts. This is any method where the trainer's presentation is any technique involving mainly an **exposition** of the knowledge or skill. Consequently, these are the **expository techniques** and they include little trainee-trainer interaction or activity on the part of the trainees themselves; this is shown in the next Figure.*

TRAINER-TRAINEE "INTERACTION" IN THE
TRAINER-CENTRED STRATEGY

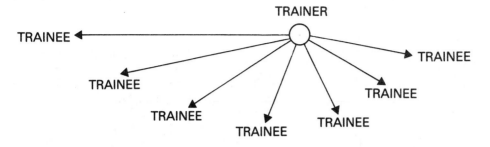

Figure 263

Worse still, the "interaction" could be thus:

EVEN LESS INTERACTION AND NO TRAINEE REACTION

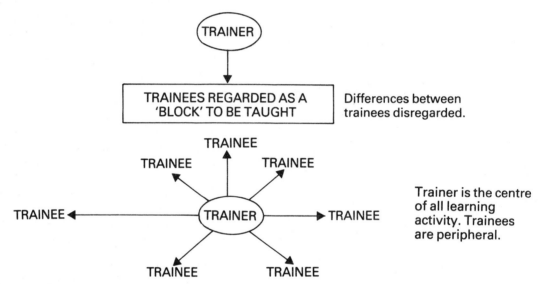

Differences between
trainees disregarded.

Trainer is the centre
of all learning
activity. Trainees
are peripheral.

Figure 264

Trainee-Centred Training Strategy

Here the **trainee is the focus of training.** They learn by
enjoying learning experiences, or discovering for
themselves and the training is more accommodating
of the individual skills and abilities of each trainee.
Active methods of learning are used, enabling the
trainee to interact directly with the trainers and the
training material as shown in the following diagram.

TRAINEE-CENTRED STRATEGIES: SOURCES OF INTERACTION

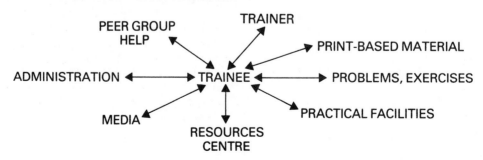

Figure 265

▨▨▨

In Figure 265, what do the terms "Peer Group Help", "Resources Centre" and "Print Based Material" mean?

Peer Group Help: *your peers are your equals, your colleagues; in this case, "peer group help" means the fellow trainees in a trainee group helping each other to learn, often by the more-advanced trainees bringing on the others.*

PEER GROUP HELP

c'mon. It's easy.

Figure 266

Resources Centre: *space set aside for storing and providing training materials and direct trainer help. The resources including books, manuals, briefs, charts, audio, videos, tape-slide etc and are accessible to anyone who wants to use them.*

Print-based Material *is the written material which we all commonly use, but also includes those materials which can be used at a distance between the trainer and the trainee, eg. distance-learning materials, such as the correspondence course. This Training Technology Programme is distance-learning material. Obviously, for firms whose trainees are scattered far and wide and who cannot attend courses, distance-learning may be the only way of training.*

We now ask you a series of questions about the **trainee-centred** strategy. The answers are shown after the questions.

IN THE TRAINEE-CENTRED STRATEGY
1. Who is primarily responsible for the learning?
2. Is the Objectives Model used?
3. Is the learning material more or less accessible than in traditional strategies?
4. Who paces the learning?
5. What choices of material are given the trainee?
6. What part does trainee-trainer contact play?
7. Can you distinguish between different types of training within the strategy?

Now you have had the chance to consider these questions you will realise that they are concerned with:

● **The advantages of the trainee-centred strategy**

Here are our answers to the numbered questions:
1. The trainer must always be primarily responsible, but the trainee has a much greater part to play in organising his or her learning. As the training is centred on the trainee, the training material should be tailored, as far as possible, to suit the personal interests and needs of the trainees.
2. Yes. All the advantages of the Objectives Model are used: the trainers and trainees have objectives which show them where they are going and assist both in checking their progress.
3. More accessible. At best, the material is readily available at all times and may be provided at the trainees' workplaces in the case of a geographically widespread firm using distance learning. (see Figure 268).
4. The trainee, under the trainer's guidance. Self pacing is an important feature of the trainee-centred strategy.
5. As wide as possible. Ideally they should have a choice of options and be able to pick what benefits them most.

DISTANCE-LEARNING REACHES THE PARTS OTHER TRAINING CAN'T TEACH

Figure 267

245

ACCESSIBILITY OF LEARNING MATERIALS:
THE "COME-AND-GET-IT" PRINCIPLE

Figure 268

6. Usually, contact between trainers and trainees is closer than in traditional training methods. Because the trainees are pursuing their training more independently, trainer guidance and counselling is very important, especially in distance-learning work.

7. There seems to be two main types to us.

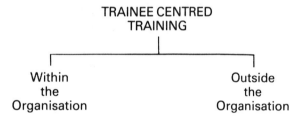

Figure 269

Within-the-organisation training concerns courses which are attended by trainees in the georgaphical area of their place of work. This training is usually organised on the firm's premises, but may take place at a local college or other training institution.

Outside-the-organisation training happens when the firm's employees are geographically scattered. Distance-learning is one example of this type.

We shall now go on to examine:
● **The disadvantages of the trainee-centred strategy**
There are quite a few of these and they are substantial.
● Setting up the system is hard work for the trainers, who have to plan, write and revise materials, distribute them, spend a lot of time counselling trainees, offering help, marking scripts, etc, and giving feedback to the trainees.

● All of this effort and all of these new or re-organised materials are costly in terms of money and trainer time and skills (often new skills which have to be learned). Further costs are incurred in updating the materials.
● The trainer has to change his or her role with this strategy. Instead of the dominant leader controlling and distributing information, he or she becomes a provider and a support. The trainer may have to be trained to accept this change.

CHANGE OF ROLE MAY BE DIFFICULT TO ACCEPT

Figure 270

The trainees might not be happy to accept more responsibility for their own learning either. Administrators providing support for the new strategy may find the changes difficult to accommodate, too.

● As a consequence of all of this change in attitudes and operations, motivation on the part of the trainers, trainees and administrators has to be very high. If it isn't the strategy doesn't work well.

- The final drawback of the trainee-centred strategy is one of the biggest: the range of training and courses to which it can be applied is limited.

What types of courses do you consider would not be suitable for this strategy?

Training with a high skill or practical element is a problem. Examples are:
- *laboratory work*
- *practical manipulative work*
- *skills training*

If you have to spend a great deal of time in your training in demonstrating laboratory techniques, in showing how physical manipulative tasks are accomplished and especially if you are training in skilled procedures, you really cannot let the trainees "do their own thing". Relating this to the taxonomic domains which we studied previously, you come up with a table like this.

RELATING DOMAINS TO THE STRATEGIES

STRATEGY \ DOMAIN	COGNITIVE	PSYCHOMOTOR	AFFECTIVE
TRAINER-CENTRED STRATEGY	(1) MEDIUM	HIGH	MEDIUM
TRAINEE-CENTRED STRATEGY	HIGH	(2) LOW	HIGH

Suitablility of strategy shown in boxes

(1)   Suitability in this box varies from HIGH to LOW, depending on the level of skill, expertise and experience of the trainer.

(2)   Suitability in this box varies from MEDIUM for simple skills to LOW for complex skills.

Figure 271

Obviously you pick your strategy to suit your task

So within the trainee-centred strategy, which methods of training and learning would you use?

We suggest:
- *Directed Reading: reading manuals and literature with the help of a study guide provided by the trainer.*
- *Assignments and longer pieces of work like Projects.*
- *Resource Centre Work, where the trainee works through a course using the materials available in the Resource Centre guided by briefs and work guides prepared by the trainer.*
- *Programmed learning materials.*
- *A-V learning programmes, especially those where the trainee can interact with the media, whether it be audio or video tape, tape-slide or a combination of these.*
- *Language laboratories.*
- *Radio and television broadcast material.*
- *Computer based instruction.*
- *Interactive video.*
- *Open and Distance-learning schemes.*
- *Discussion Groups.*
- *Games and Simulations.*
- *Case Studies.*
- *Action Learning and Quality Circles.*

The Systematic Design of Training Courses

● *Tutorials.*
● *All forms of Individualised Instruction.*
We haven't given you detail of the methods, because that really is for later Packages of the Training Technology Programme.

Let's see if you can illustrate what we've been saying.

Draw diagrams which show trainer-trainee interaction in the trainee-centred strategy.

Our illustrations follow:

TRAINER-TRAINEE INTERACTION IN THE TRAINEE-CENTRED STRATEGY

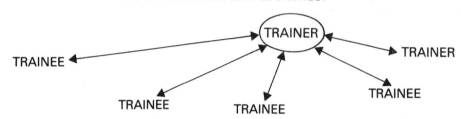

Figure 272

EVEN MORE INTERACTION AND MUCH TRAINEE REACTION

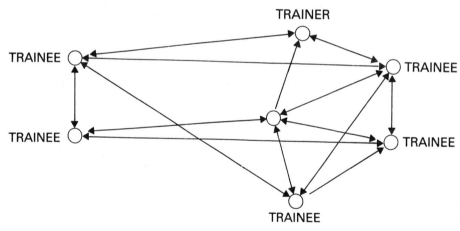

Figure 273

Well, you could go on drawing lines on Figure 273 for ever if you included more trainees, but you'll get the drift of what we mean. In the trainee-centred strategy there is a great deal of interaction between trainer and trainees and amongst the trainees. The trainees are active. This is a "Golden Rule of Training"; we'll put it in a picture frame for you.

GOLDEN RULE OF TRAINING

Figure 274

Hang Figure 274 up in your minds; there are more Golden Rules to follow!

This point about **activity** is an important one and makes a distinction between our two training strategies, as shown below.

Trainer-Centred Strategy involves EXPOSITORY TRAINING METHODS through exposition by the trainer.

Trainee-Centred Strategy involves DISCOVERY TRAINING METHODS through discovery by the trainees.

Figure 275

Let us explain what we mean by these terms.

● **Expository training methods.** These are those mentioned already in our consideration of the trainer-centred strategy and are based on the trainer presenting knowledge and skills by an exposition. The trainees receive the knowledge, mostly passively; consequently, this is often called reception learning.

Now, what are the steps used by most training methods employing this strategy? They are shown in the next Figure.

EXPOSITORY LEARNING (RECEPTION) PROCEDURE

Step 1   PRESENT INFORMATION AND/OR SKILL. Usually, this Step concentrates on general principles and the presentation may be an explanation or the demonstration of a skill.

Step 2   TEST FOR UNDERSTANDING. Here you want to find out, usually by question and answer techniques, if the first exposition, or presentation, has been understoood, if it has been received by the trainees, and if they can recall it by restating in their own words and giving accurate examples. If they can't, you re-present the information or skill, perhaps in a different form.

Step 3   PRESENT OPPORTUNITIES FOR TRAINEE PRACTICE. Ask the trainees to apply your general information to particular examples, or see how far they can apply the skill, or parts of the skill, which you have demonstrated (or had demonstrated by a skilled performer).

Step 4   TEST FOR CORRECT PRACTICE. Check the accuracy of the trainees' skill practice, find out if they have applied their knowledge correctly; ensure trainee performance is accurate when practised.

Step 5   PRESENT OPPORTUNITIES FOR APPLICATION. Give trainees the chance to use their new skills on the actual job, and/or to apply their newly learned knowledge to real-life situations.

Figure 276

● **Discovery methods.** These are those used in the trainee-centred strategy and they are concerned with trainees finding out for themselves and learning through their own direct experience. As we mentioned before, these methods are less useful for training in advanced skills procedures.

Here the trainees find out, or discover, the knowledge for themselves by experiencing the situation with trainer guidance. Consequently, this is often called discovery or experiential learning.

These are the steps used in this strategy.

DISCOVERY LEARNING PROCEDURE

Step 1	OFFER OPPORTUNITIES FOR DISCOVERY. Give the trainees a chance of doing something and seeing how it works out. Set them problems, or questions, let them try out a single skill or the first parts of a more complex skill and see what happens. Hopefully, by seeing the effects of their actions the trainees will be able to establish a relationship between cause and effect.
Step 2	TEST FOR UNDERSTANDING. Find out if the trainees have established the link between cause and effect and if they understand the consequences of their actions. Try questioning, or observing a skill. Offer more opportunities for discovery if necessary until they have an idea of how to fulfil a goal by acting a certain way.
Step 3	TEST FOR LEARNING. The learning which you are after here is whether or not the trainees understand the basic principles of the knowledge which they've been offered, or have grasped the basics of a skilled procedure.
Step 4	OFFER OPPORTUNITIES FOR APPLICATION. Check to ensure that the trainees can apply their new knowledge, or skills, in practice and whether they understand the basic principles sufficiently well enough to deal adequately with real problems and situations, or perform a skilled job properly.

Figure 277

As you can see, expository and discovery learning techniques follow procedures which partly reverse each other. Look again at Figure 259 and compare with the next Figure.

SLICING THE (TRAINING) CAKE A DIFFERENT WAY

Figure 278

Your comparison of Figures 259 and 278 should encapsulate the difference between trainer and trainee-centred strategies and consequently between expository and discovery approaches. Discovery methods entail learning through experiencing something.

Selecting a Training Strategy

As we explained previously, in this Component, we are providing you here with an outline of the material contained in Packages Two, Three and Four of the Programme. So we set out to show you the difference between the two major **strategies** of training, trainer-centred and trainee-centred and indicated some of the different **methods** which you may employ under each strategy.

It really all depends on what you are training for as to which strategy and what methods you use, but do remember the Golden Rule; this is of fundamental importance. Quite often one syllabus topic may involve the trainer in using both strategies, eg. "Effective use of visual aids."

This survey of training strategies and methods completes the System Activity of Synthesis. We now move on to the next step in our design system: Implementation.

IMPLEMENTATION OF THE TRAINING

> **Considered in this part of the Component**
> **System Activity: Implementation**
> **System Function:**
> **Implementation of the Training**

In this section of this Component we move to Step 10 of our systematic approach. Notice that we make this move in the middle of a Component and although we are changing from one of the major parts of our design system to another, i.e. from one Activity to the next, the system is really a continuous process, a series of interdependent and overlapping parts, so interlinked that we could have made this change in the middle of a sentence, if that had been appropriate.

There is much detail to be embraced in the study of

the Implementation of the Training, including a consideration of the events of instruction; question technique; writing lesson notes; methods of motivating the trainees; reinforcement of the learning; timetabling; allocating of staff and resources and so on. However, once again we offer only a preview here of material to be examined in detail in Packages Two, Three and Four, of the Programme.

In this part of the Component, we would like to focus on the fundamentally important issue of the **events of instruction**, or the general format which a good instructor follows in his or her lessons. The structure of this part of the Component is:

> **The Events of Instruction: Expository Method**
> **The Events of Instruction: Discovery Method**

Think over a couple of lessons which you have given recently and follow through in your mind the order in which you placed the learning events. If you can, consider both trainer-centred and trainee-centred lessons. Use Figure 276 as a basis for the greater detail which is to follow.

We present our table of learning events in the next Figures, beginning with a typical expository lesson. The table is modelled upon the work of the American psychologist, R. M. Gagné.

THE EVENTS OF INSTRUCTION: EXPOSITORY METHOD

1. Gaining attention
2. Informing the trainee of the objectives
3. Stimulating the recall of pre-requisite learning
4. Presenting the stimulus material
5. Providing learning guidance
6. Eliciting the performance
7. Providing feedback about the correctness of the performance
8. Assessing the performance
9. Enhancing retention and transfer

Figure 279

As you can see, we are involved here in a series of events which are largely controlled by the trainer and which influence and support the teaching-learning process.

The order of the events shown in Figure 279 can be changed to suit the training requirement.

We shall now examine each of these events of training instruction in outline.

The Events of Instruction: Expository Method

1. **Gaining attention.** There are various ways of doing this: by asking an interesting question; carrying out the first stage of a skill; making a statement saying what the trainee will make when the skill is acquired; showing the equipment or machinery which is involved in the skilled procedure; asking a question about the procedure for a mental skill; doing something unusual like organising a novel physical event e.g. running an electric spark from a plug to the engine casing. You are really making a change of stimulus to catch the attention of the trainees.

GAINING ATTENTION

Figure 280

2. **Informing the trainee of the objectives.** You know the advantages of setting objectives and of describing them to the trainees. It is only fair the trainees should know where they are going from the outset. You may support your oral statement of your objective(s) with a written explanation, a diagram or a picture.

INFORMATION ABOUT OBJECTIVES

Figure 281

251

3. **Stimulating the recall of pre-requisite learning.** You know from your Analysis of Entering Behaviour what knowledge, skills and attitudes your trainees possess (see Figure 92 and text) and what they need to possess before training. As so much new learning is the continuing of ideas and the attachment of new material to what a person knows already (changing the cognitive structure) obviously, you need to stimulate trainees to recall this information so that knowledge and those skills are available to take an active part in the events of instruction and of learning.

RECALLING THE PRE-REQUISITES

Figure 282

4. **Presenting the Stimulus Material.** This is the very heartland of the Implementation of Training. You give out your material, put across your content, go through your skilled process, do your training thing as required by all of the design system steps considered so far. Especially, you fulfil and help your students fulfil the performance objectives. This bit is about communication between the trainer and the trainees.

You support the material which you present by offering a variety of examples and emphasise the most significant features to enhance the stimulative effect. Such enhancement could include text with italics, bold print, underlining; pictures and diagrams, sometimes with important information enlarged, identified by name, or of a bizarre nature which stimulates retention. In skills training you would repeat and emphasise important cues, go over essential and/or difficult parts of the process again and again.

PRESENTING THE STIMULUS MATERIAL

Figure 283

We've left the box in Figure 283 blank for you to fill in. The stimulus material which you are presenting differs widely, of course, so you can certainly make a more appropriate and relevant diagram than we can.

5. **Providing Learning Guidance.** Throughout the presentation of the stimulus material, or content, the trainer guides the learners, often by sets of written or pictorial instructions in skills training; correction of skills procedures by trainer observation of trainees practising and then demonstration to individuals; individual questioning in both skills and knowledge areas. All of this guidance is, of course, to keep the trainees on the right track and trainer competence in guiding learning is a vital part of any instructor's repertoire of training skills and of being able to communicate with the trainees.

PROVIDING LEARNING GUIDANCE

Figure 284

6. **Eliciting the Performance.** Here the trainer asks the trainees to show that they know how to carry out the performance, or show they have the required knowledge. The trainer is communicating again, as he or she did in providing learning guidance, but here the question is "Now can you do the job?" You pitch your request at an appropriate level, of course; if the job performance, or the skill, whether mental of physical, or the knowledge is complex, you elicit (draw out) the

response in stages. If the performance is simpler, you may ask for the whole demonstration of performance competency by the trainees at once.

build on strengths. Assessment by marks isn't so important here as stating the correctness of the performance and an exact description about how the learning has gone.

ELICITING THE PERFORMANCE

Figure 285

PROVIDING FEEDBACK

Figure 286

7. **Providing "Feedback".** Here the trainer provides information to the trainees about the correctness of their performance. So the trainer feeds back to the learners an assessment of the degree of accuracy of each skilled performance, the extent to which knowledge has been assimilated by the trainees or a measure of change of attitude. This feedback is a personal thing. Each trainee needs to have individual feedback about their personal performance, so that each can remedy faults and

8. **Assessing Performance.** The first indication which the trainer had of the quality of the trainee performance was when he or she elicited the performance. Here the trainer is strengthening that first assessment. Sometimes this may take the form of a test, but really the type of assessment conducted here is usually less formal and is a careful examination by the trainer of the degree of success the trainees have had in fulfilling the specific objectives of the lesson. This assessment must always be made, by questioning or by observation of a skill being performed by the trainees and should be as **valid** and **reliable** as possible.

ASSESSING PERFORMANCE

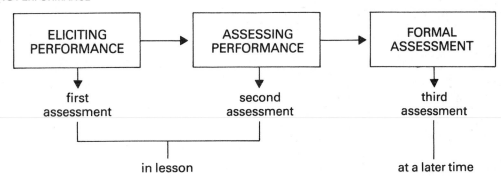

Figure 287

All of the three assessments shown in Figure 287 are part of the same system of checking trainees achievement and of drawing a picture of their progress.

9. **Enhancing Retention and Transfer.** When enhancing **retention** of the material or skilled process which has been learned by the trainee, the trainer offers

the learners a chance to recall the information, or skill, at intervals during the lesson by questioning them, by having them repeat the skill and by applying what they have learned to new situations, where appropriate. If the training is in the form of a course, then opportunities for reviewing the knowledge, or skill, should be given subsequently in the days which follow. These reviews offer the trainees opportunities for practising retrieval of knowledge, or skill, and for using what they have learned.

Transfer of learning is assured by setting a variety of tasks which require application of what has been learned in situations different from that in which the learning took place. So in the case of learned knowledge, the trainee would use the learned information to, say, solve a variety of problems not met before. In the case of a skill, the trainee would use his or her new skill on the shop floor, as distinct from the training area; a decorator, say, would redecorate part of the firm's buildings for real, rather than continuing to practise in the training department.

ENHANCING RETENTION AND TRANSFER

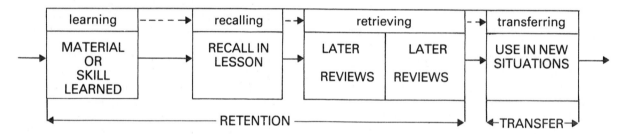

Figure 288

Remember that these events of instruction are organised flexibly. The routine is not standardised. You can change it around at will to achieve the best use of it. However, you should try to use each event when training.

Using the table below, show the events of instruction by filling out the columns for a knowledge (cognitive) lesson and for a skills lesson. Show what happens for each event in each lesson. Pick actual lessons, eg. for the knowledge lesson, a topic like "Health and Safety at Work" would be suitable. For a skills lesson, something like "Using a Lathe" would be appropriate.

INSTRUCTIONAL EVENT	KNOWLEDGE LESSON	SKILLS LESSON

Our completed table is shown in the next Figure.

EXAMPLES OF INSTRUCTIONAL EVENTS

INSTRUCTIONAL EVENT	KNOWLEDGE LESSON	SKILLS LESSON
GAINING ATTENTION	Make a change of stimulus, eg. show a diagram.	Change stimulus, eg. show machinery.
INFORMING TRAINEE OF THE OBJECTIVE(S)	Make a statement of the objectives.	Make a statement of the objectives and give a demonstration of the performance expected.
STIMULATING RECALL OF PREREQUISITES	Question the relevance and context of the knowledge and the material the trainees know already. Stimulate recall of previous learning by discussion.	Check out those skills which the trainees have already. Let them have a go or demonstrate and question.
PRESENTING THE STIMULUS MATERIAL	Present knowledge in as stimulating a form as possible. Use different techniques and types of stimulus, eg. oral, written, pictorial, realia etc.	Provide chance for trainees to see machinery, tools, etc, handle them and try out one or two introductory techniques. Emphasise cues, repeat process and demonstrations of the skill.
PROVIDING LEARNING GUIDANCE	Give oral and written instructions, question trainees and offer correction on use and understanding of knowledge.	Give trainees practice, check their skilled procedure, correct, offer feedback.
ELICITING THE PERFORMANCE	Check the way the trainees perform with the knowledge you have presented; try question and answer, or short written statements in their own words etc.	Ask for a full operation of the skilled performance by the trainee.
PROVIDING FEEDBACK	Let the trainees know how their acquisition and use of the knowledge is progressing; preferably tell each one individually.	Give information to each trainee about the quality of their skilled performances and how correctly each one is following the skilled procedure.
ASSESSING PERFORMANCE	Check out how far the trainees, and each trainee if possible, have reached the lesson objective(s).	Check out how accurately each trainee performs the total skill in accordance with the lesson objective.
ENHANCING RETENTION AND TRANSFER	Offer chances for trainees to recall information (and review later in course at repeated intervals).	Trainees continue to practise the skill.

Figure 289

Now, we have concentrated here on the events of instruction for an expository lesson and you will certainly have realised the similarity between the order of the events as shown in Figure 279 and the expository learning procedure of Figure 276.

The Events of Instruction: Discovery Method

Using Figure 277 as a basis, write down the order of instructional events for a discovery learning lesson.

Our order is shown in the next Figure.

THE EVENTS OF INSTRUCTION: DISCOVERY METHOD

1. Gain attention and stimulate recall, if necessary
2. Present the stimulus material
3. Elicit the performance
4. Provide feedback (and learning guidance if necessary now)
5. Assess the performance
6. Inform the trainees of the objectives
7. Enhance retention and transfer

Figure 290

Remember that Figures 276 and 277 showed general procedures for expository and discovery training methods, whilst Figures 279 and 290 are concerned with detailed procedures for implementing instructional events in either expository or discovery lessons.

Summary

In this Component we have been concerned with two separate System Functions: Synthesis of Training Methods (System Activity, Synthesis) and Implementation of Training (System Activity, Implementation).

Training approaches are broadly divisible into Trainer-Centred strategies and Trainee-Centred strategies. The trainer-centred approach is a traditional one and focuses on the trainer as the central fount of knowledge and skills and the purveyor of learning.

In the trainee-centred approach, it is the trainee who is the focus of training.

The Trainer-centred strategy incorporates training methods which are expository and depend upon reception learning and even rote learning. Nevertheless, the method is efficient in the use of resources and consequently, it is cost-effective. It is often effective as a learning method, but increasingly trainers are using the trainee-centred strategy, as teachers are in other areas of education.

The trainee-centred strategy uses discovery training methods which encourage the trainees to find out for themselves and whilst these methods are very **effective** in training, they are sometimes only moderately **efficient,** requiring both time and considerable resources.

Whilst the trainee-centred strategy is particularly successful in training in the cognitive and affective domains, it has drawbacks in psychomotor areas, where training in skills of a middle and high complexity is best carried out by an expository method within the trainer-centred strategy.

Whichever method is used, a Golden Rule is that **the more the trainees are active, then the more effective the training will be.**

Both expository (reception) and discovery learning methods have procedures which may be followed and an examination of these procedures gives a basis for considering the events of instruction when training is implemented. These events may be presented in different sequences and the sequences depend upon whether an expository or a discovery method of instructing is being used in the lesson. The sequence of the events of instruction are specific in nature, following the broad paths set out by the trainer-centred or trainee-centred strategies. Consequently, the discovery method uses a different order from the expository method.

There are three Components remaining in this Package, the next dealing with Assessment and Evaluation.

Before you begin it, consider how you would persuade a colleague, who only trains by using very expository methods, to change his approach and try out some trainee-centred work. If you have such a colleague, you might even try out your arguments on him, in person! Write down your arguments.

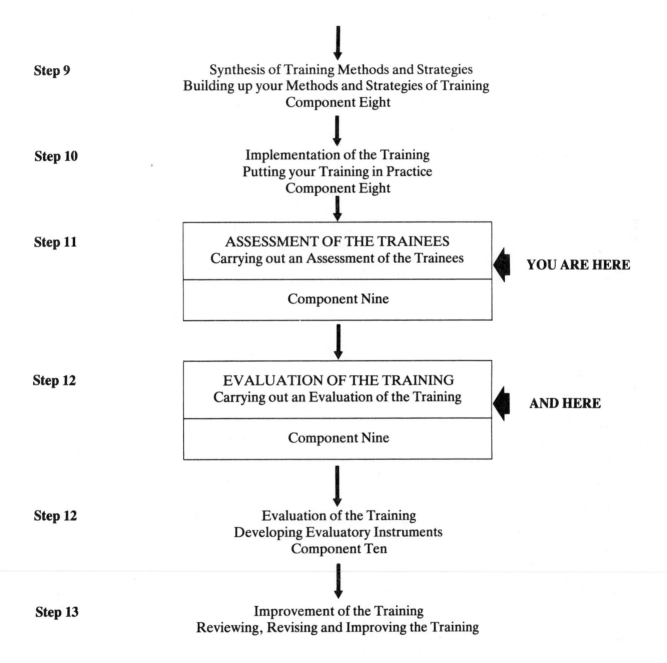

Step 9

Synthesis of Training Methods and Strategies
Building up your Methods and Strategies of Training
Component Eight

Step 10

Implementation of the Training
Putting your Training in Practice
Component Eight

Step 11

ASSESSMENT OF THE TRAINEES
Carrying out an Assessment of the Trainees

YOU ARE HERE

Component Nine

Step 12

EVALUATION OF THE TRAINING
Carrying out an Evaluation of the Training

AND HERE

Component Nine

Step 12

Evaluation of the Training
Developing Evaluatory Instruments
Component Ten

Step 13

Improvement of the Training
Reviewing, Revising and Improving the Training

Component 9:

Carrying out Assessment of the Trainees, and Carrying out an Evaluation of the Training

Key Words

Assessment: assessment of trainees; characteristics of good assessment; validity; reliability; effectiveness; practicality; functions of assessment: diagnostic; grading; comparative and predictive assessment; curve of normal distribution; norm referenced assessment; diagnostic and absolute assessment; criterion-referenced; informal assessment.

Evaluation: formative evaluation; summative evaluation; functions of evaluation; cost-effectiveness; elementary errors; cyclic process; criterion of competence; norm and criterion-referenced tests; pre and post-tests; skills tests; informal evaluation; evaluatory instruments.

Introduction

First we must distinguish between the function of assessment and that of evaluation. In "assessment" we are finding out how well the **trainees** are doing; in "evaluation" we are checking out how the **trainer** is doing and how good the course is.

WHAT IS ASSESSED? WHAT EVALUATED?

ASSESS	———	TRAINEES
EVALUATE	———	TRAINERS

Figure 291

You should note that if you are reading American books on course design, the Americans use the words assessment and evaluation as virtually synonymous. Our suggestion that evaluation is concerned with checking the **trainer** is a little unusual: mostly the statement is that you evaluate a **course**. True, but who designed the course, did the training, carried out the administration? So, whilst evaluation is a process of checking everything about the training, clearly the

person(s) who structured and organised that training is also being examined.

Assessment shows how successful the trainee is; evaluation shows how successful the trainer(s) is.

ASSESSMENT OF THE TRAINEE

Considered in this part of the Component
System Activity:
Assessment and Evaluation
System Function: Assessment

In considering the System Function of Assessment we shall examine:

The characteristics and qualities of Assessment Testing.

The main functions of Assessment.

The Types of Assessment.

Methods of Assessment.

What happens to Assessment material?

▨ Checkpoint

Before we begin our detailed examination, make out a definition of "Assessment".

Ours is in the next Figure.

ASSESSMENT: DEFINITION

> 'Assessment is the testing and appraisal of trainees performance or achievement, resulting from a training experience'.

Figure 292

Just one further point: the Training Technology Programme has a Package devoted to assessment and evaluation in training; this deals in detail with the techniques you require for fulfilling these training functions. Here we are interested with showing **in a general way** how assessment and evaluation fit into our design system.

The Characteristics and Qualities of Assessment Testing

Effective Assessment procedures, which consist mostly of some form of test, should be:-

1. **Valid.** You will remember that this quality is whether or not a test serves its purpose and we describe the meaning of validity in Component Five, Study Unit Two.
2. **Reliable.** You'll recollect we also described reliability in Component Five, see Figure 209, emphasising that reliable test scores do not depend upon chance.
3. **Practical.** Trainers and trainees must consider the assessment procedure to be appropriate to the objectives, the training content and method. In general, trainees should be tested the way they have been taught.

    Additionally, testing should be realistic in terms of time which it takes, ease of use and cost.
4. **Effective.** An assessment test procedure is effective if it is both valid and reliable. Note, however, that an examination or test, may be completely reliable and yet have low validity, or vice versa. In this case the assessment would be ineffective.

Before we consider the main functions of assessment, write down what you consider them to be.

Our answer is in the next section.

The Main Functions of Assessment

The main functions are shown in the next Figure.

ASSESSMENT FUNCTIONS

In general terms, we carry out assessment to

- Maintain training standards
- Keep the trainees "on their toes", ie motivate them
- Inform trainees of their progress
- Inform trainers of trainee progress
- Inform trainers of how well the training itself is working
- Aid selection of trainees and grade them
- Test the "temperature" and check the "pulse" of the trainees (and the training to some degree)
- Check on task competency often with a view to licensing trainees to practise

Figure 293

JUST TESTING

Figure 294

Types of Assessment

If you examine these functions of assessment, you ought to be able to discern two major purposes which include the rest of the purposes. What are these purposes?

Assessment is for
— **diagnostic purposes**
— **grading purposes** (grading also assists selection of trainees).

Let's examine each of these now.

Assessment for Grading Purposes.

Here the trainer is involved in labelling each student with a grade. There are two ways of looking at testing of this type:

— **Comparative Grading**
— **Predictive Grading**

In **Comparative Grading** you are using tests which discriminate between trainees and divide them up into classes. Sometimes, external examining bodies require these divisions to be made and "traditional" examination instruction often relies heavily on

discrimination of this nature. Frequently, the assessors aim to produce "normal distribution" test results with just over two thirds of the trainees marked within plus or minus a standard deviation (S.D.) of 1. Such a distribution produces a typical curve, called the "curve of normal distribution" as illustrated in the next two Figures.

Put in other terms, the test results shown by the curve identify, amongst a large group of trainees, a few very good students, some good students, the majority of average students and the rest below average and poor, or even fail.

A CURVE OF NORMAL DISTRIBUTION

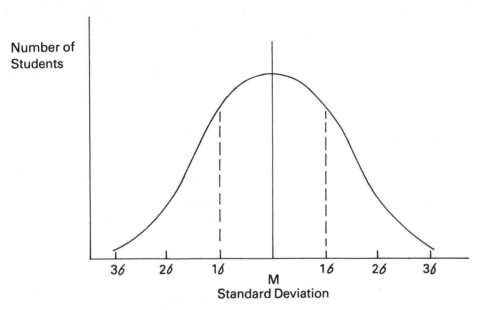

6 = Standard deviation
M = Mean Mark
||
|| = + or − S.D. 1
||

Figure 295

CURVES DISTRIBUTED NORMALLY

Figure 296

The **Standard Deviation** is worked if you:
1. Calculate the deviation, or difference, from the mean for each individual mark.
2. Square the difference (deviation).
3. Add these squares.
4. Divide by the total number of marks.
5. Square root the final figure.

Comparative assessment, as you can see, is entirely directed towards assessing each trainee and comparing him of her with the rest of the trainees. Often in training, particularly where an external award is to be made, there is an adjustment made of marks to conform to this distribution; this is called "marking on the curve".

In **Predictive Grading** the marking is also based on a comparison of trainees, provides grades, and is used to predict future performance on the basis of past work and ability which has been demonstrated. Aptitude tests and manual dexterity tests and other skilled performance tests come into this class, as do some pre-tests showing degree of "trainability". Predictive assessment is useful in selection, where the trainer and the firm wish to pick out the top ten from a hundred trainees, for example.

Assessment conducted for grading purposes which establishes the performance of trainees relative to that of other trainees is said to be **Norm-Referenced.** The grades awarded rely upon discrimination between trainees and the comparison of one trainee's achievement with that of the others.

This rank-ordering of trainees has priority over their actual competency and capabilities. The trainer and the organisation know more about where the trainees appear on the rank-order list and how they compare with each other than they do about their actual calibre.

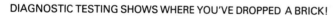

Say what you think the term "norm referencing" actually means. Give some examples of "norm-referenced" tests.

A "norm" is a "standard" so "norm referencing" is making reference to the standard of others.

"Norm-referenced" tests are those in which you grade and rank-order the examinees. These include any intra-organisational exam which produces graded lists of candidates and extra-organisational examinations where awards are made, eg. G.C.S.E., 'A' Level, BTEC, City and Guilds and degree and diploma examinations.

Assessment for Diagnostic Purposes

When assessments are made for diagnosis, the trainer is identifying, by careful observation, the extent to which a trainee has mastered a skill, developed interests or attitudes, or acquired a particular knowledge or ability. Assessment of this nature is made with reference to external standards, or **criteria,** for example, by the measurement of the degree to which a trainee has attained the performance or behaviour required by a specific objective.

This measurement of trainees' competencies is called **criterion-referenced.** A "criterion" is a means of judging. We examined this principle in Component 5, where we saw how a criterion test can be attached to each specific objective to find out how far the trainee had achieved that objective.

There are two types of Assessment under this heading: **Diagnostic Assessment** itself and **Absolute Assessment.**

Diagnostic Assessment follows the lines which we have just described and we must emphasise that the purpose is to give the trainer information on trainees' progress at a certain point in the training. The idea is that once a trainee's strengths and weaknesses have been identified this information can then be fed back ("feedback") to each trainee immediately, so that suitable training action can be taken to remedy the failings. No classification of trainees is made in these tests.

An important aspect of diagnostic testing is that the trainer is provided directly with information about the effectiveness of his or her training. If most, or many of the trainees fail to achieve a particular specific objective, then the likelihood is that there is something wrong with the training which is supposed to be making them proficient in that area.

DIAGNOSTIC TESTING SHOWS WHERE YOU'VE DROPPED A BRICK!

Figure 296a

There is an element of grading in diagnostic testing. What is this?

Well, in Absolute Assessment we have seen that the trainees are graded Pass or Fail. However, a large proportion of failures is a clear diagnosis of poor training. Don't blame the trainees; it's probably not their fault if so many have failed! Even in "pure" Diagnostic Assessment you will have a group who achieve the objectives, hopefully 80 or 90% of them, and a small group who do not; this distinction is a crude grading in itself.

The other type of assessment for diagnosis is Absolute Assessment. This method is common in training for certain professions where the trainee has to achieve a minimum level of competence at the job. This minimum level of competence, laid down by the trainer, is the criterion. The principle is that you either have the necessary mastery of the job performance, in which case you can do the job, or you do not, in which case you can't.

All skilled performances have a certain criterion level of skill which has to be achieved before the operator can be regarded as a skilled person, competent to perform the job, e.g. sheet metalworking, word crafting, watch repairing, film processing, bricklaying, mixing prescriptions accurately, completing a circuit board, finalising a profit and loss account, typing within time and error limits, the driving test.

Tests are structured to assess competence on a pass or fail basis and absolute assessment often shows a "skewed" distribution of marks as shown in the next Figure.

When looking at this graph, do remember that the distribution of marks which it shows is only a reflection of the quality of the training and of the ability of the trainees. Achieving a high number of competent people depends on effective training and trainees who are of sufficient calibre to benefit from it and achieve the pass mark.

A SKEWED DISTRIBUTION

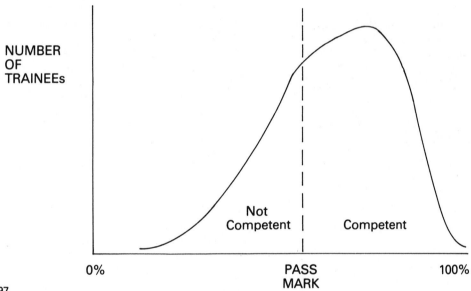

Figure 297

So you can see that all types of assessment contain elements of diagnosis and of grading. We summarise what we have said so far by means of a diagram.

TYPES OF ASSESSMENT

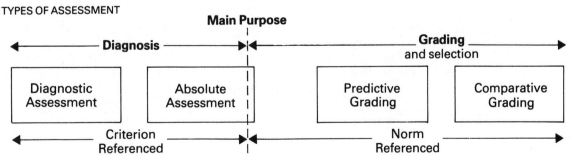

Figure 298

263

What range of qualities, capacities and abilities is being assessed, anyway?

The range which could be tested includes trainees' achievement and levels of skill, knowledge, mental skills and attitudes.

Methods of Assessment

We have gone into this already in Component Five, "Building up Criterion Tests". If you glance back at Figure 210, you will see an array of Criterion Tests and their characteristics. Jot down as many of these as you can remember, before you revise the Figure.

There seems to be a contradiction here. We seem to be advocating the test methods shown in Figure 210 which are described as **Criterion** Tests for all assessment purposes, including grading testing. How can this be?

There are two factors involved:
- *The way the assessment instruments are constructed.*
- *The use to which the test results are put.*

*Obviously, the tests, which are the instruments of assessment, are formulated according to a basic design (ie they are essay, objective tests, practicals or whatever). In the case of criterion referenced tests they **cover** the designated criteria, say, a competency laid down in a specific objective, very closely, whilst in the norm referenced tests they usually cover part of the content/ objectives only and are a **sample** of the ground covered by training. The **methods** are the same; the actual use and construction, e.g. questions asked, etc., differ.*

This leads us into the next section, concerned with what we do with this material from assessment, but before we do so, answer the following Checkpoint.

There is yet another type of assessment. Review carefully what we have said so far in this Component and see if you can detect what it is.

*"**Informal assessment**" is the answer. We all use this type of assessment in which we judge the quality of our trainees by informal conversations during training and at tea breaks. You must be careful not to let this type of assessment prejudice you against a trainee, who is expressing unguarded views in an informal moment. So don't carry it too far!*

LIMITS OF INFORMAL ASSESSMENT

Figure 299

What happens to the Assessment Material?

We can begin by showing a diagram of what you do with assessment material.

USES OF ASSESSMENT MATERIAL

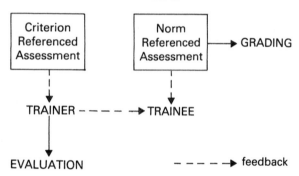

Figure 300

Interpret Figure 300.

Norm referenced assessment material is used for grading purposes mainly; obviously it also feeds back to the trainee, whose grades give an indication of progress.

Criterion referenced information provides detailed feedback to both trainer and trainee about progress. However, an important part of criterion-referenced material is used by the trainer for evaluatory purposes; this function we shall consider next.

EVALUATION OF THE TRAINER AND OF THE TRAINING

> **Considered in this part of the Component**
> **System Activity:**
> **Assessment and Evaluation**
> **System Function:**
> **Evaluation**

In this Component we are trying to give you a blueprint which shows how assessment and evaluation fit into our systematic approach. Step 11 of our design system is the making of an assessment of the trainees. **Step 12 is the evaluation of training and therefore of the work of the trainer.**

In our description of the System Function of Evaluation, we shall examine:

The Types of Evaluation
The Main Functions of Evaluation
What is Evaluated?
Methods of Evaluation
How does all this material fit together?

Before we start, attempt a definition of "Evaluation". Look for a word within the word "evaluation" itself and base your definition on the word which you have found.

Our definition is shown in the next diagram.

DEFINITION OF EVALUATION

> "Evaluation is a system designed to value the effectiveness, efficiency, and effects of training and of the trainer."

Figure 301

Clearly, trainee assessment is part of the system of evaluation. The other parts appraise the efficiency and effectiveness of the design system itself and the ways in which you use this system when implementing the training.

Types of Evaluation

There are two main types of evaluation; these are:
● **Formative Evaluation**
● **Summative Evaluation**
Before we consider the functions of these types of evaluation we had better have a look at each, describing what they are in general terms.

Formative Evaluation takes place during the training and at the end of the training. It is concerned with modifying the **form** and **processes** of training whilst the **training** is happening and after it is completed.

Summative Evaluation sums up the results of a course, mostly after the training is finished and it has

little effect on the structure and processes of the training which has just taken place.

Examine the next drawings. What process of evaluation working in practice do you think may be shown by the two illustrations?

TRAINING: EARLY STAGES

TRAINING: LATER STAGES

We believe that the improvement shown by the trainee could have been initiated especially by Formative evaluation and checked by Summative.

Formative evaluation would diagnose faults in the trainee's performance and in the training. Consequently, the weaknesses of both would have been highlighted **when they occur** *and remedied.*

Summative evaluation would confirm both the improvement in the trainee's performance and in the training itself.

We are going on to consider the purposes of evaluation next and we must view them from these two differing aspects of formative and summative evaluation.

The Main Functions of Evaluation

Functions of Formative Evaluation – These are to:

● Measure the effectiveness of the training in total.

● Show where we need to improve our design system, both from the point of view of the way we structured it and how we carried out each of the Systematic Functions in practice.

● Appraise our effectiveness as trainers when instructing.

● Measure the extent to which the trainees reached each of their objectives, ie. judge the effects of training on the learner.

● Show us where the training system is failing, allowing us to carry out "on-the-job" repairs as we go along, eg when an objective has not been realised to either change the objective, provide remedial training, or both.

● Identify procedures which we can use to improve the design of training, eg provide increased resources.

● Judge all the effects of training, in general, by producing feedback from both trainees and the training system, for the trainer.

● Check on the predictive value of the selective process and of the tests for trainability.

Write a few sentences, in your own words, describing the functions of formative evaluation.

We consider that formative evaluation, which is carried on throughout a course, provides information about just how the training is going, how well the trainees are achieving each of their objectives, where the training is failing and what we can and ought to be doing about it. Training is an active system and formative evaluation allows us to monitor the 'health', or efficiency and effectiveness of the training as it is happening. It also helps us to estimate the attitudes of the trainees to the course and the high or low value which they place upon it.

FORMATIVE EVALUATION: CHECKING THE DESIGN SYSTEM

KEY   Steps of the System Functions numbered, eg

1	=	Needs Analysis;
6	=	Aims and Objectives Analysis;
9	=	Synthesis of Training Methods;
10	=	Implementation of the Training.

Complete the identification of the numbers, referring to Figures 10 and 12 if you wish to check.

Figure 302

Functions of Summative Evaluation – These are to:

● Cover a wider range of issues than formative evaluation.

● Identify the outcomes of training, for the purpose of grading and certificating trainees.

● Help the trainer make judgements about the **overall** effectiveness of the training.

● Make reports to clients about the success of the training.

● Value the training in terms of cost-effectiveness. An organisation has an evaluative report on the training. This enables it to judge the value of the training in terms of comparing the improvement in operational efficiency after training with pre-training performance. Accounting for the cost of training and setting that cost against the post-training gains in profitability is also possible.

● Consider the effect of any innovations which have been made in training and provide information which makes further innovation more effective.

● Generate information about the structure of training which gives insight into the difficulties and problems of designing the training. This is a research function.

● Check on the predictive value of the selection process and trainability tests.

Describe the differences between formative and summative evaluation, in general terms.

Whilst formative evaluation is on-going throughout the training, summative evaluation is mainly completed after the course, although the enquiry which is part of it is carried out during and after training. It is the results of this enquiry which are evaluated summatively after training. So whereas action is taken on the products of formative evaluation immediately, action on the results of summative evaluation is largely a matter for after-training consideration.

Just as assessment looks at the trainees, summative and formative evaluation sum up the results of looking at the effectiveness of the whole of the training.

All aspects of assessment and evaluation are inter-linked and there really are no hard and fast boundaries between the different functions. To pretend there are would be to make artificial distinctions which would hinder the overall aim of producing efficient, effective and better training, trainers and trainees.

Perhaps, we can show these relationships in a simple fashion in the next diagram.

ASSESSMENT AND EVALUATION:
OVERLAPPING RELATIONSHIPS

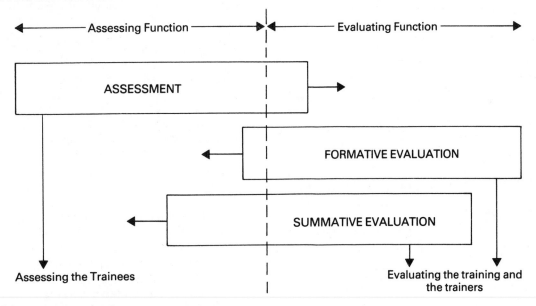

Evaluation is a way of checking; later on we shall produce an Evaluation Checklist. You might like to begin thinking now how you would put together such a list and then compare yours with ours.

Figure 303

What is Evaluated?

Just as assessment is a check on trainee attainment of skills, knowledge and sometimes attitudes, we have seen how evaluation judges the training and the trainers, their efficiency, effectiveness and effects.

However, we have included a separate small section on what is evaluated to underline one function which we have mentioned before: **cost-effectiveness.** When you have added up the total costs of operations, time off, machinery down-time, materials, staff, resources, equipment and all other training costs, it has to be worth it for the firm.

The cost benefits of training have to be quantified and this can be an awkward task. However, the aim is to prove that the training benefits and is of value to the firm. Most firms spend less than 1% of their annual turnover on training. Some European countries and America spend four or five times the British average and the Japanese up to 15%. Proving that your training is financially worthwhile is something which you should try to do, even in a simple form.

Now we move onto the big one; how do we do this evaluation?

Methods of Evaluation

There are several aspects to evaluation and each carries with it ways of evaluating which are special to it. We shall use the two major aspects which we have identified already, formative and summative evaluation as our bases and then examine each, in turn, for methods of evaluation special to them. First, however, we will make some general comments on evaluatory systems.

Evaluation in General. Evaluation is basically a simple process of eliminating errors in training and can be illustrated in the following diagram.

EVALUATION: THE BASIC PROCESS FOR
ELIMINATING ERRORS IN TRAINING

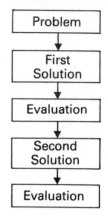

Figure 304

As you can see from the last Figure, we have a **problem** such as poor or inadequate operator performance, lack of knowledge or skills, which has been identified by Needs Analysis and which is capable of a training solution.

Following our design system gives us our **first solution** to the problem, which is the training itself. We then **evaluate** our training, finding out what is right and what is wrong with it and produce a **second solution.** This is training which is modified through our experience and what evaluation has told us. We then evaluate this second solution, our modified training, find out how well that training has worked (ie the adequacy of training as a solution to our original problem) and produce another solution.

This process goes on indefinitely; all training and all courses are evaluated and modified, so improving all the time. Consequently, all training continues to improve through time and each solution provides us with better training than that which went before. We can show this system as follows:

EVALUATION: THE CONTINUING PROCESS

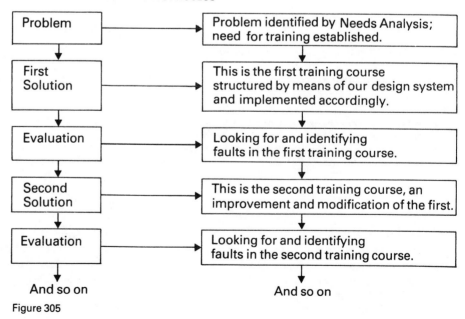

Figure 305

268

The last Figure shows the process of evaluation in a linear form, but it can be shown differently, in a way which identifies its cyclic nature.

Try to construct such a diagram, using Figure 305 as a guide.

Our diagram is shown in the next Figure.

EVALUATION: THE CYCLIC PROCESS OF ELIMINATING ERRORS

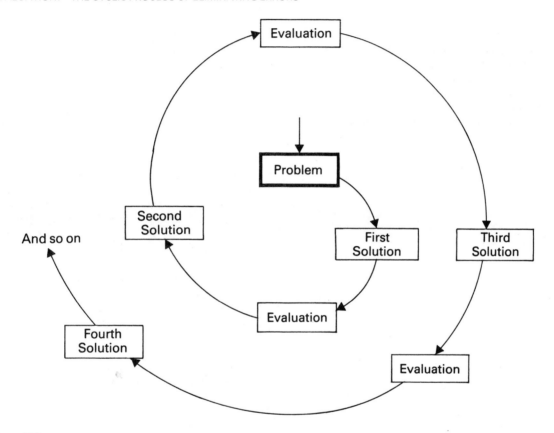

Figure 306

Notice that our evaluatory system moves in an outward spiral and continues as long as the training is being provided, whether that period is of years or months. This continuous process constrasts with the next Figure!

UP YOURS!

Figure 307

Methods of Summative Evaluation. Partly, the methods of summative evaluation are those of norm referencing. Therefore, grading tests are summative and most marking follows the curve of normal distribution. Trainee marks are compared with each other, a few do very well, a few badly and the majority are scattered in-between, clustering around an average mark. In summative evaluation, you are collecting and collating the marks which the trainees gained in Comparative and Predictive grading. You are summing up the information which you gained primarily for grading purposes. This evaluation is carried out often after the training is completed.

Typically, grading tests include:
- Phase tests, held after each phase of training.
- All normative (norm referenced) tests.
- Final examinations and tests.

Such grading tests are often similar in type to those given for formative evaluation, but the essential difference is that they only **sample** trainees' achievement and test **parts** of the knowledge which they have gained. A typical example of this sort of test is the examination paper, where the candidate answers three of four essay questions in two or three hours, the essays covering only a small proportion of the training content.

Objective tests, such multiple-choice questions may be set, but once again they cover say, 25% of the syllabus. Their prime purpose is grading and providing feedback to trainers and the firm only in the sense that the pass rate achieved gives a rough indication of the success of the training. Such feedback provides an evaluatory warning note when a question is answered badly overall, or omitted by most candidates.

Methods of Formative Evaluation. By contrast, the methods of formative evalutation are mainly those of criterion referencing. Thereafter, most diagnostic tests are formative and the information which you glean for this purpose comes from Diagnostic and Absolute Assessment. These tests show the degree of mastery which the trainees have achieved in attaining the performance and behaviour specified and they cover all aspects of the training content, as far as possible.

The aim of formative tests of this nature is that a large proportion of the trainees, say 80% or 90% will achieve 90% of the required mastery (the **90 - 90 principle**) and any who attain less will be given immediate remedial training which will bring them up to the required level. Full mastery is indicated by 100%.

Some trainers use criterion tests to produce a **profile** of the trainee's progress. This profile may be taken into account during the process of evaluation. If this is intended, then the trainees should be alerted to this part which the criterion tests are to play in the evaluation.

So these tests measure against a **criterion of competence** indicated in, say, a specific objective, whether the competence be a skilled process, knowledge, a mental skill or an attitude. Tests of this nature, you will remember, are shown in Figure 210 and include:
- Criterion Tests, ie "critical" or "criterion-referenced" tests.
- Pre-Tests.
- Post-Tests.
- Skills Tests.

Pre-tests you will recollect, are set at the beginning of training and show what the trainees know at that early stage. Post-tests are set after the learning has happened and carry on throughout training and at the end of training. We can show how they work in the diagram which follows and which shows how six trainees A, B, C, D, E, and F, fared in pre- and post-testing.

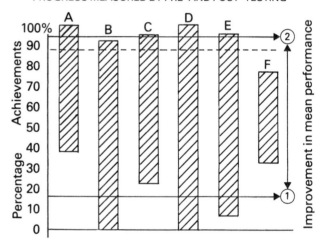

PROGRESS MEASURED BY PRE- AND POST- TESTING

Key:
1 = Pre-test Mean
2 = Post-test Mean
90% = Required Level of Competency – . – –
100% = Mastery
←→ = Improvement in mean performance

Figure 308

▨▨

What does Figure 308 tell you about the trainees' level of achievement and your training?

Each column represents one trainee. The bottom of the column represents the mark gained in the pre-test, eg. trainee A got 40%, B got 0%. The top of the column represents the mark achieved after training, eg. A got 100%, B got 93%.

Five out of the six trainees achieved the required level of competence, ie 90%. One, F, failed; this trainee now requires remedial training.

The greatest achievement was by D, who made a 100% improvement, starting by knowing nothing and finishing with mastery (100%). F achieved the least, showing a 45% improvement by moving from a pre-

test of 35% to a post-test of 80%. C, for example achieved a 70% improvement (25% to 90%).

You can conclude that your training is satisfactory: the mean moved from just over 18% to nearly 95% and only one trainee failed. As that trainee, F, began at quite a high level, and only improved by 45%, a much smaller improvement than the rest, you can conclude that this fault lies with F, rather than the training.

Although Figure 308 does not show it, the marks columns are made up by aggregating all of the marks achieved from various parts of the pre and post-tests. So, you will be able to identify the actual improvements in performance for each part of the tests and you will have a clear idea of where your training was successful and where it was less so. The latter parts can then be improved by modification in later training. Accordingly, you have evaluated your training very closely.

Criterion Tests we have considered already in great detail.

Skills Tests examine a skilled process and are characteristically criterion-referenced because the trainee has to achieve a high level of competence, or even mastery, on the grounds that you can either perform a skill, or you can't. So you either achieve the criterion of competency, as specified, or you do not. In the latter case such trainees need more training. A satisfactory level of competency for skills training might be 90% to 100%; where knowledge is tested the level might be regarded as adequate at 80% to 90%. Depends on what process or procedure you are training for.

In considering formative evaluation there are two other important sources of information:
● Informal Evaluation.
● Evaluatory Instruments.
Informal Evaluation is based upon Informal Assessment and consists of information derived from informal contact with trainees. Have a look at what we said about informal assessment and you will see that there is much material to be gathered about the comments which your trainees make about the training as you go along. Be careful, though, as we suggested previously, not to take unfair advantage of unguarded comments, as shown in the next Figure.

OVERDOING INFORMATION EVALUATION

Figure 309

How does all this material fit together?

Now have a look at the next Figure, which shows all that we have said about assessment and evaluation in summary form and how it fits together. This figure acts as a Summary for this Component.

ASSESSMENT AND EVALUATION

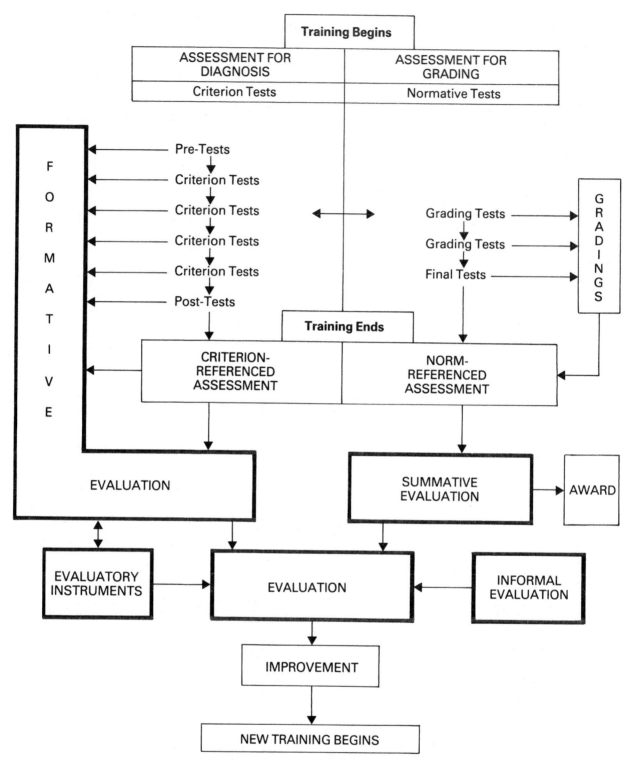

Remember that criterion tests may be converted into grading tests
simply by awarding marks.

Figure 310

As we suggested, Figure 310 acts as a Summary for
this Component.

272

There is, however, one area we have not examined in detail yet which is an important part of formative evaluation. Can you identify this area by studying the last Figure and the text of this Component?

The area which we have to consider is that of **Evaluatory Instruments.** *These are special techniques, organised to give us information about our training methods, the trainers in action and what everyone thinks about the training. Much of the most valuable evaluatory material is gathered in this way.*

Before you begin the next Component in this Package, think about techniques which you could develop to tell you about these things. You can then compare your conclusions with our suggestions in Component 10.

Just one preparatory word: much of the information provided by evaluatory instruments is about feelings, reactions to the training and processes, rather than on the competency of the trainees and the course.

Paradoxically, you can have a trainee who achieves highly on the course, yet reckons he or she wasn't taught well. Our next illustration shows this contradiction, where a trainee is receiving the trophy for being top, but thinks that the training itself was poor.

Finally, there is yet another area of evaluation which we have not yet considered. Any ideas as to what this is?

The area is **self-evaluation.** *This is evaluation of their progress and achievement by the trainees themselves. This is ensured partly by the trainer giving constant feedback to the trainees, but mainly by the trainees checking their progress against checklists, for example. A simple method of achieving this is for trainees to tick off their successful attainment of each objective on a list of the specific objectives of the course. Alternatively, the trainer can provide other checklists of topics, or parts of a skilled process, for example, which the trainees check off on accomplishment.*

Other methods of self-evaluation can be evolved from these techniques. Develop some suitable for your own training.

GOOD RESULTS, BUT BAD VIBES

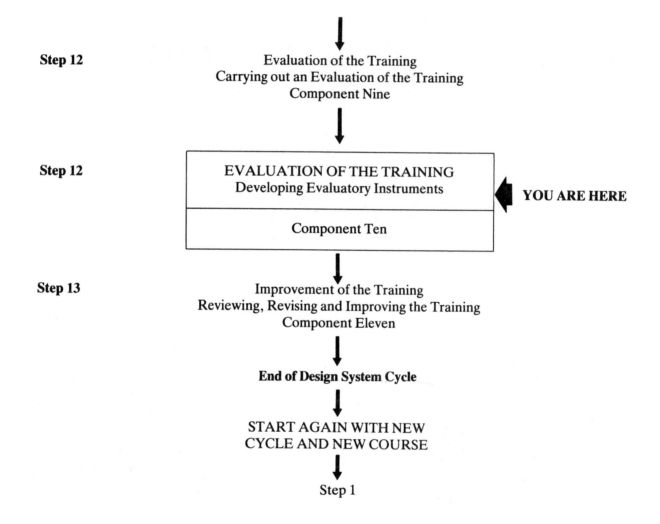

Step 12

Evaluation of the Training
Carrying out an Evaluation of the Training
Component Nine

Step 12

EVALUATION OF THE TRAINING
Developing Evaluatory Instruments

YOU ARE HERE

Component Ten

Step 13

Improvement of the Training
Reviewing, Revising and Improving the Training
Component Eleven

End of Design System Cycle

START AGAIN WITH NEW
CYCLE AND NEW COURSE

Step 1

Component 10:

Developing Evaluatory Instruments

Key Words

Evaluatory instruments; questionnaires on nature of training; course content; objectives; training methods; trainer performance; recording information on evaluation; informal evaluation.

Introduction

> **Considered in this Component**
> **System Activity:**
> **Assessment and Evaluation**
> **System Function: Evaluation**

So far the information which we have used for the purpose of formative evaluation has been drawn mainly from criterion-referenced testing. Amongst other things, this material helps us to:

- identify those parts of the course where the trainees achieved their objectives.

- identify those parts where the trainees were unsuccessful.
- show the general effectiveness and effects of the training.

Some of this information is statistically based. All of it shows whether certain standards or criteria have been attained. What it does not do is to give us insight into what the trainees themselves and the trainers **think** and **feel** about the training. This is a vitally important area; evaluation of training cannot just be about numbers, it must also focus closely on the feelings of those directly involved, as well. Our next Figure summarises this situation.

TWO ASPECTS OF FORMATIVE EVALUATION

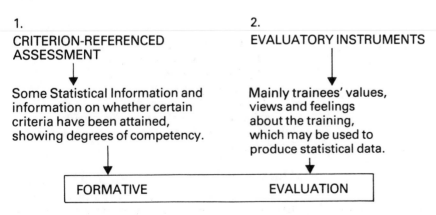

1.
CRITERION-REFERENCED
ASSESSMENT

Some Statistical Information and
information on whether certain
criteria have been attained,
showing degrees of competency.

2.
EVALUATORY INSTRUMENTS

Mainly trainees' values,
views and feelings
about the training,
which may be used to
produce statistical data.

| FORMATIVE | EVALUATION |

Figure 311

▨▨▨ Checkpoint

At the end of the last Component we asked you to consider what may be the special techniques used by evaluatory instruments and how they might provide us with information on training methods, and about the trainers in action. We have now mentioned the importance of trainees' values, views and feelings about the training.

What are those **evaluatory instruments** and what do you think is the basic principle upon which they are constructed?

The basic principle is that if you want direct information from the trainees then
ASK THEM!
Evaluatory instruments *are merely techniques for asking your questions directly of the trainee. Consequently, they take the form of questionnaires mainly. They are aided by other techniques which we shall mention, but fundamentally, if you want to ask questions, use questionnaires.*

EVALUATORY INSTRUMENTS: USING QUESTIONS

Figure 312

We have met questionnaires of the type we use in evaluation before, in our design system. If you have a look back through the text of Component 7, Study Unit 1, you will see that we used them extensively in Entering Behaviour Analysis, especially the Semantic Differential (Figures 107, 108 and 111) and the Adjective Rating Scale (Figure 109).

Before we give you a few examples of these questionnaires, let's examine which areas of our training we can focus them on.

Which areas do you think these are?

Our suggestion is that, through **Questionnaires,** we can find out about:

The Training in General
The Content of the Training
The Objectives of the Training
The Training Methods
The Trainer's Performance
What happens to the evaluation material?

OK. Let's use these areas as headings for this Component.

Questionnaires on the Training in General

We have made out a questionnaire already in Figures 109 and 111 which we can modify to suit our purpose here. The next Figures show these simple modifications.

276

QUESTIONNAIRE: NATURE OF THE TRAINING

HOW DID YOU FIND THE TRAINING WHICH YOU HAVE JUST COMPLETED?

To give us an idea of how you found your recent training let us know how you feel about it by putting a letter in each of the boxes against each adjective. Use this code:

A = EXTREMELY   B = VERY   C = SLIGHTLY   D = NOT AT ALL

I found the training to be:

INTERESTING		RELEVANT
USELESS		DEMANDING
BORING		HELPFUL

Etc., Etc.

(You would use all of the boxes shown in Figure 109.
A useful additional large box could be added as follows)

NOW WRITE COMMENTS BELOW, GIVING REASONS FOR THE LETTER GRADINGS WHICH YOU HAVE USED IN THE BOXES ABOVE.

Figure 313   (Modified version of Figure 109)

QUESTIONNAIRE: NATURE OF THE TRAINING

HOW DID YOU FIND THE TRAINING WHICH YOU ARE NOW FINISHING?

For each pair of words below, fill in ONE box with a tick which shows your general feelings now about the training.

"I found the training to be:"

| | | | | AVERAGE | | | | | |
	8	7	6	5	4	3	2	1	
INTERESTING									UNINTERESTING
USEFUL									USELESS
EXCITING									DULL
ETC.									

(Complete as shown in Figure 111 adding the box below)

WRITE COMMENTS ON YOUR TRAINING BELOW

Figure 314 (Modified version of Figure 111)

The numbers above the boxes can be used to give an overall rating for each pair of adjectives.

If your training course was divided into units or modules, you can use these questionnaires for each of those parts individually, to define your focus more sharply.

You will notice that we added a box to each questionnaire so that the trainees can say what they think about the training in their own words. If you believe it worthwhile you can add a whole sheet to the questionnaire for this purpose, so that they can readily have a go!

An alternative form of questionnaire is simply to issue a sheet of paper headed with, "WRITE WHAT YOU THINK ABOUT THE TRAINING IN THE SPACE BELOW". Whilst this may give your graffiti experts a great chance, such a questionnaire has a valid basis in psychology. When responding, most trainees will **write first what is uppermost in their minds,** so you'll have a good perspective on what they think is the most important. Such responses are difficult to collate, however.

Some trainees write very little and these questionnaires do not allow you to compare what they wrote when they entered the training with what they said when they finished it. This you can do with the questionnaires in Figure 313 (compare with Figure 109) and Figure 314 (compare with Figure 111).

Usually, it is best not to ask the trainees to sign the questionnaires, although you may wish to offer them that choice if they complete the questionnaire **after the training is finished** and they have been notified of their results. The reasons for this are obvious.

What type of questionnaires are shown in Figures 313 and 314?

Figure 313 is an adjective rating scale; Figure 314 is a semantic differential scale.

Questionnaires on the Content of Training

We have already shown you how trainees can rate the course content in Figure 107, which showed their expectations of training topic by topic. If you examine that Figure you'll be able to see how a slight amendment to that questionnaire can serve the purpose of providing feedback about how your trainees rated each piece of the content. Change the words, **"Do you consider the topics to be important to you?"** to **"How important was this topic to you?"**. The rest of the questionnaire remains the same.

You might want to ask not only how "important" it was, but also how "interesting", "useful", "difficult", varying your question in accordance with what you want to find out.

We are wondering if you have recollected that we used another form of questionnaire right at the beginning of our examination of the design system. Can you remember what it was?

We used questionnaires extensively in Needs Analysis and examples are shown in Figures 34, 40, 41 and 42. They can be modified for finding out about course content as the next Figure shows; this is a modification of Figure 42.

QUESTIONNAIRE: COURSE CONTENT

STATEMENT: The section of the course on the overhead projector was

IMPORTANT

| TRUE | 5 | 4 | 3 | 2 | 1 | UNTRUE |

USEFUL

| TRUE | 5 | 4 | 3 | 2 | 1 | UNTRUE |

EASY TO UNDERSTAND

| TRUE | 5 | 4 | 3 | 2 | 1 | UNTRUE |

TAUGHT ME A LOT

| TRUE | 5 | 4 | 3 | 2 | 1 | UNTRUE |

CIRCLE THE NUMBER WHICH YOU THINK SHOWS THE APPROPRIATE DEGREE OF TRUTHFULNESS FOR THE STATEMENT.

Figure 315

Questionnaires on the Objectives of Training

You will wish to check out your specific objectives in particular. You can use any of the questionnaires suggested by modifying them suitably. Try replacing the topic of course content by writing out the actual specific objective or by substituting the actual wording of the objective for the statements about the nature of training. In Figure 314 you could substitute the words **"I found the objective, will be able to use an OHP efficiently"** for the statement, **"I found the training to be"**. You would then lay out the rest of the form as you did before, making the other small amendments necessary.

As we wish to illustrate as many different types of questionnaire as possible, so that you have a wide variety of techniques and can pick those which suit you best, here is another layout for a questionnaire which you may use. We will use a General Objective from Component 2, Study Unit 2.

QUESTIONNAIRE: GENERAL OBJECTIVES

"After the training programme, trainees will, efficiently and effectively carry out simple programming on computers".

STATE YOUR OPINION ABOUT THE STATEMENT ABOVE BY PLACING AN X
IN THE APPROPRIATE BOX

How USEFUL was this part of the training?

	Highly useful
X	Very Useful
	Useful
	Not very useful
	Useless

How DIFFICULT was this part of the training?

	Easy
	Not very difficult
	Fairly difficult
X	Difficult
	Extremely difficult

How far have you UNDERSTOOD this part of the training?

	Completely
X	Well
	Fairly well
	Partly
	Very little

How INTERESTING was this part of the training?

X	Very interesting
	Fairly interesting
	Not very interesting
	Uninteresting

Did you have enough TIME in which to complete the training?

	Too much time
	About right
X	A little short of time
	Very short of time

How was the PACE of work of this part of the training?

	Much too quick
X	Too quick
	About right
	Slow
	Very Slow

Were you CLEAR about the scope of the work in this part of the training?

	Very clear
X	Clear
	Unclear

How much did you LEARN in this part of the training?

	A great deal
X	Quite a lot
	A satisfactory amount
	Not enough
	Very little

Are you generally SATISFIED with this part of the training?

	Very highly satisfied
X	Very satisfied
	Satisfied
	Fairly satisfied
	Not satisfied
	Dissatisfied
	Very dissatisfied

Figure 316

You can vary the questions you ask about training to accommodate what it is you wish to find out. Additionally, you will want to record the results of your questionnaires and we suggest the sort of format shown in the next Figure.

RECORD SHEET FOR QUESTIONNAIRE, FIGURE 316

USEFULNESS											TOTAL	%
Highly useful			√								1	10%
Very useful	√	√		√		√				√	5	50%
Useful					√			√	√		3	30%
Not very useful						√					1	10%
Useless											0	0%

DIFFICULTY											TOTAL	%
Easy									√		1	10%
Not very difficult							√				1	10%
Fairly difficult			√		√						3	30%
Difficult	√	√				√		√			4	40%
Extremely difficult				√							1	10%

UNDERSTANDING											TOTAL	%
Completely							√	√	√		3	30%
Well	√	√				√					3	30%
Fairly well			√		√					√	3	30%
Partly				√							1	10%
Very little											0	0%

You could continue with other headings, eg.
INTEREST
TIME
PACING
CLARITY
LEARNING
SATISFACTION

Figure 317

This record sheet is for a class of 10 trainees, so there are 10 boxes. Vary the number of boxes to equal the number of trainees.

The % column represents the % of total marks gained for each horizontal line of boxes. So, under "Usefulness", 10% of the trainees thought the course was highly useful and 50% thought it was useful.

These record sheets do give you a clear evaluation of your training from the point of view of the qualities which you have considered, e.g. usefulness, difficulty etc. The percentages are especially useful, even for a small class of ten.

The questionnaire and record sheet shown in Figures 316 and 317 can be used for checking other parts of your training, e.g. content, if you modify the questionnaire suitably.

Do remember to be selective in your use of questionnaires and the number of questions you ask on each. You must be judicious in their use, otherwise you'll find that you have a mass of material which is difficult to organise and use.

REFLECT ON YOUR USE OF QUESTIONNAIRES

Figure 318

Questionnaires on training methods

Here you examine how well your methods of training have gone down with the consumers. These are very important evaluatory instruments because such a great deal depends on your methods for the success of your training, as you know. When you design these questionnaires you ask questions about those methods which you have used in the training which you are in the process of evaluating. As usual, you have each one of your trainees answering the questions.

We have completed the questionnaire in Figure 319 as it might have been filled in by a trainee. You must next enter the marks allotted by all of your trainees onto a record sheet similar to that shown in Figure 317; this is shown in our next diagram, Figure 320.

TRAINING METHODS QUESTIONNAIRE

TRAINING METHODS
How successful have been the methods which have been used during your recent training?
By "successful" we mean how well did they help you to learn?

Grade each method according to the following scale:

Extremely successful	5	Moderately successful	2
Very successful	4	Not very successful	1
Successful	3	Unsuccessful	0

CIRCLE THE APPROPRIATE NUMBERS

PRACTICAL DEMONSTRATION	5	④	3	2	1	0
'HANDS-ON' SESSIONS	⑤	4	3	2	1	0
DISCUSSION GROUPS	5	4	③	2	1	0
LECTURES	5	4	3	2	1	⓪
VIDEO FILMS	5	4	3	②	1	0
TAPE-SLIDE	5	4	③	2	1	0
OHP	5	④	3	2	1	0
BLACKBOARD	⑤	4	3	2	1	0
WRITTEN BRIEFS	5	4	③	2	1	0
GAPPED HANDOUTS	5	4	3	2	①	0
SIMULATIONS	5	4	3	②	1	0
CASE STUDIES	5	4	③	2	1	0
PRACTICAL TESTS	5	④	3	2	1	0
WRITTEN TESTS	5	4	3	2	①	0
ASSIGNMENTS	5	4	3	②	1	0
CLASS EXERCISES	5	4	③	2	1	0
READING LISTS	5	④	3	2	1	0
SET BOOKS	5	4	3	2	①	0
COURSE MANUAL	⑤	4	3	2	1	0

ANY TRAINING METHOD YOU WOULD HAVE LIKED TO HAVE BEEN INCLUDED?

— Visits to industry (3 replies)

Figure 319

RECORD SHEET FOR QUESTIONNAIRE, FIGURE 319, TRAINING METHODS

RECORD SHEET: TRAINING METHODS	Responses (individual trainees)										TOTALS 0	1	2	3	4	5	T	N	A	R
PRACTICAL DEMONSTRATIONS	4	3	5	4	5	4	3	5	4	4				2	5	3	41	10	4·1	2
'HANDS-ON' SESSIONS	5	3	5	5	4	5	4	4	5	5				1	3	6	45	10	4·5	1
DISCUSSION GROUPS	3	3	2	1	4	3	4	2	2	4		1	3	3	3		28	10	2·8	=8
LECTURES	0	2	1	1	3	0	2	1	1	0	3	4	2	1			11	10	1·1	=18
VIDEO FILMS	2	2	3	3	2	2	4	3	2	4			5	3	2		27	10	2·7	=12
TAPE-SLIDE	3	4	3	2	3	3	4	2	2	2			4	4	2		28	10	2·8	=8
OHP	4	4	3	2	4	4	5	3	4	2			2	2	5	1	35	10	3·5	5
BLACK BOARD	5	2	2	1	2	4	3	1	2	3		2	4	2	1	1	25	10	2·5	=14
WRITTEN BRIEFS	2	4	3	4	2	2	4	3	2	1		1	4	2	3		27	10	2·7	=12
GAPPED HANDOUTS	1	4	3	2	2	1	1	1	1	1		6	2	1	1		17	10	1·7	17
SIMULATIONS	2	–	3	4	5	4	5	2	5	–			2	1	2	3	30	8	3·8	3
CASE STUDIES	3	2	4	3	4	5	3	2	2	–			3	3	2	1	28	9	3·1	=6
PRACTICAL TESTS	3	3	4	2	4	2	4	3	3	3			2	5	3		31	10	3·1	=6
WRITTEN TESTS	1	3	2	2	3	2	2	2	3	1		2	5	3			21	10	2·1	16
ASSIGNMENTS	2	3	2	4	2	2	3	3	4	3			4	4	2		28	10	2·8	=8
CLASS EXERCISES	3	4	2	3	4	2	2	3	2	3			4	4	2		28	10	2·8	=8
READING LISTS	4	1	2	3	2	2	3	2	4	1		2	4	2	2		24	10	2·4	=14
SET BOOKS	1	0	3	2	1	0	2	1	–	0	3	3	2	1			10	9	1·1	=18
COURSE MANUAL	5	2	4	3	4	4	4	3	5	2			2	2	4	2	36	10	3·6	4

KEY: T = Total score of answers   N = Number of trainees answering (10)   A = Average $\left(\frac{T}{N}\right) = \frac{T}{10}$ R = Rank order from average column

MOST successful: 1. "Hands-on" sessions   2. Practical Demonstrations   3. Simulations
LEAST successful: 1. Gapped Handouts   2. Lectures   3. Books.

Any Training Method you would like to have been included?
Visits to industry were suggested by three trainees.

Figure 320

Describe briefly, in your own words, what the record shown by Figure 320 tells you.

The record tells you the most and the least successful teaching methods which you employ on the course. The Average gives an idea of the success of your methods relative to each other.

Seemingly two of your trainees either did not take part in the simulation which you ran, as only eight answered; one does not seem to have done the case study and one doesn't have any views on the set books.

You should also note the high regard in which your course manual is held and the fact that three of your trainees believe that visits to industry are worthwhile, see Figure 319, under "Any Training Method you would have liked to have been included?"

You should now set about to find out why gapped handouts, lectures and the set books are not considered successful and we will recommend ways of doing this later in this Component.

This type of questionnaire and record sheet does provide an excellent evaluation for your training methods, but it does take some time. We believe the information which you gain is very worthwhile.

We now reach a sensitive area: the evaluation of

The Trainer's Performance

Naturally, you have to be careful here: some of the trainers involved in a course may wish to keep the trainees' views about their instruction to themselves. This makes it more difficult for the trainer in charge of a course to know how everyone is performing, so you need to discuss with those concerned how far the results of a trainer's evaluation questionnaire are to be restricted to the trainer himself, or herself, or the extent of which they may be seen by others, especially the person in charge.

Having sorted out how you are to use the information, use a questionnaire on the lines which we show in the next Figure; obviously you can modify the questions so that they provide the exact information you require, which will probably vary from course to course.

TRAINER'S PERFORMANCE QUESTIONNAIRE

Please help me to gauge my job performance as a trainer by completing this questionnaire. Show how far you agree or disagree with the following statements by ticking the appropriate box (√) 0 to 4, in the right hand columns.

Agree strongly	4	Disagree	1
Agree	3	Disagree strongly	0
Neither agree/disagree	2		

THE TRAINER, MR B. WILSON:

	0	1	2	3	4
Presents the training understandably and clearly					
Covers all the facts/skills to be learned					
Stresses the basic skills and knowledge					
Keeps continuity of course					
Shows relevance of training to the job					
Sets interesting exercises/operations					
	0	1	2	3	4
Is well-organised					
Invites questions					
Answers questions satisfactorily					
Stimulates learners to think for themselves					
Encourages trainees to participate actively					
Uses the blackboard/O.H.P./feltboard effectively					
Uses a-v equipment effectively					
	0	1	2	3	4
Is confident					
Is at ease with trainees					
Has a sense of humour					
Can be heard clearly					
Is enthusiastic					

Figure 321

As we did for the questionnaire on training methods, we must record the information produced by Figure 321. Our next diagram, Figure 322, shows how the record may be laid out, although we haven't completed the details as we did for Figure 320.

RECORD SHEET FOR QUESTIONNAIRE, FIGURE 321, TRAINER'S PERFORMANCE

										Totals					
										0	1	2	3	4	T	A
Presents the training understandably and clearly																
Covers all the facts/skills to be learned																
Stresses the basic skills and knowledge																
Keeps continuity of course																
Shows relevance of training to the job																
Sets interesting exercises/operations																
Is well-organised																
Invites questions																
Answers questions satisfactorily																
Stimulates learners to think for themselves																
Encourage trainees to participate actively																
Uses the blackboard/OHP/feltboard effectively																
Uses a-v equipment effectively																
Is confident																
Is at ease with trainees																
Has a sense of humour																
Can be heard clearly																
Is enthusiastic																

Key: T = Total Score of Answers
A = Average Score = T/N i.e. T/10 for this Figure
Number of trainees answering = 10 (i.e. 10 boxes, one for each trainee).

Figure 322

The Average column is the important one, as it gives you an idea of how well you are doing in each area. If you wish you can keep a cumulative, summary record of your performance for a number of different training groups as the next diagram shows.

SUMMARY RECORD SHEETS: TRAINER'S PERFORMANCE

TRAINING GROUP	A	B	C	D	E
Presents the training understandably and clearly	2.2	2.1	2.3	2.9	3.0
Covers all the facts/skills to be learned	2.2	3.3	2.8	2.9	3.5
Stresses the basic skills and knowledge	1.6	2.1	1.7	2.0	1.8
Etc.					

Figure 323

The figures you fill in are the Averages taken from the Record Sheets, Figure 321. Accordingly, each column (A, B, C, D, E) represents a different training group of trainees and five different Record Sheets, collated.

From the three questions summarised for the five groups of trainees, A to E above, Figure 323, have you any cause for concern?

It seems that your presentation and coverage are good, but you do not stress all of the basic facts and skills to be learned effectively. Averages of 2.0 or less indicate areas of your instruction which need attention and improvement. It is these low scores which tend to make trainers want to keep the results of trainer performance questionnaires to themselves, at least until they've seen what they have to say.

However, as the trainer in charge of a course you will frequently wish to know how other trainers are performing. In this case, apart from sharing the information in detailed questionnaires of the type shown in Figure 321, you have to insert questions about trainer performance in general questionnaires which also ask for other types of information.

Here is an example of an end-of-training questionnaire, which includes several sorts of information and several types of questions.

END-OF-TRAINING QUESTIONNAIRE

NAME OF COURSE ....

CIRCLE THE NUMBER WHICH SHOWS YOUR ANSWER TO THE QUESTION

● QUESTION 1 Was the skilled procedure demonstrated in training easy to understand?

VERY EASY 10 9 8 7 6 5 4 3 2 1 0 VERY DIFFICULT

● QUESTION 2 How sure are you that you have learned the skill sufficiently well to use it on the job?

VERY SURE 10 9 8 7 6 5 4 3 2 1 0 VERY UNSURE

● QUESTION 3 How useful did you find the "hands-on" practice in training?

VERY USEFUL 10 9 8 7 6 5 4 3 2 1 0 USELESS

● QUESTION 4 How useful did you find the practical demonstrations of the skill?

VERY USEFUL 10 9 8 7 6 5 4 3 2 1 0 USELESS

● QUESTION 5 How helpful was the use of audio-visual aids in the training?

O.H.P.
VERY HELPFUL 10 9 8 7 6 5 4 3 2 1 0 UNHELPFUL

VIDEO
VERY HELPFUL 10 9 8 7 6 5 4 3 2 1 0 UNHELPFUL

AUDIO CASSETTES
VERY HELPFUL 10 9 8 7 6 5 4 3 2 1 0 UNHELPFUL

● QUESTION 6 How difficult to understand did you find the written operating instructions?
Tick the appropriate box.

	DIFFICULT
	MEDIUM
	EASY

● QUESTION 7 Was the demonstration of the skill:

Superficial/about right/too detailed?
(Delete inappropriate comment)

● QUESTION 8 Was the pace of the training:

Too slow/about right/too fast?

(Delete inappropriate comment)

● QUESTION 9 Do you think any sections of the training should be omitted? If you do, state why.

● QUESTION 10 Is there anything which you would like to see added to the training?

● QUESTION 11 There were four trainers on the course: AB; CD; EF and HG. Place the initials of each trainer in the box below which shows best his contribution to the course.

PART A

Gave very good demonstrations	Answered question very well
Gave good demonstrations	Answered questions well
Gave adequate demonstrations	Answered questions adequately
Gave poor demonstrations	Answered questions poorly
Gave very poor demonstrations	Answered questions very poorly

PART B

Is well organised	Can be heard clearly
Is adequately organised	Can be heard adequately
Is badly organised	Cannot be heard clearly

PART C

Stresses the basic cues	Is enthusiastic
Does not stress the basic cues	Is unenthusiastic

● QUESTION 12   Any other comments on the training?

THIS QUESTIONNAIRE IS CONFIDENTIAL

Figure 324

The last Figure was intended to show different question formats as examples for you to add to your variety of question techniques and also to show how you can slip in queries about other trainers. You should, however, **clear these questions with them**, before you have the trainees complete the questionnaire.

Finally, you should remember that using questionnaires as evaluatory instruments can take place at any part of the training; not only at the end of the course, but also at the completion of a sub-unit, a module or a session. We now give a final example of a questionnaire suitable for us at the end of a discrete part of the training and answered quickly on a "yes/no" basis.

QUESTIONNAIRES EVALUATING PART OF A COURSE

NAME OF PART OF COURSE "Task Analysis"

Answer "YES" or "NO" to the questions following on the topic which you have just covered in training: "Task Analysis". Circle the suitable answer.

Was the topic covered adequately?	YES/NO
Was the depth of coverage suitable?	YES/NO
Did you get enough opportunity to practise?	YES/NO
Did you find the topic difficult?	YES/NO
Was the pace of the training right?	YES/NO
Did the trainer present the topic clearly?	YES/NO
Do you feel confident that you can carry out a Task Analysis?	YES/NO
Did you receive a lot of new information during this part of the training?	YES/NO
Did the trainer answer you questions clearly?	YES/NO
Did the trainer help when required?	YES/NO

Figure 325

At the beginning of this Component we mentioned that there are **other types of evaluatory instruments** used for gaining information about training from the trainer. Suggest what these might be.

Here is a selection:

Trainee diaries
At the beginning of training, the trainees are issued with a diary book in which they are required to state what each thinks at that time about the training each day. A short time, usually 15 minutes is set aside for this purpose at the end of the day and the diaries are collected on completion of the course.

Group discussion
Views about training are stated, explained and justified.

Observation
This is the informal evaluation mentioned previously. If carefully done it can be close to reality because the trainees may not know what you are looking for, or even that they are being observed; therefore their reactions are both natural and spontaneous.

EVALUATION BY OBSERVATION

Figure 326

Interviews
Often held after group discussion to probe the opinions of the trainees more deeply by asking them to expand on what they have said in public. It's possible to cover a lot more ground in this way, but the results may be imprecise and difficult to record.

Staff Views

The views of other trainers on the course are usually friendly and frank, highlight particular difficulties and offer solutions, are based on frequent contact with the students and show sharp awareness of the quality of the training.

A FRANK AND FRIENDLY EXCHANGE OF VIEWS BETWEEN COLLEAGUES

Figure 327

By glancing back at Figure 310, you will see that we have now covered the ground involving assessment and evaluation. Don't forget that to obtain a balanced view of your training you need to use as many sources of information as feasible and as you have time for. Evaluatory instruments do provide insights into the trainee view of training, but they do require the support of statistical evidence from testing. Be as precise as you can in your questionnaires; some are formulated in such general terms that they tell little except whether the trainee has enjoyed the course, consequently they are called "happiness sheets!" So ask accurate questions which are as specific as possible.

Now for our final section on this topic.

What Happens to the Evaluation Material?

All of the statistical, objective information which you have collected, together with that provided by your evaluatory instruments, which is mainly subjective, is now used as the basis for the next, and final step in our systematic approach, system Step 13, Improvement of the Training.

Step 13 is described in the next Component, which is the last of this Package. Before you read it, try making out a few evaluatory questionnaires for use in your own training.

Summary

In addition to the material provided by formative evaluation, it is necessary to develop special evaluatory instruments which give you an insight on the trainees' views, values and feelings about your training.

Such evaluatory instruments give information about the nature of the training in general, the content, objectives and methods of training and the actual performance of the trainers. The instruments include a wide variety of questionnaires, which must ask precise questions to avoid becoming inaccurate "happiness sheets".

Results from the questionnaires must be recorded and supported by informal evaluation, eg. trainee diaries, group discussion, observation, interviews and taking staff views about the training.

Evaluation refines your system continuously. It is an important part of the cycle of designing training courses systematically.

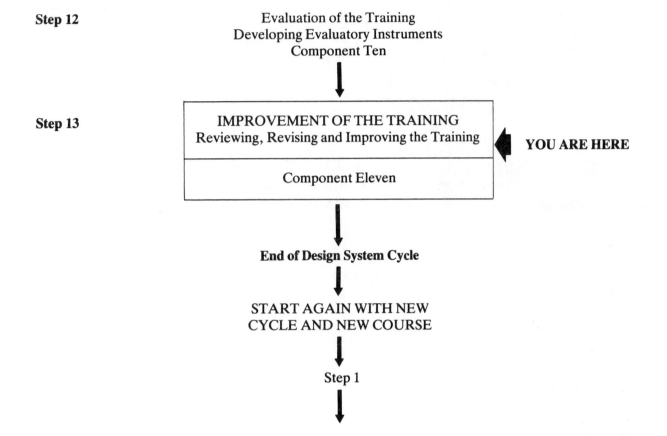

Step 12

Evaluation of the Training
Developing Evaluatory Instruments
Component Ten

Step 13

IMPROVEMENT OF THE TRAINING
Reviewing, Revising and Improving the Training

YOU ARE HERE

Component Eleven

End of Design System Cycle

START AGAIN WITH NEW
CYCLE AND NEW COURSE

Step 1

Component 11:

Reviewing, Revising and Improving the Training

Key Words

 review; revision; 'feedback'; correcting faults in the training; recording and revision chart; 'green', 'red' and 'amber' priority; responsibility; cyclic improvement.

Introduction

> **Considered in this Component**
> **System Activity:**
> **Improvement of the Training**
> **System Function: Improvement**

Our last system function of **Improvement** involves two basic processes as shown in the next diagram.

IMPROVEMENT OF THE TRAINING

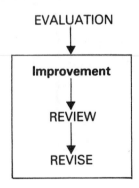

Figure 328

We will deal with the processes of **Reviewing** and **Revising** in turn.

Reviewing the Training

Review consists of drawing together all of the information which has been provided for you by the system activity of evaluation and then considering all aspects of your design system in the light of your knowledge about what is going on. If you glance back at Figure 310 you will be able to see again the type of material which is provided throughout summative and formative evaluation – this material is "feedback" to the trainer from the system and the training.

In reviewing the material, you are identifying and investigating three possible findings from evaluation. These are shown in the next diagram.

POSSIBLE REVIEW FINDINGS

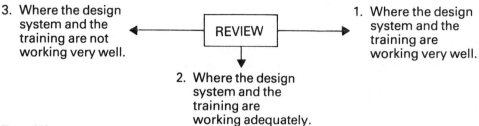

3. Where the design system and the training are not working very well.

1. Where the design system and the training are working very well.

2. Where the design system and the training are working adequately.

Figure 329

Under 1, where the training and the design system are working very well, your consideration is how you might build upon these strengths in future courses with a view to ensuring a continuation of these good points and a building up of your training upon techniques and approaches which are successful.

Under 2, you watch these areas with care, monitor their future performance, bearing in mind that you should be able to make improvements when you have time and opportunity to do so.

Under 3, where the design system and the training are not working well, you must be prepared to take your major actions towards modifying and improving the training. In a way, evaluation acts like a digital display in motor cars, where a malfunction in the vehicle system is highlighted by the digital display, or a system of warning lights, which alerts you to specific parts which are not working properly. **In the same manner, evaluation alerts you to the malfunctions in your training**. And to the good bits, too!

This system is shown in the diagram following.

EVALUATION: THE CYCLIC PROCESS

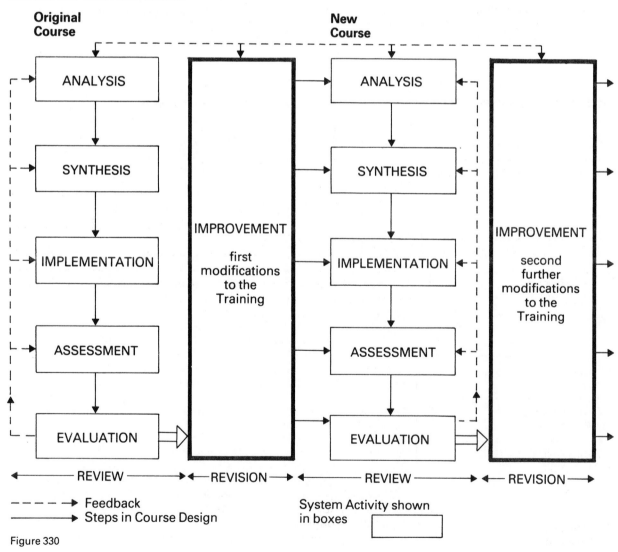

Figure 330

▰▰▰ **Checkpoint**

Why is evaluation described as part of a cyclic process?

Because the process is **continuous***: you are evaluating, modifying and producing 'new' or amended courses as a continuous cycle. Every course which you provide, subsequent to the first, is an improvement on the original training and on the courses before it; the* **process is a never-ending one***. It is unlikely that you will ever achieve the perfection of a course which does not need improving, partly because monitoring always shows aspects which can be bettered and partly because training is given to meet demands and needs which alter continuously.*

You will notice that we evaluate the **training**, which is a major activity and the design system. Often evaluation is considered to be of a valuing of the training alone, i.e. the implementation of the training and the content, aims and objectives and methods of training. However, as those aspects form part of an overall design system, **we check out how the whole system is working** to see if every part, every system activity and function is working satisfactorily, or unsatisfactorily.

You should even check your evaluatory mechanism itself, to ensure that your techniques are working efficiently, giving the correct results, can be relied upon and are valid.

Reviewing, then, is the process of saying to yourself, "What does the information which I have gained from evaluation tell me about my training? Which parts of my training system does it identify as needing improvement? What about my personal performances as a trainer?"

▰▰▰

Outline some areas of training and of your design system which might show weaknesses.

Our suggestions are shown in Figure 331.

Having made your identification you move on to Revision, the next part of the system activity involved in Improvement.

Revising the Training

You now set about improving affairs by revising the identified weaknesses in your training. The areas of weakness to which you might have to apply remedial action, i.e. where the system hasn't produced satisfactory results, adequate information, or expected outcomes, are shown next in Figure 331.

POSSIBLE TRAINING AND SYSTEM WEAKNESSES

System Function	Possible Weaknesses Requiring Remedial Action
NEEDS ANALYSIS	Goals not identified. Goals not ordered. Needs not measured accurately. Rank of need priorities not ordered well.
TASK ANALYSIS	Number of Levels of Analysis unsuitable. Type and number of Units of Analysis unsuitable.
ENTERING BEHAVIOUR ANALYSIS	Adequacy of Sources of recorded and research information doubtful. Test results – reliability and validity doubtful. Questionnaires – adequacy uncertain. Pre-testing – comprehensiveness dubious. Pre-Course expectations not identified.
RESOURCES ANALYSIS	Resources Checklists and resources inadequate. Action and responsibility for providing resources unclear.
CONSTRAINTS ANALYSIS	Identification of Constraints inadequate. Constraints not accommodated.
AIMS AND OBJECTIVES ANALYSIS	Identification/statements of Aims unsound. Identification/statements of General Objectives unsound. Identification/statements of Specific Objectives unsound. Coverage of Specific Objectives inadequate. Fulfilment of objectives by trainees not complete/failed. Objectives wrongly sequenced.

SYNTHESIS OF CRITERION TESTS	Selection of appropriate tests not made. Poor links between tests and objectives. Test characteristics not taken into account.
SYNTHESIS OF CONTENT	Content mapping badly executed. Links with Task Analysis not made. Content wrongly sequenced. Coverage of content inadequate. Taxonomies not used effectively. Advance organisers absent. Change not accommodated.
SYNTHESIS OF TRAINING METHODS	Wrong methods selected for training task. Excessively trainer-centred strategies used. Little trainee interaction with trainers and materials. Learning mainly by rote and reception. Poor trainer techniques.
IMPLEMENTATION OF THE TRAINING	Sequence of instructional events confused. Little variation of stimulus. Recall not encouraged. No learning guidance. Performance not elicited. Poor trainer performance. Insufficient learning activities. Inadequate reinforcement. Poor summarising. Unsuitable demonstrations.
ASSESSMENT OF THE TRAINEES	Tests not valid. Tests not reliable. Criteria for marking inaccurate. Tests not practical or efficient.
EVALUATION OF THE TRAINING	Insufficient diagnostic material. Evaluation not cost-effective. Ineffective evaluatory instruments. Criteria of competence inaccurate.
IMPROVEMENT OF THE TRAINING	Insufficient reviewing of previous course. Inadequate revisionary measures applied. Present course not improved on previous training. No proper organisation for improvement of future courses.

Figure 331

It is not reasonable for us to indicate all of the possible weaknesses in a training system, but we have given enough examples for you to reconsider some of the previous training which you have made and to recollect similar weaknesses. Certainly, you could double or triple the list shown in Figure 331, especially in the areas of training methods and implementation, where weaknesses abound most.

So revision of training involves acting on the weaknesses and strengths identified by evaluation. Reviewing is the first stage in the process of improvement. Revision is the second stage.

Revision = Remediation

Some revision is carried out during the training as the on-going process of formative evaluation feeds information to you about how the course is going. Most revision takes place after your review of training and involves those remedial actions which you apply directly yourself and those which you discuss with colleagues. Consultation is vital where a trainer has been identified as performing inadequately; such talks should be as friendly and positive as possible and not as shown in the next diagram.

On the other hand, evaluation will have pointed out those areas where the course has been successful. That's always worth a congratulatory word to those involved, or a pat on your own back! And it is sensible to build upon these strengths in your future training. Evaluation has both negative and positive aspects; don't forget to accentuate the positive.

ENSURING COURSE REVISION

Figure 332

As we are preparing a systematic design blueprint for training courses, we show how your Review and Revision may be charted, in Figure 333.

Fill in the chart as follows:

Review column: write down identified weaknesses and strengths.

Priority columns: place a tick in the appropriate column as follows:

> **Red** requires immediate action to remedy a serious weakness. This is a first priority action.

> **Amber** requires action to remedy a weakness, although this action is not immediate. This is a second priority action.

> **Green** identifies a strength of the course and action is required to build on that strength.

Revision column: show the revisionary correcting or strengthening action which you are to apply in practice.

Action by column: name the person responsible for taking and controlling the action.

Ended by column: show the date for completion of the action.

Approved column: sign this yourself and date it when the required action has been completed satisfactorily.

The Systematic Design of Training Courses

REVIEW AND REVISION CHART

TRAINING COURSE:

TRAINING BEGINS:

TRAINER IN CHARGE:

TRAINING ENDS:

SYSTEM FUNCTION / ACTION	REVIEW	PRIORITY		
		RED	AMBER	GREEN
NEEDS ANALYSIS				
TASK ANALYSIS				
ENTERING BEHAVIOUR ANALYSIS				
RESOURCES ANALYSIS				
CONSTRAINTS ANALYSIS				
AIMS AND OBJECTIVES ANALYSIS				
SYNTHESIS OF CRITERION TESTS				
SYNTHESIS OF CONTENT				
ASSESSMENT				
EVALUATION				
IMPLEMENTATION AND TRAINING METHODS				
IMPLEMENTATION: NON-INSTRUCTIONAL				

Figure 333

SIZE OF GROUP: LOCATION OF TRAINING:

AWARD: ANY OTHER DETAILS:

REVISION	ENDED BY	ACTION BY	APPROVED

Figure 333 continued

Having completed the reviewing and revision of your evaluation information and taken the action necessary for the correction of faults in the training, you have completed the last system function of our design system, Step 13, Improvement of the Training. Figure 334 shows these activities in diagrammatic form.

As the application of the design system to training is part of a cyclic process all you have to do now is to

START AGAIN!

EVALUATION AND IMPROVEMENT

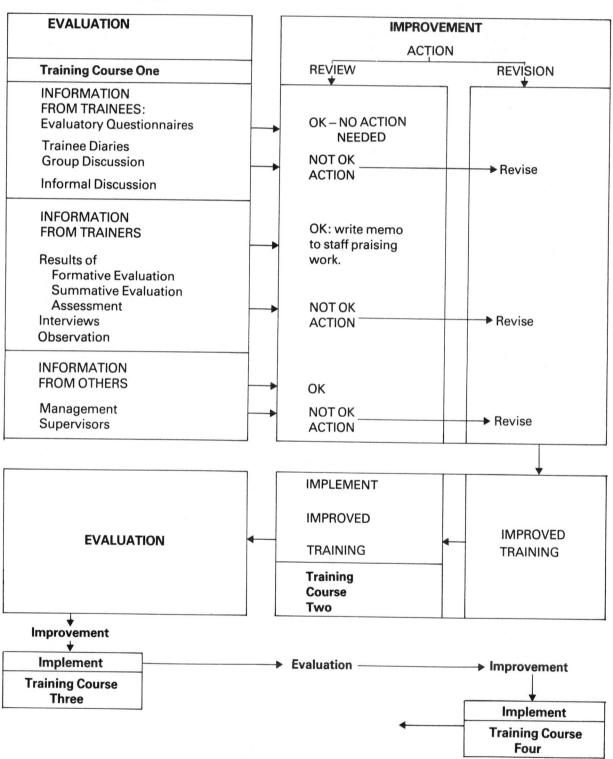

Figure 334

Summary

Improvement of the training is Step 13 in the systematic design of training courses and includes the processes of review and revision.

In reviewing the training you are concerned to collate the information provided about the training from the system activity of evaluation and to identify those strengths in your training which may be built upon and those faults which require correction.

The process of revising your training is that of remedying the weaknesses in training already identified by deciding on appropriate action and who is responsible for acting. Both review and revision procedures should be charted for record purposes.

The system function of Improvement of the Training ends the first cycle of training design and implementation. You then begin again with an improved course, carrying through your improved design and practice into a new training cycle as shown in Figure 335.

Therefore, this design system provides a systematic, self-correcting and cyclic approach to the design of training courses, as shown in the next figure.

THE DESIGN SYSTEM: A TRAINING CYCLE

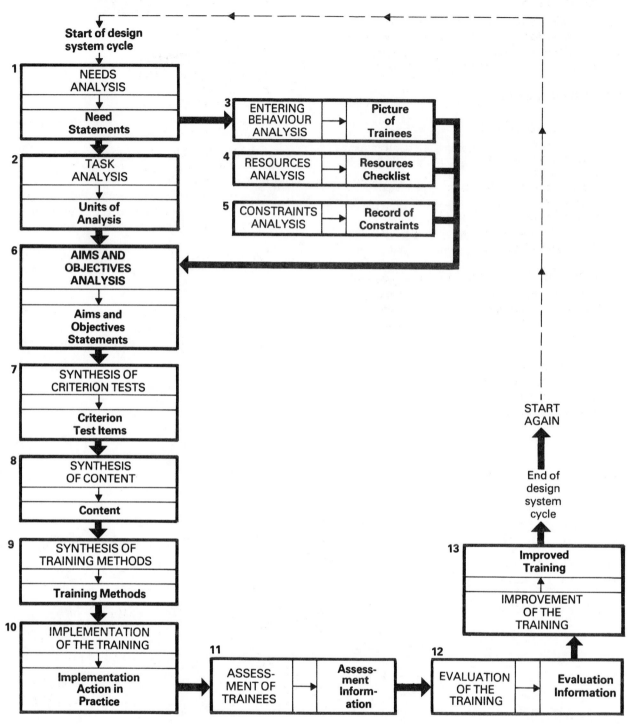

Start of design system cycle

| 1 | NEEDS ANALYSIS |
| **Need Statements** |

| 3 | ENTERING BEHAVIOUR ANALYSIS | → | **Picture of Trainees** |

| 2 | TASK ANALYSIS |
| **Units of Analysis** |

| 4 | RESOURCES ANALYSIS | → | **Resources Checklist** |

| 5 | CONSTRAINTS ANALYSIS | → | **Record of Constraints** |

| 6 | **AIMS AND OBJECTIVES ANALYSIS** |
| **Aims and Objectives Statements** |

| 7 | SYNTHESIS OF CRITERION TESTS |
| **Criterion Test Items** |

| 8 | SYNTHESIS OF CONTENT |
| **Content** |

| 9 | SYNTHESIS OF TRAINING METHODS |
| **Training Methods** |

| 10 | IMPLEMENTATION OF THE TRAINING |
| **Implementation Action in Practice** |

| 11 | ASSESS-MENT OF TRAINEES | → | **Assess-ment Inform-ation** |

| 12 | EVALUATION OF THE TRAINING | → | **Evaluation Information** |

| 13 | **Improved Training** |
| IMPROVEMENT OF THE TRAINING |

START AGAIN

End of design system cycle

KEY

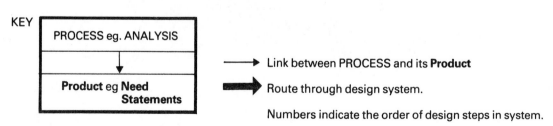

| PROCESS eg. ANALYSIS |
| **Product** eg **Need Statements** |

⟶ Link between PROCESS and its **Product**

➡ Route through design system.

Numbers indicate the order of design steps in system.

Figure 335

Package One: Aim

"To provide sufficient information and training material in the form of a distance learning package to enable trainers to undertake the systematic design of training courses both efficiently and effectively."

General Objectives

To
— introduce trainers to the design system.
— explain the way in which the design system works.
— assist trainers implement a systematic approach to solving problems in training.
— explain to trainers the design system activities of analysis, synthesis, implementation, assessment, evaluation and improvement of training.
— help trainers undertake the systematic design of training courses.

Specific Objectives (shortened list, outline form)

After completing the Package, trainers will be able, for their own training in their place of work, to implement the following design system functions efficiently and effectively:
— Needs Analysis
— Task Analysis
— Entry Behaviour Analysis
— Resources Analysis
— Constraints Analysis
— Aims and Objectives Analysis
— Synthesis of Criterion Tests
— Synthesis of Content
— Synthesis of Training Methods
— Implementation of the Training
— Assessment of the Trainees
— Evaluation of the Training
— Improvement of the Training

Voluntary Package Assignment

If you wish, carry out **one** of the exercises which follow, sending your Assignment to your Programme Tutor for comment.
1. Select one system function of the design system. Show how you would operate this function in practice, on one of your courses.
or,
2. Appraise the effects which the operation of one systematic design activity has had upon your training.
or,
3. Make a comparison between the "traditional" methods of course design and implementation and the systematic design and implementation of training.
or,
4. Undertake, in outline only, the systematic design of a training course.

THE DESIGN SYSTEM TRAINING CYCLE

Figure 336

Selected Bibliography

- DAVIES I. K. 1981

  Price Bracket: C

  'Instructional Technique'
  McGRAW HILL. New York.
  (Concise text with a wide coverage).

- BRIGGS L. J. 1977

  Price Bracket: C

  'Instructional Design'
  EDUCATIONAL TECHNOLOGY PUBLICATIONS.
  (Comprehensive, advanced text. 532 pages).

- HEATHCOTE G.,
  KEMPA R., and
  ROBERTS I. 1982

  Price Bracket: Free

  'Curriculum Styles and Strategies'
  FURTHER EDUCATION CURRICULUM REVIEW AND
  DEVELOPMENT UNIT.
  Publications Despatch Centre, D.E.S.,
  Honeypot Lane, Canons Park, Stanmore,
  Middlesex, HA7 1AZ.
  (Very clearly written text about a curriculum project. 145 pages).

- PERCIVAL F.
  ELLINGTON H. 1984

  Price Bracket: C

  'A Handbook of Educational Technology'
  KOGAN PAGE. London.
  (Very readable, general text; good glossary. 248 pages).

- ROMISZOWSKI A. J. 1981

  Price Bracket: B
  (Softback)

  'Designing Instructional Systems'
  KOGAN PAGE. London.
  (Advanced text, very detailed and comprehensive. 415 pages).

- ROMISZOWSKI A. J. 1984

  Price Bracket: C

  'Producing Instructional Systems'
  KOGAN PAGE. London.
  (A follow-on book to Designing Instructional Systems. 286 pages).

- ROWNTREE D. 1982

  Price Bracket: B
  (Softback)

  'Educational Technology in Curriculum Development'
  HARPER AND ROW. London.
  (General, readable text. 296 pages).

- VARIOUS AUTHORS,
  COUNCIL FOR
  EDUCATIONAL TECHNOLOGY

  Price Bracket:
  Usually A

  Wide range of materials concerning many aspects of education,
  available from
  Council for Educational Technology,
  3 Devonshire Street,
  London, W1N 2BA.
  (Readable, interesting texts).

The Price Brackets are approximate guides, as follows:
Price Bracket A = less than £7.
Price Bracket B = £7 to £12.
Price Bracket C = Over £12.

A very comprehensive Bibliography can be found at the end of Package 4 of this Programme.